THE WORLD'S BIGGEST BOOK OF

BRAINTEASERS &

LOGIC PUZZLES

• •

NORMAN D. WILLIS, PAUL SLOANE, DES MacHALE,

MICHAEL A. DISPEZIO, KURT SMITH, MARTIN GARDNER,

TIM SOLE, & ROD MARSHALL

Sterling Publishing Co., Inc.
New York

Library of Congress Cataloging-in-Publication Data Available

10 9 8 7 6 5 4 3 2 1

Published by Sterling Publishing Co., Inc.
387 Park Avenue South, New York, NY 10016

This book is comprised of material from the following titles:

Great Critical Thinking Puzzles © 1997 by Michael A. DiSpezio
Mind-Boggling Word Puzzles © 2001 by Martin Gardner
Challenging Lateral Thinking Puzzles © 1992 by Paul Sloane & Des MacHale
Math Logic Puzzles © 1996 by Kurt Smith
Nearly Impossible Brain Bafflers © 1998 by Tim Sole; illustrations © 1998 by Rod Marshall
Amazing Logic Puzzles © 1994 by Norman D. Willis
Challenging False Logic Puzzles © 1997 by Norman D. Willis
False Logic Puzzles © 1997 by Norman D. Willis
Mystifying Logic Puzzles © 1998 by Norman D. Willis

© 2006 by Sterling Publishing Co., Inc.
Distributed in Canada by Sterling Publishing
c/o Canadian Manda Group, 165 Dufferin Street,
Toronto, Ontario, Canada M6K 3H6
Distributed in the United Kingdom by GMC Distribution Services,
Castle Place, 166 High Street, Lewes, East Sussex, England BN7 1XU
Distributed in Australia by Capricorn Link (Australia) Pty. Ltd.
P.O. Box 704, Windsor, NSW 2756, Australia

Sterling ISBN-13: 978-1-4027-3372-7
         ISBN-10: 1-4027-3372-0

For information about custom editions, special sales, premium and
corporate purchases, please contact Sterling Special Sales
Department at 800-805-5489 or specialsales@sterlingpub.com

CONTENTS

••••••••••••••••••••••

THE WORLD'S MOST AMAZING LOGIC PUZZLES

The World's Most Amazing Duplgoose Egg Puzzle

The planet Dranac lies far beyond the known solar system. It has its own unique beings and civilization. It is apparent that Dranac is far behind Earth in technological development. As well, Dranacians have less respect for honesty. Deception and crimes are commonplace among the inhabitants. These puzzles will deal with statements by suspects of crimes. Finding the solutions will depend on determining who is telling the truth and who is lying.

Duplgooses, small farm animals, lay eggs only occasionally, although in pairs. Their eggs, an important food source on Dranac, are a highly valued commodity. A basket of duplgoose eggs has been stolen from the open market in the local village. There are four suspects, and each makes one statement, although only one of the four speaks truthfully. The guilty one can be deduced from their statements below.

   A. B did it.
   B. C did it.
   C. I did it.
   D. Either A or C is the guilty one.

DID C DO IT? IF NOT, WHO DID?

The World's Most Amazing Huffalon Theft Puzzle

Huffalons, great sturdy beasts that are used for riding, pulling carts and carrying bundles, are the chief source of transportation on the planet. There have been a number of huffalon thefts in the local village. It is apparent that there are two thieves working together. Several suspects have been identified, and two of them are the guilty ones. Each makes one statement below, and four of the six statements are truthful. Only the two guilty parties make false statements.

- A. C is guilty.
- B. F is not guilty.
- C. D is not guilty.
- D. B is guilty.
- E. A is not guilty.
- F. E is not guilty.

WHICH TWO ARE GUILTY?

The World's Most Amazing Overseer's Theft Puzzle

A crime has occurred in the home of a wealthy village overseer. A valuable collection of ancient Dranacian artifacts has been stolen, and there is no question that it was an inside job. The suspects are the cook, the housekeeper, the stable hand, and the huffalon groom, each of whom makes two statements. The statements made by the stable hand and the housekeeper are false; the huffalon groom makes one truthful statement and one false statement, though in what order is unknown; only the cook makes two truthful statements.

But which suspect is which? They are identified only as A, B, C, and D. Their statements follow:

> A. 1. I am not the housekeeper.
>   2. The huffalon groom is guilty.
>
> B. 1. I am not the huffalon groom.
>   2. The housekeeper is guilty.
>
> C. 1. I am not the cook.
>   2. The stable hand is guilty.
>
> D. 1. I am not the stable hand.
>   2. The cook is guilty.

WHICH ONE MAKES WHICH STATEMENTS, AND WHO IS THE GUILTY PARTY?

The World's Most Amazing
Purloined Prickly Plum Pie Puzzle

The inhabitants of Dranac are especially fond of their delicious prickly plum pie. A pie just out of the oven and piping hot was placed on an open windowsill to cool. It was not long before it disappeared and was illegally consumed. There are three suspects who are known to be lovers of prickly plum pie. Each makes three statements as follows, although only one of the guilty party's statements is true. As to the truthfulness of the statements made by the other two suspects, little is known.

A. 1. I was not even there.
    2. C stole the pie.
    3. B helped him eat it.

B. 1. A stole the pie.
    2. The aroma of prickly plum pie is hard to resist.
    3. I did not steal the pie.

C. 1. I do not like prickly plum pie.
    2. B stole the pie.
    3. I did not steal the pie.

WHO IS GUILTY?

The World's Most Amazing Farm Theft Puzzle

Farm tools and equipment are missing. They have been stolen, and the crime was committed by one of the four farmhands. Their statements are below. Unfortunately, none of them can be depended upon to speak truthfully; each makes one true statement and one false statement, although in which order is unknown.

Farmhand No. 1: 1. I do not trust Farmhand No. 2.
                            2. I am certainly not guilty.

Farmhand No. 2: 1. Farmhand No. 1 is guilty.
                            2. Farmhand No. 4 did not do it.

Farmhand No. 3: 1. I did not know that the theft had occurred until I heard about it the day it was discovered.
                            2. Farmhand No. 1 did not do it.

Farmhand No. 4: 1. Farmhand No. 1 is innocent.
                            2. Farmhand No. 3 did not do it.

WHO IS THE GUILTY ONE?

The World's Most Amazing Ballot Box Stuffer Puzzle

In the election for mayor of the village, the winning candidate's margin of victory was only three votes. The problem is that there were twenty more votes than there are registered voters. Someone stuffed the ballot box. Three suspects have been identified, and one of them is guilty. The three are A, the winning candidate's husband; B, the losing candidate's wife; and C, a local character. They make statements, as follows:

A. 1. B had a motive to commit the crime.
   2. C's first statement is true.
   3. B is guilty.

B. 1. My husband was the one hurt by the results; I had no incentive to commit the crime.
   2. C did it.
   3. My husband and I planned to spend several lunar periods on a region-wide tour. We would have had to cancel the trip if he had won the election; I had a motive.

C. 1. I was not near the voting booth on election day.
   2. I am innocent.
   3. B did it.

CONSIDERING THAT EACH SUSPECT MAKES ONLY ONE TRUE STATEMENT, CAN YOU IDENTIFY THE GUILTY ONE?

The World's Most Amazing Village Marketplace Theft Puzzle

The economy of Dranac is based on buying, selling, and bartering staples in village marketplaces. Produce includes such things as huffalon milk, duplgoose eggs, and prickly plums. An armload of prickly plums is taken by a thief while the owner is engaged in negotiating a sale. Three suspects have been identified, one of whom is guilty. They make assertions below, though each suspect makes at least two false statements.

A. 1. B is guilty.
    2. I have met C on several occasions.
    3. I have plenty of my own prickly plums.

B. 1. A and C have never met.
    2. I am guilty.
    3. A's third statement is false.

C. 1. I have never met A.
    2. A is guilty.
    3. B's third statement is true.

WHICH ONE IS GUILTY?

The World's Most Amazing Produce Cart Theft Puzzle

A cart pulled by a huffalon and loaded with duplgoose eggs for the village market was taken by a thief while the proprietor was busy setting up his sales booth. The stolen property was subsequently recovered, and there are three suspects. They each make assertions below, but no one of them makes all true statements.

A. 1. B is innocent.
2. Everything C will say is false.
3. I am not guilty.

B. 1. I did not do it.
2. C was in the village when it happened.
3. A's second statement is false.

C. 1. A is the thief.
2. I was not even near the village when it happened.
3. I am innocent.

ONE OF THE THREE IS GUILTY, BUT WHICH ONE?

The World's Most Amazing Attempted Sabotage Puzzle

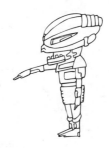

A group of space travelers landed on the planet, but were not welcomed by all inhabitants. Someone tried to damage one of the airlocks on the travelers' spaceship. There are three suspects, and each is questioned regarding the crime. One makes three truthful statements, one makes no truthful statements, and how one suspect responds is unknown. From the following statements made by the three suspects, determine which one is guilty.

A. 1. I did not do it.
    2. I always speak truthfully.
    3. I do not believe it is natural to travel in space.

B. 1. I did not do it.
    2. My statements are all false.
    3. I do not believe it is natural to travel in space.

C. 1. I did not do it.
    2. Only one of my statements is false.
    3. I would like to go with the space travelers when they leave.

WHICH ONE IS GUILTY?

The World's Most Amazing Saddle Theft Puzzle

On several occasions recently, huffalon saddles have been discovered missing from the Village Saddle and Cart Company and there is sufficient evidence to conclude that a thief has been at work. The list of suspected thieves has been narrowed to four employees. All four were on duty during the times that the thefts occurred. The four suspects made the following statements, several of which are false. In fact, no two of the four make the same number of true statements.

A. 1. B is the guilty one.
    2. I was on a fishing trip during the last theft.
    3. No one thinks I am guilty.

B. 1. A is lying; I am not the guilty one.
    2. C has been on duty during every theft.
    3. D is guilty.

C. 1. B's first statement is true.
    2. I agree with A's first statement.
    3. I am not guilty.

D. 1. A's alibi is false.
    2. All of C's statements are false.
    3. I would not think of committing the crime.

WHICH OF THE FOUR SUSPECTS IS GUILTY?

The World's Most Amazing Lying Puzzle

Hyperborea existed long ago, at a time when there were monsters, when it was believed that the world was flat, and when the sun rose out of the eastern ocean and set in the western sea. Hyperborea was situated north of Mount Olympus, home of the gods. The Hyperboreans were much favored by the gods, especially Apollo. A happy people, they lived blissfully in a land of sunshine, abundance, and everlasting springtime. What is little known about the Hyperboreans is their unusual standards of veracity, which provide for a delightful, although sometimes frustrating, type of puzzle, as you will see.

Hyperborea is divided into three regions: those who live in the southern region are known as Sororeans and always speak truthfully; those who live in the northern region are known as Nororeans and always speak falsely, and those who live in the middle region are known as Midroreans and make statements that are alternately true and false, but in which order is unknown.

Apollo decides to visit the Hyperboreans, his most favored people, in disguise. He approaches three inhabitants and asks which region each represents. The three respond, as follows:

A.   I am a Sororean.

B.   I am a Nororean.

C.   1. They are both lying.
        2. I am a Midrorean.

ASSUMING THAT EACH REPRESENTS A DIFFERENT REGION, WHICH IS THE SOROREAN, WHICH IS THE NOROREAN, AND WHICH IS THE MIDROREAN?

The World's Most Amazing One-to-Answer-for-Three Puzzle

In order to establish meaningful dialogue with the inhabitants, it would be helpful to know who is speaking truthfully and who is not. With this in mind, Apollo, perplexed after his meeting with three Hyperboreans, decides on a slightly different tack. He approaches three more inhabitants and directs his attention to one of them, hoping for a more lucid response this time. The three are known to be a Sororean, who always speaks truthfully; a Nororean, who always speaks falsely; and a Midrorean, who makes statements that are alternately true and false, but in which order is unknown. Apollo, much to his consternation, receives this response:

A.   1. I am not the Sororean.
          2. B is not the Nororean.
          3. C is not the Midrorean.

CAN YOU DETERMINE WHICH OF THE THREE IS THE SOROREAN, WHICH IS THE NOROREAN, AND WHICH IS THE MIDROREAN?

The World's Most Amazing Three Fishermen Puzzle

Three Hyperborean fishermen are known to be a Sororean, who always speaks truthfully; a Nororean, who always speaks falsely; and a Midrorean, who makes statements that are alternately true and false, but in which order is unknown. Upon returning from a day of fishing, the three fishermen are engaged in conversation with a visitor. Although one of the fishermen apparently does not feel like speaking, the other two speak, as follows:

A.   1. There were not many fish in our nets today.
      2. B's job is to throw and retrieve the nets.

B.   1. My job is to operate the boat.
      2. We brought in many fish with our nets today.
      3. If C felt like talking, he would truthfully say that he is the Sororean.

WHO IS THE SOROREAN, WHO IS THE NOROREAN, AND WHO IS THE MIDROREAN?

The World's Most Amazing Abacus Abhorrence Puzzle

Progress is coming to Hyperborea in the form of the abacus. While this will mean improved ability to count and to calculate, there is considerable concern among the inhabitants, as it will mean changes for many people. Three Hyperboreans are discussing the new technology. The three are known to be a Sororean, who always speaks truthfully; a Nororean, who always speaks falsely; and a Midrorean, who makes statements that are alternately true and false, but in which order is unknown.

A. 1. C still counts using his fingers and toes.
2. B needs to have his own abacus.
3. I am not the Nororean.

B. 1. I do not need to have my own abacus.
2. I am the Midrorean.

C. 1. I disagree with A's first statement.
2. I am the Sororean.

WHO IS THE SOROREAN, WHO IS THE NORONEAN, AND WHO IS THE MIDROREAN?

The World's Most Amazing Chariot Race Winner Puzzle

Chariot racing is a favorite sport among Hyperboreans, and is very competitive. In a highly contested race, little distance separated the first three finishers, and there was disagreement as to which one was the winner. Hyperboreans are either Sororeans, who always speak truthfully; Nororeans, who always speak falsely; or Midroreans, who make statements that are alternately true and false, but in which order is unknown. Regarding the three chariot racers, which group or groups they represent is uncertain.

BASED ON THE FOLLOWING STATEMENTS, WHO WON THE RACE AND TO WHAT GROUP OR GROUPS DO A, B, AND C BELONG?

A. 1. I was the winner.
    2. B was second.
    3. C was third.

B. 1. I was the winner.
    2. I was well out in front all the way.
    3. C was behind A and me.

C. 1. I was the winner.
    2. A was far behind when I crossed the finish line.
    3. B finished before A.

The World's Most Amazing Disagreeable D Puzzle

Four Hyperboreans are asked to which group or groups they belong. They respond below, although one of them is being disagreeable.

Inhabitants of Hyperborea belong to three groups: Sororeans, who always speak truthfully; Nororeans, who always speak falsely; and Midroreans, who make statements that are alternately true and false, but in which order is unknown.

A. 1. We each belong to a different group.

B. 1. We are all in the same group.

C. 1. We are not at all in the same group.
   2. I am in the same group as B.

D. 1. I disagree with A's statement.
   2. I disagree with B's statement.
   3. I disagree with C's first statement.

WHAT GROUP OR GROUPS ARE REPRESENTED BY THE FOUR HYPERBOREANS?

The World's Most Amazing
Two-Times-Four Shepherd Puzzle

In every group of shepherds in Hyperborea, at least one is a Sororean, who always speaks truthfully, and at least one is a Nororean, who always speaks falsely. A visitor approached four shepherds on a hillside and asked each how many of the four were Sororeans. These answers were given:

  –Three of us are Sororeans.
  –One of us is.
  –There are two of us.
  –None of us are Sororeans.

The visitor approached four more shepherds on another hillside and asked how many were Nororeans. Their answers follow:

  –We are all Nororeans.
  –One of us is.
  –Three of us are.

The fourth shepherd declined to speak.

HOW MANY OF THE SHEPHERDS ON THE TWO HILLSIDES WERE SOROREANS?

The World's Most Amazing Mars Temper Puzzle

Four Hyperboreans were conversing with a visitor, who was actually Mars, god of war, in disguise. The visitor inquired as to their group or groups. Hyperboreans are: Sororeans, who always speak truthfully; Nororeans, who always speak falsely; and Midroreans, who make statements that are alternately true and false, but in which order is unknown. At times the answers to questions put to Hyperboreans can be very frustrating. Mars, who had a short temper, turned all four into frogs. Following are the responses that Mars received to his inquiry:

  A. 1. I am either a Sororean or a Nororean.
      2. B is a Sororean.

  B. 1. I am either a Sororean or a Midrorean.
      2. A is a Midrorean.

  C. 1. I am neither a Nororean nor a Midrorean.
      2. B claims falsely to be either a Sororean or a Midrorean.

  D. 1. I am a Sororean and A is a Nororean.
      2. I disagree with C's second statement.

TO WHAT GROUP OR GROUPS DO A, B, C, AND D BELONG?

The World's Most Amazing Transfer Puzzle

Hyperborea is beginning trade with Ethiopia, which is located in the part of the known world that is south of Mount Olympus. It is rumored that, to establish a trade base, one or more Hyperboreans will be transferred to Ethiopia. Four Hyperboreans are discussing the subject. At least one is a Sororean, who always speaks truthfully; at least one is a Nororean, who always speaks falsely; and at least one is a Midrorean, who makes statements that are alternately true and false, but in which order is unknown. Their statements follow:

A. 1. C said that D is going to be transferred.
    2. The food in Ethiopia is very good.
    3. I applied for the transfer, but I am badly needed here.

B. 1. The food in Ethiopia is not very good.
    2. C said that D is going to be transferred.
    3. A is a Sororean.

C. 1. I did not say that D would be transferred.
    2. D is a Nororean.

D. 1. A is going to be transferred.
    2. The food in Ethiopia is not very good.
    3. C said that I am going to be transferred.

WHICH EMPLOYEE IS THE SOROREAN, WHICH IS THE NOROREAN, WHICH IS THE MIDROREAN, AND TO WHICH GROUP DOES THE FOURTH EMPLOYEE BELONG?

The World's Most Amazing Outlier Puzzle

The land of Hyperborea has several well-established conventions to which all Hyperboreans should adhere. Certainly, their unusual standards of veracity are important to the land's traditions. There are the few odd inhabitants, though, who do not accept the value of conventions. The following statements are made by four inhabitants, who are engaged in a discussion. One is a Sororean, who always speaks truthfully; one is a Nororean, who always speaks falsely; one is a Midrorean, who make statements that are alternately true and false, but in which order is unknown. Some would say that one of the four is not a true Hyperborean. At any rate, this individual does not follow the customary rules of veracity and must be considered an Outlier.

WHICH ONE IS THE SOROREAN, WHICH ONE IS THE NOROREAN, WHICH ONE IS THE MIDROREAN, AND WHICH ONE IS THE OUTLIER?

A. 1. My statements are not all truthful.

    2. We are overworked.

    3. We are all lucky to be here.

    4. We Hyperboreans are favored by the gods.

B. 1. I agree with A's third statement.

    2. Every time I see a visitor, I think maybe it is one of the gods, in disguise.

    3. I am doing more than my share of the work.

    4. My statements are all truthful.

C. 1. My statements are all truthful.

    2. D's second statement is false.

    3. The gods do not visit us in disguise.

    4. We are all overworked.

D. 1. C's first statement is truthful.

    2. B's third statement is truthful.

    3. My statements are all truthful.

    4. The gods frequently visit us in disguise.

The World's Most Amazing Hyperborean Hero Puzzle

Hyperboreans recognized heroes as those warriors who had single-handedly vanquished monsters. Each of five Hyperboreans, Actaeon, Ceyx, Minos, Nisus, and Pyramus, had accomplished this feat. They defeated one sea serpent, two griffins (whose bodies were lions and heads and wings were eagles), and two chimaeras (whose foreparts were lions and hindquarters were dragons).

All Hyperboreans are either Sororeans, who always speak truthfully; Nororeans, who always speak falsely; Midroreans, who make statements that are alternately true and false, but in which order is unknown; or those few Outliers who do not abide by the land's traditions.

How truthful an Outlier's statements are is unknown, except that they are not the same as those who are Sororeans, Nororeans, or Midroreans. As to the five heroes, little is known of their standards of veracity, except that one of them, and only one, is an Outlier.

BASED ON THEIR STATEMENTS BELOW, DETERMINE THE GROUP OF EACH HERO, AND WHAT TYPE OF MONSTER EACH DEFEATED.

Actaeon: 1. Everything Minos states is false.
2. I did not defeat a griffin.
3. Ceyx defeated a griffin.
4. I agree with Nisus' first statement.

Ceyx: 1. I defeated a sea serpent.
2. Minos did not defeat a chimaera.
3. Nisus defeated a chimaera.
4. Actaeon defeated a griffin.

Minos: 1. I agree with Actaeon's first statement.
2. Ceyx did not defeat a chimaera.
3. Actaeon is not a Sororean.
4. I defeated a sea serpent.

Nisus: 1. Minos' third statement is false.
2. I defeated a chimaera.
3. Actaeon did not defeat a griffin.
4. Pyramus defeated a chimaera.

Pyramus: 1. Nisus defeated a sea serpent.
2. Minos is a Midrorean.
3. Actaeon is not a Nororean.
4. Ceyx defeated a chimaera.

The World's Most Amazing Multiple-Level-Living Puzzle

This is a land of the future. The Knowheyan civilization is an advanced one, and the inhabitants are observed to be of great height and intelligence. A peculiarity of Knowheyans, however, is that they always speak in negative sentences, which, in itself, can be puzzling. Because of the strange language spoken by the Knowheyans, an interpreter is provided to serve as a guide in this section and to respond to questions that might be asked.

The land of Knowhey is small and has a large population. Because of limited space Knowheyans live in multiple-level residential buildings. Six inhabitants each occupy a different level in a six-level building. The interpreter explains, in typical Knowheyan fashion, which inhabitant lives on which level, as follows:

1. A does not live above the third level.
2. Neither C nor E lives above either D or F.
3. F does not live below A or B, and does not live above D.
4. E does not live below B or above A.

WHICH INHABITANT LIVES ON WHICH LEVEL?

The World's Most Amazing Knowheyan Job Puzzle

Five Knowheyans, A, B, C, D, and E, work in a metropolis as Airfoil Technician, Communications Consultant, Space Planner, Lunar Energy Engineer, and Synthetic Food Nutritionist. No two of them are the same age.

The Knowheyan interpreter explains about the jobs and ages of these five inhabitants, as follows:

1. The Communications Consultant is not younger than any of the other four.

2. D is not as old as A and not as young as B, who is not as old as the Lunar Energy Engineer, but not as young as C.

3. The Airfoil Technician is not younger than the Space Planner, who is not younger than the Synthetic Food Nutritionist.

4. C is not the youngest of the five.

WHAT IS THE JOB OF EACH OF THE FIVE KNOWHEYANS?

The World's Most Amazing Knowheyan Art Fair Puzzle

Knowheyans are not negative by nature; it is just that their way of expressing themselves, using negative sentences, makes it appear that way. Several fortunate visitors have an opportunity to attend the Midseason Art Fair, in which they are able to observe a variety of Knowheyan art forms. An artists' competition was held as a part of the fair and awards were given for the top four entries, which were collage painting, holography, laser etchings, and reconstituted materials sculpture. The interpreter is explaining the results of the competition to the visitors:

1. A, who was not the first-place winner, did not enter a holograph.
2. The fourth-place winner did not enter a sculpture or a holograph.
3. The one who entered the collage painting, who was neither A nor C, did not win first or second place.
4. Neither B, nor the one who entered the laser etching, was the fourth-place winner.
5. The third-place winner was neither B nor C.
6. The one who entered the laser etching, who was not A, was not the second-place winner.

WHAT WAS THE ART ENTRY OF EACH OF THE FOUR AND IN WHAT ORDER DID THEY FINISH?

The World's Most Amazing Gulf Game Puzzle

Gulf is a popular game on Knowhey. It is played by hitting a small ball over long distances. The objective is to put the ball into a small hole with a minimum number of hits. The name of the game is derived from the land's terrain, which includes many extended inlets, or gulfs, over which balls must travel. In an attempt to explain the game, the Knowheyan interpreter is describing, in negative Knowheyan fashion, the results of a game played by four inhabitants, A, B, C, and D. Each lost a different number of balls, and no player lost fewer than one or more than four.

1. The player with the highest score did not lose the fewest or the most balls.
2. The one with the second-lowest score, who was not D, did not lose more than three balls.
3. The player with the lowest score did not lose four balls.
4. The one with the highest score lost more than two balls.
5. B did not lose more than three balls or fewer than two balls.
6. The player who lost only one ball was not the one with the lowest score.
7. Neither D, who was not the one with the highest score, nor A, lost more than three balls.

WHAT WAS THE SCORING ORDER OF THE FOUR PLAYERS AND HOW MANY BALLS DID EACH LOSE?

The World's Most Amazing Leisure Time Puzzle

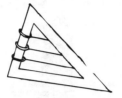

The advanced technology in the land of Knowhey affords the inhabitants considerable leisure time. Four Knowheyans, A, B, C, and D, each enjoys one of four leisure time activities: boating, music, reading, and gulf (a game that involves hitting a small ball long distances, frequently over inlets, or gulfs, over which balls must travel). The time from dawn to dusk is referred to as SP (Solar Period) and is measured in hundredths of SP. No two of the four spend the same amount of time in their leisure time interests.

In response to a question regarding the four Knowheyans' leisure time interests, the interpreter makes the following statements:

1. Neither A nor C plays gulf or is the one who spends .75 SP in leisure time interests.
2. The one who spends .6 SP in leisure time interests does not like boating.
3. The one who spends .9 SP in leisure time interests does not enjoy boating or music.
4. D does not play gulf, nor does A enjoy reading.
5. The one who enjoys boating is not the one who spends .5 SP in leisure time interests.
6. B does not spend .9 SP in leisure time interests.
7. The gulfer does not spend .5 SP in leisure time interests.

CAN YOU DETERMINE WHICH KNOWHEYAN ENJOYS WHICH LEISURE TIME INTEREST AND THE AMOUNT OF TIME EACH DEVOTES TO THE ACTIVITY?

THE WORLD'S MOST CHALLENGING LATERAL THINKING PUZZLES

The World's Most Challenging Apple Puzzle

There were six apples in a basket and six girls in the room. Each girl took one apple, yet one apple remained in the basket. How come?

The World's Most Challenging
President Puzzle

The twenty-second and twenty-fourth presidents of the United States had the same mother and the same father, but were not brothers. How could this be so?

The World's Most Challenging Game, Set, and Match Puzzle

....

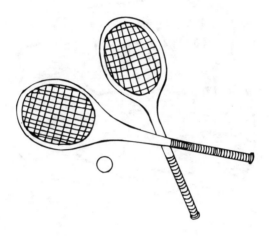

Two men were playing tennis. They played five sets, and each man won three sets. How did they do this?

The World's Most Challenging Wondrous Walk Puzzle

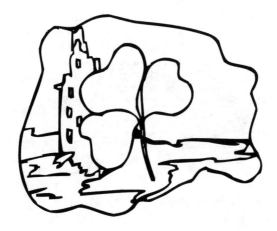

A man walked all the way from Dublin to Cork along main roads without passing a single pub. How did he manage that? (Pubs or "public houses," that is, bars, are very common in Ireland.)

The World's Most Challenging Father-and-Son Puzzle

William's father was older than his grandfather. How did that happen?

The World's Most Challenging Amazing Fall Puzzle

A man who was not wearing a parachute jumped out of a plane. He landed on hard ground yet he was unhurt. Why?

The World's Most Challenging Good Shopping Puzzle

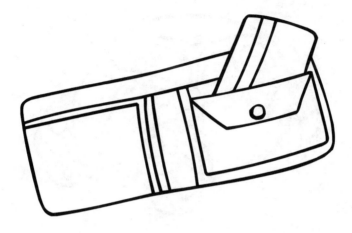

A man got up at 9 A.M. He became so engrossed in his newspaper, he did not have time to go out and shop as he had planned. At 11 A.M. he went for a flying lesson. He carefully followed all the instructions given to him by his instructor until he came in to land. He then ignored his instructor and crashed the plane, killing them both. The accident would not have happened if he had gone shopping, which just goes to show how important shopping can be. Why should this be so?

The World's Most Challenging Turn-to-Drive Puzzle

Two brothers were talking. One said, "I am fed up with living in Birmingham because I have to drive all the time. Why don't we move to London?" His brother replied, "But that would mean that I would have to drive all the time." Why was this true?

The World's Most Challenging See-Saw Puzzle

A deaf man needed to buy a saw to cut some wood. He went into a hardware store. How did he indicate to the storekeeper that he wanted to buy a saw?

The World's Most Challenging Lookout Puzzle

Two sentries were on duty outside a barracks. One faced up the road to watch for anyone approaching from the north. The other looked down the road to see if anyone approached from the south. Suddenly one of them said to the other, "Why are you smiling?" How did he know that his companion was smiling?

The World's Most Challenging Deadly Drive Puzzle

A man drove to and from work every day along a dangerous and twisty mountain road. However, he knew the road very well, so he could drive quickly yet safely. One day, while he was at work, his car was broken into and several items were stolen. As the car was not damaged, the man got in and started driving. He never reached home. His car swerved off the road and he was killed. Why?

The World's Most Challenging
Man-in-an-Elevator Puzzle

Bill was on holiday. He stayed on the fifth floor of a hotel. Every morning at 8 A.M. he took the elevator down to the lobby on the first floor, had breakfast, and then took the elevator back up to the fifth floor. Every evening at 8 P.M. he took the elevator down to the lobby and then he walked up the five flights of stairs and went back to his room. He did not like walking up all those stairs, so why did he do it?

The World's Most Challenging
Growing Younger Puzzle

Ben was twenty years old in 1980 but only fifteen years old in 1985. How come?

The World's Most Challenging Habitual Walker Puzzle

A deaf man was very regular in his habits. He arose every morning at 7:35 A.M. and set off for his half-hour morning walk at 7:45. In the course of this walk he went over a level railroad crossing, but he knew that he was quite safe because the first train did not come by until 9 A.M. One morning, although he followed his routine exactly, he was run over by a train at the crossing. What went wrong?

The World's Most Challenging Greenland Puzzle

Greenland is a huge country covered with snow and ice. Why did the man who discovered it call it Greenland?

The World's Most Challenging Radio Puzzle

A young girl was listening to the radio. Suddenly it went off for a minute and then came back on again. There was nothing wrong with the radio or with the program transmission from the radio station. She did not touch the radio controls. Why did it go off and on?

The World's Most Challenging Boxing Match Puzzle

At the end of a long, hard boxing match, one boxer was knocked out by the other. The judges agreed it was a completely proper victory. Yet during the course of the match, no man threw a punch. What happened?

The World's Most Challenging Nephew Puzzle

A man and his sister were out shopping one day when the man said, "That boy over there is my nephew." "That is right," replied his sister, "but he is not my nephew." How come?

The World's Most Challenging Barrel Trouble Puzzle

A man filled an empty barrel. It was then lighter than when he started. What did he fill it with?

The World's Most Challenging Rival Fan Puzzle

··

One day, in a crowded room, a supporter of the Brazilian soccer team saw a supporter of his team's great rivals, Argentina. The Brazilian fan walked over to the Argentinian fan and struck him a fierce blow. The Argentinian fan who had been knocked flat got up from the floor, turned around, and then thanked the man who had hit him. Why?

The World's Most Challenging Coming-Up-for-Air Puzzle

As part of a school experiment, a girl was sent to the middle of a nearby city with instructions to collect a sample so that pollution levels could be measured. She was given a glass container with a removable but tight-fitting lid. Of course she noticed that the jar contained comparatively clean air from the school environment. How did she ensure that she excluded this air and retrieved an absolutely accurate sample of the city air?

The World's Most Challenging Nuts Puzzle

A man was changing a wheel on his car when the four nuts used to hold the wheel in place fell into a sewer drain and were lost. He was afraid he was stuck there, but a passing boy made a very useful suggestion which enabled the man to drive off. What was the boy's idea?

The World's Most Challenging Golf Pro Puzzle

Although there are very few golf-tour professionals who are left-handed, most clubs prefer to have left-handed golf pros as instructors. Why?

The World's Most Challenging Deduction Puzzle

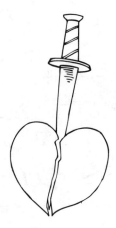

A man suspected his wife of having an affair. One day he told her that he had been suddenly called away on business and would be out of town for a few days. He then left the house, but returned an hour later. His wife was not there, but he quickly discovered the name and address of her lover. How?

The World's Most Challenging Penny Black Puzzle

The famous Penny Black, the world's first postage stamp, was introduced in England in 1840. The idea of postage stamps was a great success and was taken up worldwide. Yet the Penny Black was in use for only one year before it was replaced by the Penny Red. Why?

The World's Most Challenging Flat Tire Puzzle, I

A man woke up one morning to find that one of the wheels of his car had a completely flat tire. Despite this, he set off in his car and drove 100 miles to visit a customer. He then drove 100 miles home. He did not repair or inflate the flat tire. How did he manage to make the journey?

The World's Most Challenging Flat Tire Puzzle, II

Four college students arrived late for a lecture, explaining to their instructor that their car had suffered a flat tire on the way there. How did the clever lecturer immediately show those assembled that the late arrivals were not telling the truth?

The World's Most Challenging Bottled-Fruit Puzzle

We all know that there's a way to get a ship into a bottle. How would you get a full-sized pear into a bottle without damaging the pear, or breaking or cutting the bottle?

The World's Most Challenging Cowboy Fate Puzzle

Cowboys who lived in the Wild West led a dangerous existence. They were at risk from cattle stampedes, Indian attacks, rattlesnakes, disease, and gunfights. However, none of these was the usual cause of death, which was something routine but deadly. What was the most common cause of death among cowboys?

The World's Most Challenging Village Idiot Puzzle

Visitors to a scenic mountain village were often amused by the village idiot. When offered a choice between a shiny fifty-cent piece and a crumpled five-dollar bill, he would always happily choose the half-dollar. The bill was worth ten times as much, so why did he never choose it?

The World's Most Challenging Island Fire Puzzle

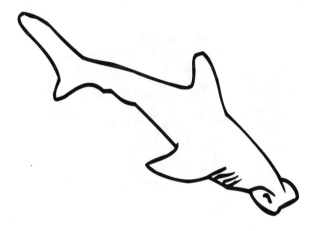

A man is on an island which is one mile long and about 100 yards wide. The grass and shrubs are very dry from a long drought. Suddenly, a fire starts at one end of the island. It is racing toward him along the width of the island fanned by a strong wind blowing in his direction. He cannot take refuge in the sea because it is infested with sharks. There is no beach, just sheer cliffs. What can he do to avoid being consumed by the flames?

The World's Most Challenging Sleepy Kings Puzzle

On one occasion King George II of England went to sleep on the night of September 2 and did not wake up until the morning of September 14. His doctors and advisors were not particularly worried by this. Maybe this was because they knew that a similar sort of thing had once happened to King Henry III of France. He had fallen asleep on December 9 and not woken until December 20. We know that monarchs in those days had a pretty easy life, but what was going on here?

The World's Most Challenging Portrait Puzzle

A man stands looking at a portrait and says, "Sons and brothers have I none, but this person's father is my father's son." Who is in the portrait?

The World's Most Challenging "Winning Isn't Everything" Puzzle

Three friends, Alf, Bert, and Chris, played golf every Saturday for a year. The games were friendly but competitive. They all had the same handicap so whoever took the least strokes won the game and whoever took the most strokes came last. At the end of the year they compared scores to see who was the best, and a furious row broke out. Alf pointed out that he had finished ahead of Bert more often than he had finished behind him. Bert countered that he had finished ahead of Chris more often than he had finished behind him and that Chris had finished ahead of Alf more often than he had finished behind him. How could this be so?

The World's Most Challenging Reluctant Diner Puzzle

....

A businessman came home as usual at 5 P.M. He normally ate dinner as soon as he arrived home. This evening he was very hungry as he had had no lunch. However, despite the fact that all his favorite foods were available and ready to be eaten, he waited until exactly 8 P.M. before dining alone. Why did he wait?

The World's Most Challenging Death-in-a-Car Puzzle

A man went out for a drive. A day later he was found dead in the car. The car had not crashed. How had he died?

The World's Most Challenging Last Cord Puzzle

A man lies dead in a field. Next to him is a long piece of cord. How did he die?

The World's Most Challenging Saturday Flight Puzzle

A man flew into Los Angeles on Saturday. He stayed for three nights at the Beverly Hills Hotel, then spent one night in the Santa Monica Hilton. He then flew out again on Saturday. Between the two flights he never left the Los Angeles area and he did not stay anywhere except those two hotels. How could he arrive and leave on Saturday, yet stay only four nights?

The World's Most Challenging Train Puzzle

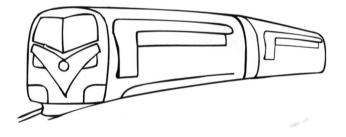

A single train track runs through a tunnel which goes from east to west. One afternoon two trains run along the track at the same speed and enter the tunnel, one going east and the other going west. Neither stops or changes speed, yet they do not crash. Why not?

The World's Most Challenging Copyright Puzzle

How do the publishers of dictionaries or atlases protect themselves from pirates who would copy their work?

The World's Most Challenging Ransom Puzzle

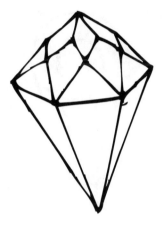

A rich man's son was kidnapped. The ransom note told him to bring a valuable diamond to a phone booth in the middle of a public park. Plainclothes police officers surrounded the park, intending to follow the criminal or his messenger. The rich man arrived at the phone booth and followed instructions but the police were powerless to prevent the diamond from leaving the park and reaching the crafty villain. What did he do?

The World's Most Challenging Moving Part Puzzle

Two common objects carry out the same function. One of the objects has many thousands of moving parts while the other object has no moving parts. What are the objects?

The World's Most Challenging Early Burial Puzzle

John Brown died on Thursday, December 6, and was buried the same week—on Wednesday, December 5, to be precise. How did that happen?

The World's Most Challenging Trouble-and-Strife Puzzle

Mrs. White was happily knitting while her husband watched television. Suddenly the phone rang. Mr. White answered it. He was angry because it was a wrong number, but she was even more angry. Why?

The World's Most Challenging Bath Water Puzzle

....

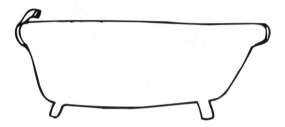

Some time ago, before central heating and water boilers, people would heat water on stoves. At that time, a scullery maid was heating a large pan of water in order to add it to a bathtub which contained some water at room temperature. When the butler saw it, he told her off. "Don't you realize," he said, "that the longer you heat that water on the stove the colder the bath will be when you pour the hot water in?" He was right. Why?

The World's Most Challenging Hold Up Puzzle

A man parked his car outside a bank and rushed in. He held up twenty-five people and ran out with $200. A policeman who saw the whole incident stopped the man. He told him off and then let him go. Why?

The World's Most Challenging Worst Sailor Puzzle

Jim was one of the worst sailors onboard ship. He was surly, lazy, untrustworthy, uncooperative, and always causing trouble. Yet the ship's captain often said of him, "I wish we had ten men like Jim." Why?

The World's Most Challenging Valuable Book Puzzle

A man had a book which was worth $40,000. Why did he deliberately destroy it?

The World's Most Challenging Cuddly Bear Puzzle

At a children's hospital the patients loved to play with the cuddly teddy bears they had there. Unfortunately, the children liked them so much that the bears were disappearing at an alarming rate, as the young patients took them home. How did the hospital solve this problem?

The World's Most Challenging High-Society Dinner Puzzle

···

At a fancy, upper-class dinner party a precious gold coin was being passed around the table for inspection when suddenly the lights went out. When the lights came on again the coin was missing. A search of each guest was ordered. One man refused to be searched. The police were called, but before they arrived the missing coin was found under a saucer. Why did the guest refuse to be searched?

The World's Most Challenging Eight-Year-Old Puzzle

····································

A girl was eight years old on her first birthday. How could that be?

The World's Most Challenging Hole-Covering Puzzle

....

A manhole is a hole which allows someone to gain access to the sewers or other pipes which are below ground. Our local town council recently decided that all the town's manhole covers should be changed from square to round ones. We are used to the town council making silly decisions, but this time they were absolutely right. Why?

The World's Most Challenging
Protagoras Paradox Puzzle

Protagoras was a lawyer in ancient Greece. As an act of kindness, he took on a poor but promising young man as a pupil. He agreed to teach him law, but make no charge until the student had won his first case, when the student would repay his tuition fees. The young man gladly agreed to this plan. The student completed his training, then decided that he did not wish to practice law. Instead, he retired to the countryside to keep goats. Protagoras was disgusted at this waste of talent and training, and dismayed that he would not be reimbursed for the tuition. He decided to sue his pupil in order to recover his fees. If the two men met in court to argue the case, who do you think would have won?

The World's Most Challenging Hand-in-Glove Puzzle

A French glove manufacturer received an order for 5,000 pairs of expensive sealskin gloves from a New York department store. He then learned that there was a very expensive tax on the import of sealskin gloves into the United States. How did he (legitimately) get the gloves into the country without paying the import tax?

The World's Most Challenging School Superintendent Puzzle

A visiting school superintendent noticed that whenever he asked one class a question, all the children would put up their hands. Moreover, although the teacher always chose a different child to answer, the answer was always correct. Why?

The World's Most Challenging Trump Puzzle

....

Can you resolve this argument which arose at a recent bridge match? Spades were trumps. Which is more likely: that a pair of players will have no spades dealt to them, or all the spades dealt to them?

The World's Most Challenging How-to-Beat Nick Faldo Puzzle

••

A man challenged the Masters golf champion to a round of golf on the condition that he be allowed to chose the time and place of their contest. The champion accepted the challenge, but was easily defeated by the challenger. Why?

The World's Most Challenging How-to-Beat Carl Lewis Puzzle

A man challenged the Olympic 100-meter sprint champion to a race over a short distance on the condition that he be allowed to choose the course. How does the man manage to beat the champion? (N.B.: The solution to the preceding problem won't help you here.)

The World's Most Challenging Missing-Furniture Puzzle

A man was doing his job, but was killed because he lacked a certain piece of furniture. Why?

The World's Most Challenging Dead-Man Puzzle

A man lies dead in a room, with a cord tied tightly around his neck. The door has been locked from the inside. Outside of the body, there is nothing else in the room. Remembering that one cannot choke oneself (one would pass out before dying), how did he die?

The World's Most Challenging Busy Hospital Puzzle

St. James Hospital handled all the accident cases for the city. They were kept especially busy by the large number of drivers and passengers injured on the city's roads. To improve road safety, a law was passed making the wearing of seat belts mandatory. Drivers and passengers now started to wear seat belts in their cars. The frequency of road accidents remained exactly the same. However, the hospital was now even busier handling road-accident victims than before. Why?

The World's Most Challenging Fallen Sign Puzzle

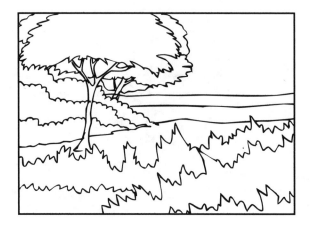

A man was walking in countryside unfamiliar to him. He came to a crossroads where he found that the signpost showing the directions of the roads had fallen over. How did he find out which way to go?

The World's Most Challenging False Fingerprint Puzzle

A man stabbed his wife to death. He was alone with his victim before and after the crime. To throw the police off the scent, he suddenly decided to leave false fingerprints on the murder weapon. How did he do it?

The World's Most Challenging
Found, Lost, Found Puzzle

A man threw something away. He then paid someone else twenty dollars to try to find it, but the search was unsuccessful. Later the man found it easily himself. How?

The World's Most Challenging Disabled Child Puzzle

....

A child was born with his legs so wasted that he would never be able to walk. When they learned this, the child's parents were especially happy that the child was disabled rather than normal and healthy. Why?

The World's Most Challenging Insurance Puzzle

A man's lifelong ambition was to achieve a certain goal, yet he insured himself against achieving it. What was the goal?

The World's Most Challenging Egg Puzzle

Ornithologists now agree that there is a very good reason why birds' eggs are generally narrower at one end than the other. What is the reason?

The World's Most Challenging Guard Dog Puzzle

A landowner boasted that nobody could enter his orchard because of the fierce dog he had guarding it. How did a crafty boy safely gain entrance without damaging the dog in any way?

The World's Most Challenging Last Message Puzzle

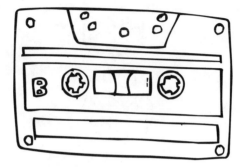

A man was found shot dead in his study. He was slumped over his desk and a gun was in his hand. There was a cassette recorder on his desk. When the police entered the room and pressed the play button on the tape recorder they heard, "I can't go on. I have nothing to live for." Then there was the sound of a gunshot. How did the detective immediately know that the man had been murdered?

The World's Most Challenging Japanese Speaker Puzzle

A Los Angeles businessman took great pains to learn Japanese from a native speaker of the language. He became fluent; his vocabulary and grammar were excellent and his accent was good. When he later went to Japan and started speaking Japanese with a group of businessmen there, they could hardly contain their surprise and amusement at the way he spoke. Why?

The World's Most Challenging Cellar Door Puzzle

A little girl was warned by her parents never to open the cellar door or she would see things that she was not meant to see. One day while her parents were out she did open the cellar door. What did she see?

The World's Most Challenging Deadly Shot Puzzle

A man lay dead in a field. Next to him was a gun. One shot had been fired, and because of that shot the man had died. Yet he had not been shot. In fact, there was no wound or mark on his body. How had he died?

The World's Most Challenging Flat-Out Puzzle

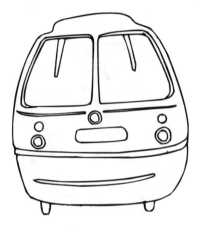

A driver whose car had no brakes was approaching a level crossing at 60 miles per hour while a train was approaching the same crossing also at 60 miles per hour. The crossing was unmanned and had no barriers. The train was 100 yards long and it was 50 yards from the crossing. The car was 100 yards from the crossing. Neither train nor car stopped or changed direction or speed. The driver did not get out of his car. How did he survive the crossing?

The World's Most Challenging Odd-Story Puzzle

Three men went into a café and each had a single cup of coffee. Each put an odd number of lumps of sugar into his cup of coffee. In total they put twelve lumps of sugar in their cups. How many lumps did each consume?

The World's Most Challenging Free-Map Puzzle

At some stage between the two World Wars, the British government decided that it would be desirable to produce accurate maps of the whole country by using the new technique of aerial photography. They were very concerned that the cost of the project would be high, as it involved many flights, much film, and long hours of painstaking matching of photographs. In the end the whole process ended up costing the government nothing. Why not?

The World's Most Challenging Shock Puzzle, I

A man woke up. He lit a match. He saw something and died of shock.
What was going on?

The World's Most Challenging Shock Puzzle, II

A man was searching a trunk in the attic when he found something that caused him to drop dead of fright. What did he find?

The World's Most Challenging Deadly Party Puzzle

A man went to a party and drank some of the punch. He then left early. Everyone else at the party who drank the punch subsequently died of poisoning. Why did the man not die?

The World's Most Challenging Speechless Puzzle

Two men who were good friends had not seen each other for several years. One afternoon they met, but they did not speak to each other. Neither was deaf nor dumb and there was no prohibition on speaking in the place where they met. Why did they not speak to each other?

The World's Most Challenging How-to-Hug Puzzle

A boy was about to go on his first date. Since he had never embraced a girl before, he was anxious to learn a little about how to do it. He went to his local public library and saw a book entitled *How to Hug*. He took it home to read and was greatly disappointed; it gave him no useful advice at all. Why not?

The World's Most Challenging Healthy Dairymaids Puzzle

In the eighteenth century a disease called smallpox was responsible for the deaths of millions of people worldwide. The man whom we can thank for defeating the scourge of smallpox is Edward Jenner, an English country doctor who lived from 1749 to 1823. He noticed that dairymaids never caught smallpox. From this observation he went on to develop a treatment to prevent smallpox and thereby became one of the world's most famous doctors. Why did dairymaids never catch smallpox?

The World's Most Challenging Toothache Puzzle

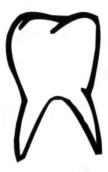

A man was suffering from a toothache, so he went to a dentist and had two bad teeth removed. The dentist had done a good job and the man was pleased that he was no longer in pain. Some time later, in a court case, judgment was rendered against the man and he was forced to pay damages to a third party because he had had those teeth removed. Why should that have been so? (Incidentally, the dentist was not at fault and was not involved in the court case.)

The World's Most Challenging Lake Problem Puzzle

There is a large irregularly shaped lake on your estate. It is of variable and unknown depth. There are no rivers or streams entering or leaving the lake. How would you find the volume of water in the lake?

The World's Most Challenging Realization Puzzle

A man was walking downstairs in a building when he suddenly realized that his wife had just died. How?

The World's Most Challenging Deadly Dish Puzzle

Two men went into a restaurant. They both ordered the same dish from the menu. After they tasted it, one of the men immediately got up from the table, went outside of the restaurant, and shot himself. Why?

The World's Most Challenging Men-in-Uniform Puzzle

Two men are in the back of a van which is parked on a country road. Both men are in uniform. One is dead. The other is angry and frustrated. What happened?

THE WORLD'S MOST
NEARLY IMPOSSIBLE
BRAIN BAFFLERS

··

The World's Most Nearly Impossible
Brain Baffler, One

....

FAREDCE

WHAT WORD, EXPRESSION, OR NAME IS DEPICTED ABOVE?

The World's Most Nearly Impossible Brain Baffler, Two

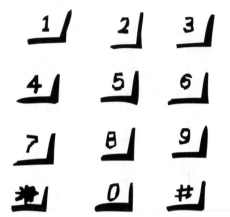

Find a ten-digit number containing each digit once, so that the number formed by the first n digits is divisible by n for each value of n between 1 and 10.

The World's Most Nearly Impossible Brain Baffler, Three

When the examination results were published, one college found that all thirty-two of its students were successful in at least one of the three exams that each of them had taken. Of the students who did not pass Exam One, the number who passed Exam Two was exactly half of the number who passed Exam Three. The number who passed only Exam One was the same as the number who passed only one of the other two exams, and three more than the number who passed Exam One and at least one of the other two exams.

HOW MANY STUDENTS PASSED MORE THAN ONE EXAM?

The World's Most Nearly Impossible Brain Baffler, Four

If eighty-nine players enter a single elimination tennis tournament, how many matches would it take to decide the winner, excluding byes?

The World's Most Nearly Impossible Brain Baffler, Five

....

Using exactly two 2s and any of the standard mathematical symbols, write down an expression whose value is five.

The World's Most Nearly Impossible
Brain Baffler, Six

....

M E
A L

WHAT WORD, EXPRESSION, OR NAME IS DEPICTED ABOVE?

The World's Most Nearly Impossible Brain Baffler, Seven

This puzzle was devised by Dr. Karl Fabel and published in 1949 in "T.R.D.'s Diamond Jubilee" issue of the *Fairy Chess Review*. Squares are numbered 8 to 1 down, and a to h across.

WHITE TO PLAY AND MATE IN SIXTY.

The World's Most Nearly Impossible
Brain Baffler, Eight

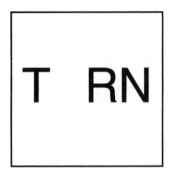

WHAT WORD, EXPRESSION, OR NAME IS DEPICTED ABOVE?

The World's Most Nearly Impossible
Brain Baffler, Nine

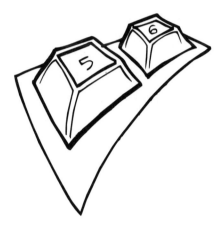

Find a ten-digit number whose first digit is the number of ones in the number, whose second digit is the number of twos in the number, whose third digit is the number of threes in the number, and so on, up to the tenth digit, which is the number of zeros in the number.

The World's Most Nearly Impossible Brain Baffler, Ten

WITHOUT USING A CALCULATOR, GUESS WHICH IS BIGGER: E(PI) OR (PI)E?

The World's Most Nearly Impossible Brain Baffler, Eleven

A selection of eight cards is dealt. with every second card being returned to the bottom of the pack. Thus the top card goes to the table, card two goes to the bottom of the pack, card three goes to the table, card four to the bottom of the pack, and so on. This procedure continues until all the cards are dealt.

The order in which the cards appear on the table is:
A K A K A K A K

HOW WERE THE CARDS ORIGINALLY STACKED?

The World's Most Nearly Impossible Brain Baffler, Twelve

Gambler A chooses a series of three possible outcomes from successive throws of a die, depending simply on whether the number thrown each time is odd (O) or even (E). Gambler B then chooses a different series of three successive possible outcomes. The die is then thrown as often as necessary until either gambler's chosen series of outcomes occurs.

For example, Gambler A might choose the series EOE and B might choose OEE. If successive throws gave, say, EEOOEOE, then A would win the game after the seventh throw. Had the sixth throw been E rather than O, then B would have won.

A has chosen the series EEE; and B, who was thinking of choosing OEE, changes his mind to OOO. Has B reduced his chance of winning the game or is it still the same?

The World's Most Nearly Impossible
Brain Baffler, Thirteen

···

R I

D   N

S K

HOUSE

WHAT WORD, EXPRESSION, OR NAME IS DEPICTED ABOVE?

The World's Most Nearly Impossible
Brain Baffler, Fourteen

Find three different two-digit primes where the average of any two is a prime, and the average of all three is a prime.

The World's Most Nearly Impossible Brain Baffler, Fifteen

··

```
        T   W   E   L   V   E
        T   W   E   L   V   E
        T   W   E   L   V   E
        T   W   E   L   V   E
        T   W   E   L   V   E
  +     T   H   I   R   T   Y
      ─────────────────────────
        N   I   N   E   T   Y
```

Each letter in the sum above represents a different digit. Can you crack the code and discover the uncoded sum?

The World's Most Nearly Impossible Brain Baffler, Sixteen

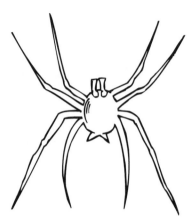

A spider is in a rectangular warehouse measuring 40 x 10 x 10 meters. The spider is on the 10 x 10 meter wall, 5 meters from the sides and 1 meter above the ground. The proverbial fly is on the opposite wall, 5 meters from the sides and 1 meter below the ceiling. What is the shortest route for the spider to walk to the fly?

The World's Most Nearly Impossible
Brain Baffler, Seventeen

···

amUous

WHAT WORD, EXPRESSION, OR NAME IS DEPICTED ABOVE?

The World's Most Nearly Impossible Brain Baffler, Eighteen

In a game of table tennis, twenty-four of the thirty-seven points played were won by the player serving, and Smith beat Jones 21 to 16. Remembering in table tennis that service alternates every five points, who served first?

The World's Most Nearly Impossible Brain Baffler, Nineteen

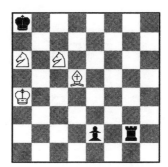

This chess puzzle by C. S. Kipping was published in the *Manchester City News* in 1911. Squares are numbered 8 to 1 down, and a to h across.

WHITE TO PLAY AND MATE IN THREE.

The World's Most Nearly Impossible Brain Baffler, Twenty

·····································

```
┌─────────────────────┐
│                     │
│       EVER          │
│       EVER          │
│       EVER          │
│       EVER          │
│       EVER          │
│                     │
└─────────────────────┘
```

WHAT WORD, EXPRESSION, OR NAME IS DEPICTED ABOVE?

The World's Most Nearly Impossible Brain Baffler, Twenty-One

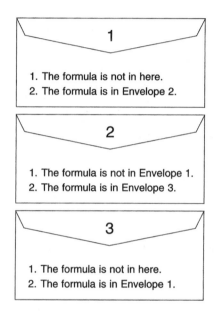

1

1. The formula is not in here.
2. The formula is in Envelope 2.

2

1. The formula is not in Envelope 1.
2. The formula is in Envelope 3.

3

1. The formula is not in here.
2. The formula is in Envelope 1.

In the three envelopes shown, the statements on one of the three are both true, the statements on another are both false, and the remaining envelope has one statement that is true and one that is false.

WHICH ENVELOPE CONTAINS THE FORMULA?

The World's Most Nearly Impossible Brain Baffler, Twenty-Two

How can eleven matches make nine, nine matches make ten, and ten matches make five?

The World's Most Nearly Impossible Brain Baffler, Twenty-Three

···

Caesar and Brutus are playing a game in which each says the next number from a well-known sequence. The first twenty terms of the sequence are given below:

1 2 3 2 1 2 3 4 2 1 2 3 4 3 2 3 4 5 3 2

THE FORTIETH TERM IS 2. IF CAESAR BEGAN THE GAME, WHO WILL BE THE FIRST TO SAY 10?

The World's Most Nearly Impossible Brain Baffler, Twenty-Four

....

WHICH PART OF THE HEART'S PERIMETER IS LONGER: THAT LYING ABOVE THE LINE OF THE ARROW, OR THAT LYING BELOW?

The World's Most Nearly Impossible Brain Baffler, Twenty-Five

BEND
DRAW
DRAW
DRAW

WHAT WORD, EXPRESSION, OR NAME IS DEPICTED ABOVE?

The World's Most Nearly Impossible Brain Baffler, Twenty-Six

....

Last week		This week	Last week		This week
Atomic	1	Atomic	Valentine	21	
Blockbuster	2		What	22	
Classic	3		Xanadu	23	Xanadu
Dizzy	4		YMCA	24	
Emma	5		Zabadak!	25	
Footloose	6		Autumn Almanac	26	
Gaye	7		Angie Baby	27	
Hello	8		Another Day	28	
Intuition	9		Angel Eyes	29	Angel Eyes
Jesamine	10		Angel Fingers	30	
Kayleigh	11		Amateur Hour	31	Amateur Hour
Lamplight	12		Angela Jones	32	New entry
Mickey	13		Ain't Nobody	33	
Night	14		American Pie	34	
Obsession	15		Ant Rap	35	
Perfect	16		Alphabet Street	36	
Question	17		Alternate Title	37	Alternate Title
Reward	18		As Usual	38	
Sandy	19		Adoration Waltz	39	
True	20		Always Yours	40	

This week's chart of the top-forty pop songs has just been published. The song that was at number thirty-five in last week's chart has dropped out, and there is a new entry at number thirty-two. There are also five non-movers, at positions 1, 23, 29, 31, and 37. Of the other thirty-four songs in the new chart, eighteen have moved up and sixteen down, but in every instance the number of positions moved, whether up or down, was a factor (greater than one, but possibly equal to the number itself) of the song's position in last week's chart.

THE TITLES OF LAST WEEK'S TOP-FORTY ARE SHOWN ABOVE. COMPLETE THIS WEEK'S CHART.

The World's Most Nearly Impossible Brain Baffler, Twenty-Seven

WHAT WORD, EXPRESSION, OR NAME IS DEPICTED ABOVE?

The World's Most Nearly Impossible Brain Baffler, Twenty-Eight

··

```
A  N  T
A  S  S
B  A  Y
C  O  Y
D  I  M
E  E  L
F  A  R
M  A  R
P  I  E
S  E  E
T  I  E
T  O  P
W  I  N
```

The above was originally a list of five-letter words, but in each case two consecutive letters (though never the first two) have been removed. The twenty-six missing letters are all different. What was the original list?

The World's Most Nearly Impossible Brain Baffler, Twenty-Nine

There is one in a minute and two in a moment, but only one in a million years. What are we talking about?

The World's Most Nearly Impossible Brain Baffler, Thirty

Find nine different integers from 1 to 20, inclusive such that no combination of any three of the nine integers form an arithmetic progression. For example, if two of the integers chosen were 7 and 13, then that would preclude 1, 10, and 19 from being included.

The World's Most Nearly Impossible Brain Baffler, Thirty-One

·······································

This puzzle was composed by Hans August and Dr. Karl Fabel, and was published in 1949 in *Romana de Sah*. Squares are numbered 8 to 1 down, and a to h across.

WHITE HAS JUST MADE HIS SEVENTEENTH MOVE. WHAT WAS BLACK'S NINTH MOVE, AND WHAT WERE THE MOVES THAT FOLLOWED IT?

The World's Most Nearly Impossible Brain Baffler, Thirty-Two

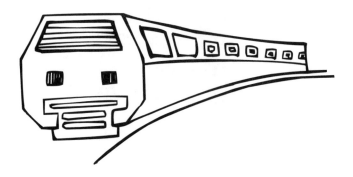

Two travelers set out at the same time to travel opposite ways round a circular railway. Trains start each way every fifteen minutes, on the hour, fifteen minutes past, half past, and forty-five minutes past. Clockwise trains take two hours for the journey, counterclockwise trains take three hours. Including trains seen at the starting point and the ones they are traveling on, how many trains did each traveler see on his journey?

The World's Most Nearly Impossible Brain Baffler, Thirty-Three

....

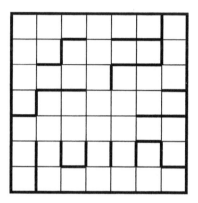

The Roman numerals still in use are I = 1, V = 5, X = 10, L = 50, C = 100, D = 500, and M = 1000. Examples of four Roman numbers are VIII = 8, LXXVI = 76, CXXXVI = 136, and MDCCCLXII = 1862.

Today, the Roman numerals IIII, VIIII, and DCCCC are usually abbreviated as IV, IX, and CM, respectively, a numeral to the left of a higher numeral denoting subtraction. Where there is an opportunity, these abbreviations are used in this cross-number, together with CD for CCCC, XC for LXXXX, and XL for XXXX. Thus 1904 would be written as MCMIV and 49 as XLIX. Note that the logical extension of this method of abbreviation, such as IL for 49, for example, was never fully developed and so is not used here. All that is used, where there is an opportunity, are the six usual abbreviations already mentioned.

In the grid above, all answers are Roman numerals and, when converted to Arabic (standard) numbers, are palindromes (none starting with zero) of two digits or more. One number occurs twice, the rest are all different.

CAN YOU FILL THE GRID?

The World's Most Nearly Impossible Brain Baffler, Thirty-Four

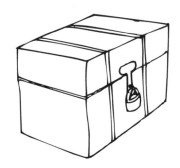

We place in a box thirteen white marbles and fifteen black. We also have twenty-eight black marbles outside the box.

We remove two marbles from the box. If they have a different color, we put the white one back in the box. If they have the same color, we put a black marble in the box. We continue doing this until only one marble is left in the box.

WHAT IS ITS COLOR?

at
the
•
of
on

WHAT WORD, EXPRESSION, OR NAME IS DEPICTED ABOVE?

The World's Most Nearly Impossible Brain Baffler, Thirty-Six

A drawer contains a number of red and blue socks. If I pull two out at random, then the chance of them being a red pair is a half and the chance of them being a blue pair is a twelfth. How many socks are in the drawer?

The World's Most Nearly Impossible Brain Baffler, Thirty-Seven

A long time ago, you could buy eight hens for a dollar or one sheep for a dollar, and cows were ten dollars each. A farmer buying animals of each type bought a hundred animals for a hundred dollars. What animals did he buy?

The World's Most Nearly Impossible Brain Baffler, Thirty-Eight

WHAT WORD, EXPRESSION, OR NAME IS DEPICTED ABOVE?

The World's Most Nearly Impossible Brain Baffler, Thirty-Nine

ARE 1997 NICKELS WORTH MORE THAN 1992 NICKELS?

The World's Most Nearly Impossible Brain Baffler, Forty

INSERT THE MISSING LETTER:

J ? M A M J J A

The World's Most Nearly Impossible Brain Baffler, Forty-One

In a league of four soccer teams, each team played the other three teams. Two points were awarded for a win and one point for a tie. After all six games were played, a final league table was prepared, as shown below:

TEAM	WON	TIED	LOST	GOALS FOR	GOALS AGAINST	POINTS
A	3	0	0	6	1	6
B	1	1	1	2	4	3
C	1	0	2	2	2	2
D	0	1	2	2	5	1

WHAT WAS THE SCORE IN EACH OF THE SIX GAMES?

The World's Most Nearly Impossible Brain Baffler, Forty-Two

Lynsey is a biology student. Her project for this term is measuring the effect of an increase in vitamin C in the diet of twenty-five laboratory mice. Each mouse will have a different diet supplement of between 1 to 50 units. Fractions of a unit are not possible.

Although the university pays for the mice's food, Lynsey has to buy the vitamin C supplement herself. The first consideration in designing this experiment was therefore to minimize the total number of supplements.

The second consideration was that no mouse should have an exact multiple of another mouse's supplement. Thus, if one mouse was on a supplement of 14 units, then this would preclude supplements of 1, 2, 7, 28, and 42 units.

WHAT SUPPLEMENTS SHOULD LYNSEY USE?

The World's Most Nearly Impossible Brain Baffler, Forty-Three

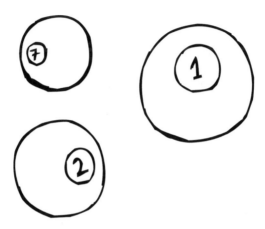

Find two ten-digit numbers, each containing the digits from 0 to 9 once and once only, with the property that successive pairs of digits, from left to right, are divisible in turn by 2, 3, 4, 5, 6, 7, 8, 9, and 10.

The World's Most Nearly Impossible
Brain Baffler, Forty-Four

··

STEP
PETS
PETS

WHAT WORD, EXPRESSION, OR NAME IS DEPICTED ABOVE?

The World's Most Nearly Impossible Brain Baffler, Forty-Five

··

1
11
21
1211
111221
312211
13112221
1113213211
31131211131221

WHAT ARE THE NUMBERS IN THE TENTH LINE OF THE ABOVE PYRAMID?

The World's Most Nearly Impossible
Brain Baffler, Forty-Six

WHAT WORD, EXPRESSION, OR NAME IS DEPICTED ABOVE?

The World's Most Nearly Impossible
Brain Baffler, Forty-Seven

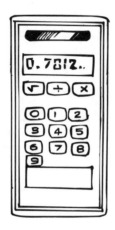

LAGER
  x 4
_____

REGAL

WHAT DIIGIT DOES EACH LETTER REPRESENT IN THE MULTIPLICATOIN ABOVE, GIVEN THAT NO TWO LETTERS STAND FOR THE SAME DIGIT?

The World's Most Nearly Impossible Brain Baffler, Forty-Eight

WHAT WORD, EXPRESSION, OR NAME IS DEPICTED ABOVE?

The World's Most Nearly Impossible Brain Baffler, Forty-Nine

Letters other than "x" each represent a different digit. An "x," however, may represent any digit. There is no remainder. Find which digits the letters and each "x" stand for:

```
                        O   N   E
        _____
T  R  Y )  T   H   I   S   x
           x   x   x
           _____
               x   x   x
               x   x   x
               _____
                   x   x   x   x
                   x   x   x   x
                   _____
```

The World's Most Nearly Impossible Brain Baffler, Fifty

The number 6 has factors (not counting itself) of 1, 2, and 3, which add up to 6. The number 28 has the same property, since its factors, 1, 2, 4, 7, and 14, add up to 28. What four-digit number has this property?

The World's Most Nearly Impossible
Brain Baffler, Fifty-One

....

Between noon and midnight, but not counting these times, how often will the minute hand and hour hand of a clock overlap?

The World's Most Nearly Impossible
Brain Baffler, Fifty-Two

WHAT WORD, EXPRESSION, OR NAME IS DEPICTED ABOVE?

The World's Most Nearly Impossible Brain Baffler, Fifty-Three

A set of building blocks contains a number of wooden cubes. The six faces of each cube are painted, each with a single color, in such a way that no two adjacent faces have the same color. Given that only five different colors have been used and that no two of the blocks are identical in their colorings, what is the maximum number of blocks there can be in the set?

The World's Most Nearly Impossible Brain Baffler, Fifty-Four

The Bowls Club has fewer than 100 members. To the nearest whole number, 28 percent of the members are former committee members, 29 percent are current committee members, and 42 percent have never been on the committee. Again, to the nearest whole number, 35 percent of the former committee members are women. What is the total membership of the club?

The World's Most Nearly Impossible Brain Baffler, Fifty-Five

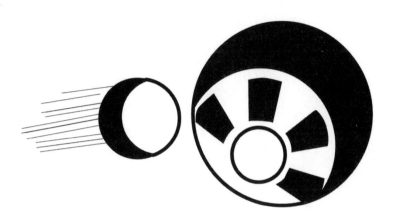

The pars for a nine-hole golf course designed by a mathematician are: 3 3 5 4 4 3 5 5 4

ON WHICH VERY WELL-KNOWN SERIES (AS WELL-KNOWN AS ONE, TWO, THREE, ETC.) ARE THE PARS BASED?

The World's Most Nearly Impossible
Brain Baffler, Fifty-Six

This may seem self-contradictory, but find three integers in arithmetic progression (that is, with equal differences, such as 230, 236, and 242) whose product is prime.

The World's Most Nearly Impossible Brain Baffler, Fifty-Seven

1248 1632 6412 8256

WHAT IS THE NEXT TERM IN THE SERIES?

The World's Most Nearly Impossible Brain Baffler, Fifty-Eight

WHAT WORD, EXPRESSION, OR NAME IS DEPICTED ABOVE?

The World's Most Nearly Impossible Brain Baffler, Fifty-Nine

The ages of Old and Young total forty-eight. Old is twice as old as Young was when Old was half as old as Young will be when Young is three times as old as Old was when Old was three times as old as Young. How old is Old?

The World's Most Nearly Impossible
Brain Baffler, Sixty

Consider a 5 x 5 version of a chessboard with one player having five queens and the other player three queens. There are no other pieces. Can you place the queens on the board so that neither player's queens can capture one of his or her opponent's queens?

The World's Most Nearly Impossible Brain Baffler, Sixty-One

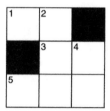

ACROSS
1. Starting piece between 3 and 4
3. 2-Down minus a perfect square
5. Three!

DOWN
2. A perfect square
4. 1.5 times 5-Across
   (or two-thirds of 5-Across)

The World's Most Nearly Impossible Brain Baffler, Sixty-Two

....

NE14
10S?

WHAT WORD, EXPRESSION, OR NAME IS DEPICTED ABOVE?

The World's Most Nearly Impossible Brain Baffler, Sixty-Three

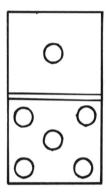

A full set of dominoes (0-0 to 6-6) has been laid out in a rectangular array. The numbers in the diagram represent the spots on the dominoes, and the puzzle is to identify the position of each domino within the pattern.

```
1 2 6 1 6 3 4 5
3 3 6 4 3 2 5 4
3 0 6 0 3 1 2 2
0 5 5 4 6 5 0 2
0 2 5 1 5 0 0 1
6 4 3 4 4 1 1 1
2 2 6 4 5 0 3 6
```

The World's Most Nearly Impossible Brain Baffler, Sixty-Four

At the end of the soccer season, every player had scored a prime number of goals and the average for the eleven players was also a prime number. No player's tally was the same as anyone else's, and neither was it the same as the average.

GIVEN THAT NOBODY HAD SCORED MORE THAN FORTY-FIVE GOALS, HOW MANY GOALS DID EACH PLAYER SCORE?

The World's Most Nearly Impossible
Brain Baffler, Sixty-Five

....

timing

tim   ing

WHAT WORD, EXPRESSION, OR NAME IS DEPICTED ABOVE?

The World's Most Nearly Impossible Brain Baffler, Sixty-Six

Allwyn, Aitkins, and Arthur are to fight a three-way duel. The order in which they shoot will be determined by lot and they will continue to shoot until two are dead. Allwyn never misses, Aitkins is 80 percent accurate, and Arthur, the cleverest of the three, hits his target just half of the time. Who has the best chance of surviving?

The World's Most Nearly Impossible Brain Baffler, Sixty-Seven

··

GR12"AVE

WHAT WORD, EXPRESSION, OR NAME IS DEPICTED ABOVE?

The World's Most Nearly Impossible
Brain Baffler, Sixty-Eight

Can you subdivide a square measuring 11 x 11 into five rectangles such that the five lengths and five widths of the rectangles are all different and integral?

The World's Most Nearly Impossible Brain Baffler, Sixty-Nine

31 62 __ 25 56 __ 19

WHAT ARE THE MISSING NUMBERS?

The World's Most Nearly Impossible
Brain Baffler, Seventy

Find three different positive integers whose factorials are each one less than a perfect square, and whose factorials sum to a perfect square.

The World's Most Nearly Impossible Brain Baffler, Seventy-One

I recently overheard a conversation that went roughly as follows:

Bob: "Here's a problem that might interest you. On my bus this morning there were only three other passengers, all of whom I knew. We discovered that the product of their ages was 2,450, and that the sum was exactly twice your age. How old are they?"

Jim: "Hang on. You haven't given me enough info."

Bob: "Oh, sorry. I forgot to mention that one of the passengers on the bus was someone older than me, and I am—"

Jim: "I know how old you are. And I now know the passengers' ages, too."

HOW OLD ARE JIM, BOB, AND EACH OF THE THREE OTHER PASSENGERS?

The World's Most Nearly Impossible Brain Baffler, Seventy-Two

This puzzle is based on a theme by W. A. Shinkman, and the mate-in-three was first solved by Sam Loyd. The puzzle above was published in the *Leeds Mercury Supplement* in 1895. Squares are numbered 8 to 1 down, and a to h across.

WHITE TO PLAY AND MATE IN THREE.

The World's Most Nearly Impossible Brain Baffler, Seventy-Three

··

Squares are numbered 8 to 1 down, and a to h across.

**WHITE TO PLAY AND MATE IN THREE. CONSTRUCT A GAME
THAT WILL LEAVE THE POSITION SHOWN ABOVE AFTER
BLACK'S SIXTEENTH MOVE.**

The World's Most Nearly Impossible Brain Baffler, Seventy-Four

In a game of poker, one of the hands of five cards had the following features:

- There was no card above a 10 (an ace is above a 10 in poker).
- No two cards were of the same value.
- All four suits were represented.
- The total values of the odd and even cards were equal.
- No three cards were in sequence.
- The black cards totaled 10 in value.
- The hearts totaled 14.
- The lowest card was a spade.

WHAT WAS THE HAND?

The World's Most Nearly Impossible Brain Baffler, Seventy-Five

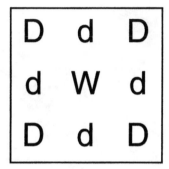

WHAT WORD, EXPRESSION, OR NAME IS DEPICTED ABOVE?

The World's Most Nearly Impossible Brain Baffler, Seventy-Six

"Bookkeeper" has three consecutive double letters. What common two-word phrase, if you remove the space, also has three consecutive double letters?

The World's Most Nearly Impossible Brain Baffler, Seventy-Seven

···

ON

THE THE

WHAT WORD, EXPRESSION, OR NAME IS DEPICTED ABOVE?

The World's Most Nearly Impossible Brain Baffler, Seventy-Eight

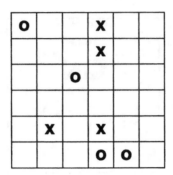

Divide the above figure into four identical parts, with each part made up of whole squares only. Each of the four parts should also contain one O and one X, but not necessarily in the same relative positions.

The World's Most Nearly Impossible Brain Baffler, Seventy-Nine

Use each of the numbers 1, 5, 6, and 7 once and once only, parentheses as required, and any combination and any number of the following symbols:

+ − x /

FIND AN EXPRESSION THAT EQUALS 21.

The World's Most Nearly Impossible Brain Baffler, Eighty

P and Q are integers that between them contain each of the digits from 0 to 9 once and once only. What is the maximum value of P x Q?

The World's Most Nearly Impossible Brain Baffler, Eighty-One

···

COTAXME

WHAT WORD, EXPRESSION, OR NAME IS DEPICTED ABOVE?

The World's Most Nearly Impossible
Brain Baffler, Eighty-Two

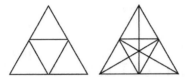

A total of five triangles can be seen in the diagram on the left.

HOW MANY TRIANGLES CAN BE FOUND IN THE DIAGRAM ON THE RIGHT?

The World's Most Nearly Impossible Brain Baffler, Eighty-Three

WHAT WORD, EXPRESSION, OR NAME IS DEPICTED ABOVE?

The World's Most Nearly Impossible Brain Baffler, Eighty-Four

....

In this long division, each "x" represents a digit. Find which digits each "x" stands for:

```
                        x   x   .   x   x   x
              _____
   x   x   )  x   x   x   x
              x   x
              _____
              x   x   x
              x   x
              _____
                  x   x
                  x   x
                  _____
                  x   x   x
                  x   x   x
                  _____
                          x   x
                          x   x
                          _____
```

The World's Most Nearly Impossible Brain Baffler, Eighty-Five

Five soccer teams, United, County, Rovers, Albion, and Thistle, took part in a league tournament. Their colors were white, yellow, green, red, and blue, though not necessarily in that order. No teams were tied in the standings at the end of the tournament. From the following information, determine for each team its captain, colors, and position in which it finished in the league.

- Rovers did not win the league, but finished higher than fourth.
- Neither Albion nor the team in green finished in the top three.
- Evans captained the team in yellow.
- Cooke's team finished ahead of County, which was captained by Dixon.
- Allen's team finished second and Boyle's team finished last.
- The team in white finished lower than both United and the team in blue, but above Evans's team.
- Albion was not the green team and United was not the blue team.

The World's Most Nearly Impossible Brain Baffler, Eighty-Six

Symphon

WHAT WORD, EXPRESSION, OR NAME IS DEPICTED ABOVE?

The World's Most Nearly Impossible Brain Baffler, Eighty-Seven

······································

5	1	4
6	3	8
2	7	9

Arrange the digits from 1 to 9 in a 3 x 3 array in such a way that the sum of a number's immediate neighbors (including diagonals) is a multiple of that number.

The example shows an unsatisfactory attempt. The three numbers bordering 9 add to 18, which is a multiple of 9 as required, and the numbers bordering 1, 2, 3, 4, and 5 also meet the condition specified. The numbers bordering 6, 7, and 8, however, do not meet the required condition.

THE WORLD'S
MOST INTENSE FALSE
LOGIC PUZZLES

·······································

The World's Most Intense Mule Puzzle

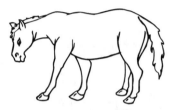

Socrates is credited with being the first known formal logic thinker. He devoted his life to expanding his knowledge, and helping others to do the same. His method was to employ a questioning technique using given propositions and arriving at answers by deductive reasoning. Since Socrates was known among his fellow Athenians as possessing great skill in analysis and deductive reasoning, he was frequently called upon to resolve disputes and to solve crimes.

Each of the puzzles in this section involves problems or crimes, and contains statements by individuals, some of which are true and some of which are false. To find the solutions it is necessary to determine which statements are false and which are not.

Three farmers who have shared the use of a mule for some time disagree as to who owns the animal. It is not certain, however, that the responsibility of ownership is desired. They have asked Socrates to settle the issue. The three make the following statements. Each makes one true and one false statement.

A. 1. It is C's mule.
   2. I can make no claim to it.

B. 1. C has no right to it.
   2. It is A's mule.

C. 1. It is my mule.
   2. B's second statement is false.

SOCRATES HESITATES FOR SCARCELY AN INSTANT AND DETERMINES THE OWNER. TO WHICH FARMER DOES THE MULE BELONG?

The World's Most Intense Writings of Homer Puzzle

Valuable writings of Homer are missing. They have been stolen from the library in the Parthenon by one of three suspects. The three are questioned by Socrates, and each makes one true and two false statements, as follows:

A. 1. I did not even know that Homer's books were in the Parthenon.
    2. C is innocent.
    3. B must be the thief.

B. 1. I did not do it.
    2. A is innocent.
    3. A's first statement is true.

C. 1. Homer's writings are not worth taking.
    2. A did it; or else it was B.
    3. I would never consider such a dishonest thing.

WHICH ONE IS GUILTY?

The World's Most Intense Open Cellar Door Puzzle

When Socrates was imprisoned for being a disturbing influence, he was held in high esteem by his guards. All four of them hoped that something would occur that would facilitate his escape. One evening the guard who was on duty intentionally left the cell door open so that Socrates could leave for distant parts.

Socrates did not attempt to escape, as it was his philosophy that if you accept society's rules, you must also accept its punishments. However, the open door was considered by the authorities to be a serious matter. It is not clear which guard was on duty that evening. The four guards make the following statements in their defense:

A. 1. I did not leave the door open.
   2. C was the one who did it.

B. 1. I was not the one who was on duty that evening.
   2. A was on duty.

C. 1. B was the one who was on duty that evening.
   2. I hoped Socrates would escape.

D. 1. I did not leave the door open.
   2. I am not surprised that Socrates did not attempt to escape.

CONSIDERING THAT, IN TOTAL, THREE STATEMENTS ARE TRUE, AND FIVE STATEMENTS ARE FALSE, WHICH GUARD IS GUILTY?

The World's Most Intense Secret Observer Puzzle

As Socrates' reputation grew, there were those who were jealous of his fame, and who had been embarrassed by his method of cross-examining to gain the truth. There was a movement to indict Socrates as a negative and disturbing influence. A citizen was chosen to secretly pose as a student of Socrates, to observe his teaching and gain evidence against him. Socrates was informed that one of four followers was, in reality, such an observer. Socrates questioned the four. Their statements follow. All statements are true except any mentioning the secret observer.

    A.   1. C is definitely a student, here to learn.
           2. D is a stranger to me.

    B.   1. A and D are not acquainted.
           2. C is not the observer.

    C.   1. B's first statement is false.
           2. A's second statement is true.

    D.   1. C's first statement is false.
           2. A's first statement is true.

WHICH OF THE FOUR SPEAKERS IS THE OBSERVER?

The World's Most Intense Statue of Athena Puzzle

A piece from the gold-and-ivory statue of Athena was stolen. There was evidence that the thief, acting alone, entered the temple in the dead of night and used a large hammer to dislodge a piece of the statue. Socrates agreed to cross-examine four suspects, all of whom were in Athens when the crime occurred. One of them is guilty. One suspect makes three true statements; one suspect makes three false statements. As to the truthfulness of the statements by the other two suspects, little is known. Their statements follow:

A. 1. I did not do it.
   2. I was in Philius when the crime occurred.
   3. B is guilty.

B. 1. I am innocent.
   2. C owns a large hammer.
   3. C was seen at the Acropolis late that night.

C. 1. I do not own a large hammer.
   2. A and B are both guilty.
   3. I went to bed early that night.

D. 1. Only one of my statements is false.
   2. C was out late that night.
   3. I am innocent.

WHICH ONE IS THE THIEF?

The World's Most Intense Victory Parade Leader Puzzle

At the successful end of the war with Persia, it was decided that there should be a parade through the main streets of Athens. At the front of the procession should be the soldier who had led the charge during the last battle, but the identity of this soldier was unclear. Socrates was asked to decide who should lead the parade, and he questioned three candidates. One of them makes one false statement; one makes two false statements, one makes three false statements, as follows:

A. 1. I led the charge in the last battle.
   2. I am clearly the choice to lead the parade.
   3. C was in the reserve ranks during the battle.

B. 1. C did not lead the charge during the last battle.
   2. I am the logical choice to lead the parade.
   3. I could keep in time with the parade music very well.

C. 1. I should be selected.
   2. B would not be able to keep in time with the parade music.
   3. I was not in the reserve ranks during the last battle.

WHICH SOLDIER SHOULD LEAD THE PARADE?

The World's Most Intense Trip of Socrates Puzzle

Socrates wanted to take a trip to Philius, and decided that one of his young followers should accompany him. Three of them expressed keen interest, and Socrates questioned them to determine which one of the three should be selected.

The disciple selected makes three true or three false statements. Of the other two, one makes two true and one false statement, and one makes one true and two false statements. Their statements follow:

A. 1. C is the oldest.
    2. B would not carry the baggage.
    3. I am the one with three true statements.

B. 1. I would carry the baggage.
    2. C will be chosen.
    3. A's first statement is false.

C. 1. I am the oldest, so I should be selected.
    2. B will be selected.
    3. B's third statement is true.

WHICH FOLLOWER DID SOCRATES SELECT TO ACCOMPANY HIM?

The World's Most Intense Statue Repair Puzzle

After the damage to the statue of Athena, Socrates was requested to select the most qualified craftsman to undertake the necessary repairs. He interviewed four recommended craftsmen. Their statements were not all truthful. However, each of the four makes the same number of true statements and the same number of false statements, as follows:

A. 1. I do not have all the necessary tools.
2. D is the most qualified.
3. C is experienced in this type of work.

B. 1. A is the most qualified.
2. D has never worked with ivory.
3. A's first statement is false.

C. 1. I am experienced in this type of work.
2. B is the most qualified.
3. A does not have all the necessary tools.

D. 1. C is the most qualified.
2. A does not have all the necessary tools.
3. I have never worked with ivory.

WHICH CRAFTSMAN SHOULD SOCRATES SELECT?

The World's Most Intense Discus Throw Puzzle

The Athenian Games involved several athletic events. Following the games one season, there was a dispute as to who had won the discus throw. Socrates agreed to question the competitors and determine the winner. The statements of four of the athletes are below. No two make the same number of false statements.

A.   1. C did not win the discus throw.
       2. I was second.
       3. C and I trained together.

B.   1. A was the winner.
       2. I placed a close second.
       3. C and I trained together.

C.   1. B was the winner.
       2. I did not train with anyone.
       3. A was second.

D.   1. A was not the winner.
       2. B was second.
       3. C and I trained together.

WHO WON THE DISCUS EVENT?

The World's Most Intense Food Produce Theft Puzzle

Five citizens were asked to deliver food to the Acropolis to provide a meal for city dignitaries who were meeting there. One delivered bread; one delivered goats' cheese; one delivered honey; one delivered milk; and one delivered nuts. Shortly after the produce was left, significant amounts of the food were found to be missing, illegally acquired, it was determined, by one of the five citizens.

Socrates agreed to cross-examine the suspects. Their statements are below. The one who delivered the milk makes three true statements; the one who delivered the cheese makes two true and one false statement; the one who delivered the honey makes one true and two false statements; and the one who delivered the bread and the one who delivered the nuts each makes three false statements.

A. 1. I did not deliver the bread.
   2. D is the one who stole the food.
   3. B delivered the honey.

B. 1. I did not deliver the cheese.
   2. I am certainly not guilty.
   3. C delivered the honey.

C. 1. I did not deliver the honey.
   2. B's second statement is false.
   3. D is not the thief.

D. 1. I did not deliver the nuts.
   2. A is the thief.
   3. E delivered the bread.

E. 1. I did not deliver the milk.
   2. C stole the food.
   3. A delivered the bread.

WHICH ONE DELIVERED WHICH FOOD PRODUCT, AND WHO IS GUILTY?

The World's Most Intense Open Market Theft Puzzle

A theft has occurred at the Athenian open market. A variety of goods has been stolen including a large quantity that would require a cart to transport.

Four suspects are questioned by Socrates and one of them is the culprit. The statements of the four are below. None of the suspects is completely truthful, and no two make the same number of true statements.

A. 1. D has been to the open market on several occasions.
    2. None of us is guilty.
    3. B, who is a visitor, has been observed at the open market.
    4. All of my statements are false.

B. 1. A is not the guilty one.
    2. D owns a cart.
    3. I have never been to the open market.
    4. D is a visitor to Athens, but has been here several times.

C. 1. A's first and third statements are false.
    2. D does not own a cart.
    3. This is D's first visit to Athens.
    4. B's statements are all true.

D. 1. I do not own a cart.
    2. B is the guilty one.
    3. This is my first visit to Athens.
    4. B's third statement is true.

WHICH OF THE FOUR IS GUILTY?

The World's Most Intense Neptune Communication Puzzle

Somewhere in the far and forlorn reaches of the North Sea is the small island of Ave, on which strange things happen. That the island is watched over by Neptune, and that some say it is enchanted, are only part of its uniqueness. The Isle of Ave is inhabited by an unusual people. Avians have their own standards of veracity.

The inhabitants of the Isle of Ave belong to three groups: Soravians, who always speak truthfully; Noravians, who always speak falsely; and Midravians, who make statements that are alternately truthful and false—in which order is unknown.

Since the Isle of Ave is under his watchful eye, Neptune would like to establish communication with Avians. To do so, it is necessary to know who has what standard of veracity. He approaches three inhabitants, A, B, and C, known to be a Soravian, a Noravian, and a Midravian, not necessarily in that order. He asks one of them two questions:

Neptune: Are you the Soravian?
    A. No

Neptune: Is B the Soravian?
    A. No.

NEPTUNE NOW KNOWS WHICH OF THE THREE IS THE SORAVIAN, WHICH IS THE NORAVIAN, AND WHICH IS THE MIDRAVIAN. DO YOU?

The World's Most Intense Two Avians Puzzle

Avians belong to three different groups: Soravians, who always speak truthfully; Noravians, who always speak falsely; and Midravians, who make statements that are alternately truthful and false, but not necessarily in that order. The two speakers below are known to belong to different groups.

    A. B is a Noravian.
    B. A's statement is truthful.

TO WHAT GROUPS DO A AND B BELONG?

The World's Most Intense Umbrella Selling Puzzle

Since it rains continually on the Isle of Ave, you would think that an umbrella purveyor would find it an ideal place to ply his trade. The problem in dealing with Avians, however, is communication. A visiting seller of umbrellas approaches three Avians and asks which group each represents.

The three are known to be a Soravian, who always speaks truthfully; a Noravian, who always speaks falsely; and a Midravian, who makes statements that are alternately truthful and false, but the order is uncertain. The three make the following statements:

A. C will answer falsely to all questions.
B. A's statement is false.
C. B's statement is false.

Frustrated by his inability to interpret the Avians' statements, the visitor leaves, deciding that it would be best to sell his umbrellas in some other place.

WHICH ONE IS THE SORAVIAN, WHICH ONE IS THE MIDRAVIAN AND WHICH ONE IS THE NORAVIAN?

The World's Most Intense Hippogriff Puzzle

The Isle of Ave seems to be a stopping place for all manner of strange beasts. There is, however, considerable excitement among the inhabitants, as a hippogriff has visited the island for the first time. This monster has the body of a horse and the wings, head, and talons of an eagle. Three inhabitants are discussing the visitor.

The three are known to be a Soravian, who always speaks truthfully; a Noravian, who always speaks falsely; and a Midravian, who makes statements that are alternately truthful and false, or false and truthful. Their statements follow:

A. 1. I have seen hippogriffs on the island several times.
   2. You cannot believe anything that B says.

B. 1. A has never seen a hippogriff before.

C. 1. If A says he has seen hippogriffs on the island before, you can count on it's being true.

WHO IS THE SORAVIAN, WHO IS THE NORAVIAN, AND WHO IS THE MIDRAVIAN?

The World's Most Intense Aspidochelon Catching Puzzle

The aspidochelon is a sea monster so huge that it resembles an island. However it is rumored to be a gastronomical delicacy. Three Avian fishermen are contemplating an aspidochelon hunt.

Avians belong to three different groups: Soravians, who always speak truthfully; Noravians, who always speak falsely; and Midravians, who make statements that are alternately truthful and false, although not necessarily in that order. As to the three fishermen, little is known as to their group or groups. Their statements follow:

A. 1. The last time we caught an aspidochelon, C and I helped hold the net.

 2. I am a Soravian.

B. 1. I am not a Midravian.

 2. We do not know for sure if aspidochelon is good to eat.

 3. A's first statement is false.

C. 1. None of us has ever seen an aspidochelon.

 2. I am a Noravian.

WHAT GROUP OR GROUPS DO THE THREE FISHERMEN REPRESENT?

The World's Most Intense
Disguised Neptune Visitor Puzzle

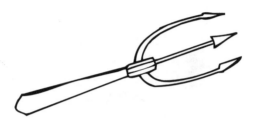

The Avians are watched over by Neptune, who occasionally visits them in disguise. Three Avians are discussing a fourth individual, who may be Neptune in disguise, although there seems to be a difference of opinion.

Inhabitants of Ave are known to be Soravians, who always speak truthfully; Noravians, who always speak falsely; or Midravians who make statements that are alternately truthful and false; or false and truthful. The group or groups of the three speakers below are unknown.

A.   1. I saw D suddenly appear from behind a tree.

     2. None of us is a Soravian.

     3. B is a Noravian.

B.   1. D is Neptune visiting us in disguise.

     2. Only one of us is a Soravian.

     3. I am not a Midravian.

C.   1. D is my next-door neighbor.

     2. A is a Soravian, as is D.

WHAT GROUP OR GROUPS ARE REPRESENTED BY THE THREE SPEAKERS?

The World's Most Intense Truthful Statement Puzzle

Neptune is finding that establishing meaningful dialogue with the Avians is not as easy as he thought it would be. Perhaps he needs to be a little more direct. Neptune steps up to four inhabitants and insists on a truthful statement.

Among the four, at least one is known to be a Soravian, who always speaks truthfully; at least one is known to be a Noravian, who always speaks falsely; and at least one is known to be a Midravian, who makes statements that are alternately truthful and false, but in unknown order. Each makes one statement, as follows:

A. I am either a Soravian, a Noravian, or a Midravian.
B. I am either a Soravian or a Midravian.
C. I am either a Noravian or a Midravian.
D. I am either a Soravian or a Noravian.

CONSIDERING THAT TWO OF THE FOUR STATEMENTS ARE TRUTHFUL AND TWO ARE FALSE, WHAT DOES NEPTUNE NOW KNOW ABOUT EACH OF THE FOUR?

The World's Most Intense Sea Monster Problem Puzzle

Three Avian fishermen are known to be a Soravian, who always speaks truthfully; a Noravian, who always speaks falsely; and a Midravian, who makes statements that are alternately truthful and false. A sea monster has been caught in their nets and the three are discussing the problem, as follows:

A. 1. This is not the first time the sea monster has gotten caught in our nets.
    2. I am going to change jobs if this does not stop happening.
    3. C speaks truthfully only part of the time.

B. 1. This is the first time a sea monster has gotten caught in our nets.
    2. C was so frightened that he fell overboard.
    3. The sea monster took more fish than we did.

C. 1. A is not going to change jobs if this does not stop happening.
    2. I did not fall overboard.
    3. The sea monster did not take more fish than we did.

NEPTUNE RESOLVED THE PROBLEM BY ADVISING THE SEA MONSTER TO LEAVE THE AREA. WHICH IS THE SORAVIAN, THE NORAVIAN, AND THE MIDRAVIAN?

The World's Most Intense Village Fair Puzzle

These puzzles involve the activities of the people who inhabited a shire within the kingdom of Lidd. The puzzles contain statements that provide limited amounts of pertinent information. They afford just enough information for you to arrive at the correct solutions. However, you will find that there is one false statement in each puzzle. To find the correct solution, first determine which statement should be discarded.

The annual village fair is a much anticipated event, and the livestock showings and awards are an important part of the festivities. This year it was necessary to have four separate showings to accommodate the large number of entries: daybreak to midmorning, midmorning to midday, midday to midafternoon, and midafternoon to sundown. One showing was for cows, one for goats, one for pigs, and one for sheep—not necessarily in that order. The animals winning the four categories were owned by Dor, Edvo, Frer, and Har, and one of their entries won the blue ribbon for best animal in the fair.

Of the six statements that follow, five are valid and one is false. Based on these statements, who owned which animals; what was the showing time for each; and which animal was awarded the blue ribbon?

(continued)

1. The sheep escaped from its owner shortly after midmorning and was not recaptured until the next day.

2. Edvo was convinced that his goat would win the blue ribbon.

3. Dor left the show with her entry at midday and did not return.

4. The blue ribbon winner was entered in the midday to midafternoon showing, immediately following the goat's showing.

5. Frer's animal was entered in a later showing than that in which the pig was entered.

6. Edvo's animal was entered in the first showing of the day.

The World's Most Intense Dragon Meduso Puzzle

A comely village lass had been captured by the dreaded dragon Meduso. This dragon was not only large and fierce, with fiery breath, but had the power to turn anyone to stone who looked directly into his eye. The village leaders appealed to the King for knightly assistance to free the lass. Sir Hector, who had the duty that day, set out on his steed.

Sir Hector made four attempts to rescue the village lass. In one attempt, he used his peripheral vision to fight the dragon. However, the smoke and fire from Meduso's breath caused irritation to his eyes and the resulting tears restricted his vision. In another attempt, he used his highly polished shield as a mirror in which to see the dragon, but clouds of smoke from the dragon's breath obscured the reflection. In one attempt, he slipped into the cave at night while the dragon was sleeping. However, the dragon, who was a very light sleeper, awoke and chased Sir Hector from the cave. In another attempt, he blindfolded himself and located the dragon by his sound. However, his lance struck a sturdy oak tree, jolting him from his mount.

As Sir Hector was preparing for a fifth attempt, his squire arrived with the news that the fair damsel had returned, having escaped while the dragon was out foraging for food.

(continued)

From the following statements, what was the sequence of Sir Hector's four attempts to rescue the village lass? Of the six statements below, five are valid and one is false.

1. At least one other attempt followed Sir Hector's attempt to use his peripheral vision.

2. Sir Hector's attempt to use a blindfold was not immediately before or immediately after the attempt to slip into the cave.

3. The attempt by Sir Hector to slip into the dragon's cave was not his fourth attempt.

4. Sir Hector's attempt to use his polished shield was immediately before his attempt to slip into the dragon's cave.

5. Sir Hector's attempt to use a blindfold was not after his attempt to use his polished shield.

6. Sir Hector's attempt to use his peripheral vision was not immediately before or immediately after his attempt to use a blindfold.

The World's Most Intense Dragon Watch Puzzle

Because of the ever present danger of dragons, the villagers took turns keeping watch. During one particular period, five people were assigned watch duty, each on one of five shifts. Their ages varied, with no two being the same age. From the statements below, determine the order in which the watches were held and the relative age of each of the five villagers. One statement below is false; the others are valid.

1. Har was not the oldest, the youngest, nor did he have the first or fifth watch.

2. The youngest of the five, who was neither Edvo nor Tolo, did not have the fifth watch.

3. Winn was younger and had a later watch than Edvo, who stood a later watch and was younger than Frer.

4. Tolo, who was not the second oldest or fourth oldest, was older than Har, and had an earlier watch than Frer.

5. Edvo's relative position in the order of the watches was the same as his relative position in age.

6. Har was next to Tolo in age and next to Edvo in the order of watches held.

7. The fourth oldest held a later watch than Tolo, but an earlier watch than Edvo, who had a later watch and was younger than Frer.

8. The one who held the second watch was the oldest of the five villagers.

The World's Most Intense New Pony Puzzle

Ponies were used for labor and were the primary means of transportation in Farmwell. Four villages, who were neighbors, each recently acquired a pony. One was black; one was palomino, one was gray; and one was white. They varied in height from nine to twelve hands, no two being the same height. The four neighbors were Boro, Jes, Kover, and Tolo. Their second names were Son of Alfo, Son of Dirk, Son of Evel, and Son of Fergy, not necessarily in that order.

From the statements below, determine the first name and second name of each of the four neighbors, and the color and height of the pony each acquired. One of the six statements is false, the rest are valid.

1. Tolo, who lived next to Son of Fergy and across from Son of Evel, did not acquire a pony that was ten hands high, nor was his new pony's color palomino or black; his pony was acquired immediately after Kover's pony.

2. Boro, whose new pony was white, was the second to acquire a pony, followed by Son of Evel, whose pony was not eleven hands high.

3. Son of Dirk's new pony was the second one to be acquired; it was neither nine hands high nor eleven hands high.

4. The last of the four to acquire a pony did not own the one that was eleven hands high.

5. Son of Alfo, who lived next to Kover, acquired a black pony.

6. The neighbor whose new pony was twelve hands high was the first of the four to acquire a pony.

The World's Most Intense Work and Recreation Puzzle

The villagers were industrious, each working hard at a particular trade. Among five of them, one was a weaver, one was a carpenter, one was a blacksmith, one was a cobbler, and one was a miller.

A happy people, they enjoyed singing, dancing, instrumental music, telling stories, and sharing puzzles. Each had a favorite and a second-favorite activity. Based on the statements below, what was the vocation of each and what was the favorite and second-favorite activity of each? No two had the same favorite and no two had the same second-favorite. One statement below is false; the rest are true.

1. The one whose favorite activity was singing was much in demand because of the simplicity and high quality of the furniture he built.

2. Dancing was the favorite activity of the cobbler.

3. Fram's second-favorite was the same as Dok's favorite; Zett's second-favorite was the same as Winn's favorite.

4. Neither the blacksmith nor the miller enjoyed telling stories.

5. Winn, who was not the miller, enjoyed storytelling most; his second-favorite activity was dancing.

6. The weaver enjoyed instrumental music most; his second-favorite activity was singing.

7. The cobbler, Hober, and the miller were good friends.

8. The second-favorite activity of the carpenter was storytelling.

The World's Most Intense Giant in the Shire Puzzle

The villagers were fortunate that relatively few monsters or other adversaries invaded their shire. When a giant looking for an easy meal began stealing livestock, a group of the people united and, presenting a formidable presence, were successful in driving the giant away. Among those in the group were Alf, Bord, Dek, Fober, and Hon. Their second names were Son of Edno, Son of Lor, Son of Quin, Son of Rup, and Son of Tas. Their occupations were as follows: two raised sheep, one raised cattle, one raised goats, and one raised pigs. In chasing the giant away, two wielded pitchforks, one wielded an ax, one wielded a club, and one wielded a spade.

From the statements that follow, what was the first name and second name of each of the five; what was the occupation of each; and what weapon was wielded by each? Of the seven statements, one is false, the rest are valid.

1. Neither Son of Rup nor Son of Tas, both of whom wielded pitchforks, raised sheep or goats.

2. Dek, Hon (who raised cattle), Alf (who was not Son of Rup), and Son of Tas were among the leaders in organizing the group to attack the giant.

3. Son of Edno and Son of Quin raised sheep.

4. Dek, who was not son of Tas, and Fober, who wielded a spade, had adjacent farms.

5. Although Son of Quin was reluctant, at the last minute he was persuaded by Son of Edno and Alf to join the group.

6. Son of Lor did not raise goats or pigs.

7. Alf, who did not raise sheep, wielded an ax.

The World's Most Intense Pony Racing Puzzle

The most important sporting events in the shire were pony races. In one series of four races, six riders competed. No rider won more than one race. From the statements below, what was the ranking of each rider in each race? ("Before" means in a higher-ranking position, not necessarily immediately before; "after" means lower-ranked, not necessarily immediately after.) Of the sixteen statements, fifteen are valid and one is false.

1ST RACE

　　1. Pro finished before Pen, who finished before Ismo.

　　2. Lak finished before Pro.

　　3. Pir finished after Ismo.

　　4. Adus finished in third place.

2ND RACE

　　5. Lak finished before Ismo, who finished before Adus.

　　6. Pro finished in the same place as in the previous race.

　　7. Pir finished in fifth place.

　　8. Pen finished before Lak.

(continued)

3RD RACE

9. Pen finished before Pro, who finished before Pir.

10. Pir finished after Lak and before Ismo.

11. Lak finished before Pen.

12. Pir did not finish in the same place as he did in either of the first two races.

4TH RACE

13. Pir finished one position better than his best position in any of the other three races.

14. Pro finished before Adus and after Lak.

15. Pen finished in fifth place.

16. Lak finished after Pir.

The World's Most Intense
Valley of Liars Visitor Puzzle

Among strange lands, the Land of Liars is unparalleled. The inhabitants all make false statements. However, they adhere to definite patterns according to the time of day. There are those who speak the truth in the morning and lie in the afternoon. The inhabitants in this group are known as Amtrus. There are also those who speak the truth in the afternoon and lie in the morning. The inhabitants in this group are known as Pemtrus.

There is a valley in the Land of Liars, in which the inhabitants have their own patterns of veracity: The Amtrus are like others in the Land except that in any statements specifically mentioning other Amtrus they lie in the morning and tell the truth in the afternoon. The Pemtrus are like other Pemtrus in the Land except that in any statements specifically mentioning other Pemtrus they lie in the afternoon and tell the truth in the morning.

To solve each puzzle, you must determine which speakers are Amtrus and which are Pemtrus, and whether it is morning or afternoon.

(continued)

A traveler enters the Land of Liars intending to visit the Valley of Liars. He is aware that Amtrus speak the truth in the morning and lie in the afternoon, and that Pemtrus speak the truth in the afternoon and lie in the morning. The visitor encounters two inhabitants. He inquires as to the time of day and as to the group or groups to which the two belong. They reply as follows:

A. 1. B and I are Pemtrus.

B. 1. A is not a Pemtru.
   2. It is either morning or afternoon.

IS IT MORNING OR AFTERNOON; AND TO WHAT GROUP OR GROUPS DO THE TWO INHABITANTS OF THE LAND OF LIARS BELONG?

The World's Most Intense Route to the Valley of Liars Puzzle

Still heading toward the Valley of Liars, the visitor approaches a fork in the road. One road leads north and the other east. Two inhabitants are asked for directions. The two reply as follows:

A. 1. Take the road leading east.
    2. It is morning.

B. 1. Take the road leading north.
    2. I am an Amtru.

WHICH ROAD SHOULD THE VISITOR TAKE?

The World's Most Intense Two Valley Liars Puzzle

The visitor reaches the Valley of Liars. He has been advised that they have their own patterns of veracity. They are like others in the Land of Liars except that when Amtrus specifically mention other Amtrus they lie in the morning and speak the truth in the afternoon; and when Pemtrus specifically mention other Pemtrus they lie in the afternoon and speak the truth in the morning.

Two Valley inhabitants are asked the time of day and to what group or groups they belong. They respond as below:

A. B and I are Pemtrus.

B. A is not a Pemtru.

IS IT MORNING OR EVENING; AND TO WHAT GROUP OR GROUPS DO THE TWO VALLEY INHABITANTS BELONG?

The World's Most Intense Two More Valley Liars Puzzle

Two Valley inhabitants, A and B, are asked to what group or groups they belong. They respond as follows:

A. 1. B is Pemtru.

   2. B and I belong to the same group.

B. 1. A's statements are false.

IS IT MORNING OR AFTERNOON; AND TO WHAT GROUP OR GROUPS DO A AND B BELONG?

The World's Most Intense Three Valley Liars Puzzle

The statements below are made by three Valley inhabitants, whose group or groups are unknown.

> A. If asked, B would erroneously claim that he and I belong to the same group.
>
> B. If you ask C the time of day, he will say it is morning.
>
> C. A's statement is false.

IS IT MORNING OR AFTERNOON; AND TO WHICH GROUP DOES EACH OF THE THREE SPEAKERS BELONG?

The World's Most Intense
Three Valley Liars Puzzle, Again

Three Valley inhabitants make statements. As to their group or groups, little is known.

- A. C and I are not both Pemtrus.
- B. C and I belong to the same group.
- C. A and I do not belong to the same group.

IS IT MORNING OR AFTERNOON; AND TO WHICH GROUP DOES EACH BELONG?

The World's Most Intense Four Valley Liars Puzzle

Four Valley inhabitants make the following statements. Of these four, little is known as to their group or groups.

- A. If you were to ask D, he would say that I am a Pemtru.
- B. I am the only one from my group.
- C. If asked, B would claim that he and I belong to the same group.
- D. B and I are Amtrus.

IS IT MORNING OR AFTERNOON; AND TO WHICH GROUP OR GROUPS DO THE FOUR VALLEY INHABITANTS BELONG?

The World's Most Intense Impostor Puzzle

Of the five individuals who make the statements below, one is a visitor from another land and not subject to the Valley standards of veracity. He is an impostor, posing as an inhabitant. As to the four inhabitants, Amtrus and Pemtrus are equally represented.

    A. C and I do not belong to the same group.
    B. It is either afternoon, or else I am a Pemtru.
    C. A is not a Pemtru.
    D. Either A is an Amtru, or else I am an Amtru.
    E. It is either afternoon, or else I am an Amtru.

WHICH SPEAKER IS THE IMPOSTOR; IS IT MORNING OR AFTERNOON; AND WHAT GROUP IS REPRESENTED BY EACH OF THE FOUR INHABITANTS?

THE WORLD'S
MOST TAXING FALSE
LOGIC PUZZLES

The World's Most Taxing Stradivarius Theft Puzzle

A famous violinist was in town for a concert. While he was away from his room for a short time his favorite violin, a Stradivarius, was stolen. The inspector took immediate action, and through diligent research was able to identify four suspects. Each of them makes one statement as follows. The guilty one's statement is false; the other statements are true.

A. I was not in town at the the time of the theft.
B. C is the culprit.
C. B's statement is false.
D. C's statement is true.

WHICH ONE IS GUILTY?

The World's Most Taxing Forest Robber Puzzle

A notorious robber has made a lucrative living by robbing travelers in the forest. Inspector Detweiler has, after extensive examination of the available clues, identified three suspects. Their statements follow. One makes two true statements; one makes one true and one false statement; one makes two false statements.

A. 1. I am not the robber.
    2. C is the robber.

B. 1. C is innocent.
    2. A is the robber.

C. 1. I am not the robber.
    2. B is innocent.

WHICH ONE IS THE ROBBER?

The World's Most Taxing Two Pickpocket Puzzle

Two pickpockets were plying their trade at the village fair. The inspector's review of the clues indicated that there were two culprits working together. He has interrogated four suspects who are known pickpockets. The two who are guilty each make only one true statement. Little is known as to the truthfulness of the statements made by the other two suspects. Determine the two who are guilty from their statements below:

A. 1. B is one of the culprits.
   2. C would never be guilty of such a crime.
   3. D is a disreputable character and certainly could be one of the culprits.

B. 1. A's first statement is true.
   2. C is one of the culprits.
   3. If C is not one of the culprits, then either A or D is guilty.

C. 1. A's second statement is true.
   2. B is not one of the guilty ones.
   3. B's second statement is true.

D. 1. A's third statement is true.
   2. B's second statement is true.
   3. C's second statement is false.

The World's Most Taxing Poacher Puzzle

A closed hunting season in the forest has been declared. Hunting has been considered a source of food for some, and, consequently, poaching has become a problem. Inspector Detweiler has been requested to bring to a halt a series of illegal appropriations of game. Clues indicate that there is one culprit, and the inspector has identified four suspects. The four make statements below. The truthfulness of their statements is unknown, except that only one of the guilty suspect's statements is true.

A.   1. D is innocent.
     2. I am not the poacher.
     3. Hunting is a source of food in these parts.

B.   1. C's being a suspect is a case of mistaken identity.
     2. A's second statement is true.
     3. Not all of my statements are true.

C.   1. I am not the poacher.
     2. D is the poacher.
     3. My being a suspect is not a case of mistaken identity.

D.   1. A's statements are not all true.
     2. At least one of C's statements is true.
     3. I do not like to eat game.

WHICH ONE IS THE POACHER?

The World's Most Taxing Property Destruction Puzzle

Five local villagers were having a late evening political discussion at the village gathering place. As the night wore on, the discussion deteriorated into a debate and then into an excessively noisy argument.

At this point, the proprietor attempted to intervene in order to quiet the disturbance. In the ensuing fracas, an expensive candelabrum was knocked over and broken. The five customers immediately vacated the premises.

Inspector Detweiler recorded the statements below in attempting to determine who broke the candelabrum. Not all of the statements are truthful. In fact, only one suspect makes no false statements.

BUTCHER

1. I was not even there.
2. The cobbler was looking for trouble; he did it.
3. The candlestick maker helped him do it.

BAKER

1. I agree with the butcher's first statement.
2. The candlestick maker did not do it.
3. I agree with the butcher's second statement.

(continued)

CANDLESTICK MAKER

1. I did not do it.
2. The butcher was there.
3. The baker did it.
4. The cobbler did not do it.

BLACKSMITH

1. If the proprietor had not intervened this would not have happened.
2. None of us is to blame.
3. The candlestick maker is innocent.
4. The cobbler did not do it.

COBBLER

1. I agree with the baker's third statement.
2. The candlestick maker did it.
3. I was not looking for trouble; I did not do it.
4. The baker did not do it.

WHICH ONE IS GUILTY?

The World's Most Taxing Guilty Two Puzzle

In a series of thefts, it was found that there were two culprits working together. The inspector was able to identify five suspects, and the five each make two statements, below. One of the thieves makes two true statements. The other guilty one makes two false statements. Little is known as to the truthfulness of the statements made by the three innocent suspects.

A. 1. I was nowhere near the scene of the crime that day.
    2. B is innocent.

B. 1. I am innocent.
    2. E's first statement is false.

C. 1. I have no idea who the guilty ones are.
    2. D's statements are both false.

D. 1. C's second statement is not true.
    2. A is not guilty.

E. 1. A and B are the thieves.
    2. At least one of D's statements is true.

WHICH TWO ARE GUILTY?

The World's Most Taxing Pickpocket Theft Puzzle

A notorious pickpocket had evaded apprehension for some time. The inspector redoubled his efforts to bring him to justice, and his keen detection work resulted in four suspects, all of whom were in town during the last known theft. One of them is guilty. Each makes three statements. If either A or C is guilty, each of the four suspects makes two true statements and one false statement. If either B or D is guilty, no two of the four suspects make the same number of true statements.

A. 1. I was out of town during the last known theft.
   2. Neither D nor I did it.
   3. C did not do it.

B. 1. A was in town during the last known theft.
   2. I am innocent.
   3. D is the guilty one.

C. 1. A is the pickpocket.
   2. B's first statement is false.
   3. B's third statement is false.

D. 1. The pickpocket deserves to be apprehended.
   2. At least one of B's statements is false.
   3. A is not guilty.

WHO IS GUILTY?

The World's Most Taxing Missing D Puzzle

A professional burglar has recently managed to actively pursue his criminal activities by targeting the homes of the most affluent villagers. The inspector is on the trail of the culprit and has identified four suspects, one of whom is missing. The other three are questioned; each makes two true statements and one false statement.

A. 1. I am not the burglar.
   2. D has no alibi.
   3. D went into hiding.

B. 1. A's first statement is true.
   2. A's third statement is false.
   3. D is not the burglar.

C. 1. I am not the burglar.
   2. D has an alibi.
   3. B's second statement is false.

WHO IS THE BURGLAR?

The World's Most Taxing Unlucky Car Thief Puzzle

A car thief who had managed to evade the authorities in the past unknowingly took the automobile that belonged to Inspector Detweiler. The sleuth wasted no time and spared no effort in discovering and carefully examining the available clues. He was able to identify four suspects, with certainty that one of them was the culprit.

The four make the statements below. In total, six statements are true and six are false.

A. 1. C and I had met many times before today.
    2. B is guilty.
    3. The car thief did not know it was the inspector's car.

B. 1. D did not do it.
    2. D's third statement is false.
    3. I am innocent.

C. 1. I had never met A before today.
    2. B is not guilty.
    3. D knows how to drive.

D. 1. B's first statement is false.
    2. I do not know how to drive.
    3. A did it.

WHICH ONE IS THE CAR THIEF?

The World's Most Taxing Oldest/Youngest Puzzle

A thief has been taking sheep from farmyards in the area, and there are four suspects. The inspector has been able to determine that the guilty one is either the oldest or the youngest of the four. They make the following statements, although each suspect makes only one true statement.

A. 1. B is the oldest among us.
    2. The youngest among us is guilty.
    3. C is innocent.

B. 1. A is not the youngest.
    2. D is the guilty one.
    3. D is the youngest.

C. 1. A is the youngest of the four of us.
    2. I am the oldest.
    3. D did not do it.

D. 1. The oldest among us is innocent.
    2. B is guilty.
    3. I am the youngest.

WHICH ONE IS GUILTY?

The World's Most Taxing Hyperborean Outlier Puzzle

According to the ancient Greeks, Hyperborea was a land to the north of Mount Olympus, home of the gods. The inhabitants were favored by the gods; they lived for a thousand years in a land of perpetual springtime, and they were free from pestilence.

Little known were the Hyperboreans' unique standards of veracity. Those who lived in the southern region of the land were known as Sororeans and they always spoke truthfully; those who lived in the northern region were known as Nororeans and they always spoke falsely; those who lived in the middle region were known as Midroreans and they made statements that were alternately truthful and false, but in which order was unknown.

There were a few rebels, called Outliers, who disdained the normal conventions of Hyperborea and refused to adhere to the accepted standards of veracity. Their statement patterns as to truth and falsehood were anything that was different from other inhabitants (that is, if three or more statements were made, there were some true statements and some false statements, but not in an alternating pattern).

Hyperboreans belong to three groups: Sororeans, Nororeans, and Midroreans. Of the three inhabitants who make the statements below, little is known as to their group or groups except that Outliers are not present.

A. 1. B and I are both Midroreans.
   2. C is a Nororean.

B. 1. A and I belong to two different groups.
   2. C and I belong to the same group.

C. 1. I am not a Nororean.
   2. A and I belong to the same group.

TO WHAT GROUP OR GROUPS DO A, B, AND C BELONG?

The World's Most Taxing Outlier Puzzle

Four Hyperboreans are engaged in conversation. One is a Sororean, one is a Nororean and one is a Midrorean. The fourth speaker is an Outlier.

From their statements below, which one is the Sororean, which one is the Nororean, which one is the Midrorean, and which one is the Outlier?

A. 1. I am the Outlier
    2. D is the Nororean.

B. 1. A's first statement is true.

C. 1. I am not the Outlier.
    2. B is not the Midrorean.

D. 1. C's first statement is true.

The World's Most Taxing One of Each Puzzle

Among four Hyperboreans one is a Sororean, one is a Nororean, one is a Midrorean and one is an Outlier. They make the following statements:

A. 1. I am the Outlier.

2. D is not more truthful than I am.

3. B is the Sororean.

B. 1. A is the Outlier.

2. C is not the Sororean.

3. I am not the Midrorean.

C. 1. A is not the Outlier.

2. B is not the Sororean.

3. I am more truthful than D is.

D. 1. B is not the Nororean.

2. A's second statement is false.

3. C's third statement is false.

WHICH ONE IS THE SOROREAN, WHICH ONE IS THE NOROREAN, WHICH ONE IS THE MIDROREAN, AND WHICH ONE IS THE OUTLIER?

The World's Most Taxing Olympic Game Puzzle

It is not commonly known that the original Olympic Games occurred not in Olympia, Greece, but in Hyperborea. Three Hyperborean Olympic athletes are discussing the results of the recent competition. Inhabitants of Hyperborea belong to three groups: Sororeans, Nororeans and Midroreans. There are also those few Outliers.

Their groups are unknown except that exactly one of the athletes is an Outlier.

    A. 1. I was the winner of the one-half league run.

        2. You can count on what C says to be truthful.

        3. I am not a Midrorean.

    B. 1. A did not win the one-half league run.

        2. I entered three events.

        3. C is the Outlier.

    C. 1. I am not the Outlier.

        2. B's second statement is truthful.

        3. A did not win the one-half league run.

WHAT ARE THE GROUPS OF THE THREE ATHLETES?

The World's Most Taxing Outlier Puzzle, Again

Outliers, although few in number, occasionally make their presence known. Hyperboreans are either Sororeans, Nororeans, Midroreans, or those few Outliers. As to the four inhabitants who make statements below, little is known as to their standards of veracity, except that exactly one of them is an Outlier.

A. 1. B is the Outlier.
    2. D is a Sororean.
    3. C is a Midrorean.

B. 1. I am not the Outlier.
    2. A is a Nororean.
    3. C is not a Midrorean.

C. 1. I am not a Midrorean.
    2. B is not the Outlier.
    3. D is a Sororean.

D. 1. I am a Sororean.
    2. B is the Outlier.
    3. A is a Midrorean.

TO WHICH GROUP DOES EACH OF THE FOUR HYPERBOREANS BELONG?

The World's Most Taxing Olive Picking Puzzle

Olives are an important staple in Hyperborea, and olive picking is an occupation engaged in by many inhabitants. Four olive pickers are having a discussion. One is known to be a Sororean, one is known to be a Nororean, one is known to be a Midrorean, and one is known to be an Outlier. Their statements follow:

A. 1. I picked more olives today than anyone else.
    2. I am the Midrorean.
    3. C is the Outlier.

B. 1. I am the Midrorean.
    2. I would have picked more olives today than A, except that I did not start until after lunch.
    3. C is the Outlier.

C. 1. D dropped more olives than he picked.
    2. I picked more olives today than A did.
    3. B picked olives all day today.

D. 1. C picked more olives today than A did.
    2. I did not drop any olives today.
    3. B would have picked more olives than A today, except that he did not start until after lunch.

WHICH ONE IS THE SOROREAN, WHICH ONE IS THE NOROREAN, WHICH ONE IS THE MIDROREAN, AND WHICH ONE IS THE OUTLIER?

The World's Most Taxing Four for the Races Puzzle

Four Hyperboreans are practicing for the upcoming chariot races. They are known to be a Sororean, a Nororean, a Midrorean, and an Outlier. They make the following statements:

A. 1. This race track is slow.
   2. D is doing so well in practice that he will win.
   3. C is the Outlier.

B. 1. A's first statement is true.
   2. I am the Midrorean.
   3. D is the Nororean.

C. 1. This race track is fast.
   2. I agree with B's second statement.
   3. I am not the Nororean.

D. 1. I am doing so poorly in practice that I will lose.
   2. B's second statement is false.
   3. A is the Sororean.

WHICH ONE IS THE SOROREAN, WHICH ONE IS THE NOROREAN, WHICH ONE IS THE MIDROREAN, AND WHICH ONE IS THE OUTLIER?

The World's Most Taxing Six Hyperboreans Puzzle

Six Hyperboreans hold the jobs of chariot maker, fishnet weaver, musician, olive grower, tax collector, and wine maker. One is known to be a Sororean; two are known to be Nororeans; two are known to be Midroreans; one is known to be an Outlier. They make statements as follows:

AGENOR

1. As olive grower I have the most important job.
2. Cadmus is the chariot maker.
3. Philemon's third statement is true.

ALPHENOR

1. Philemon is not the fishnet weaver.
2. I find my work as tax collector to be very satisfying.
3. Now that Hesperus is the chariot maker, we have been winning more races.

CADMUS

1. Agenor claims to be the olive grower, but that is my job.
2. Alphenor is the tax collector.
3. Hesperus is the chariot maker.
4. Everything that Philemon says is false.

CALLISTO

1. The last tour I took with my lyre was so successful I intend to schedule another one.
2. Everything that Agenor says is true.
3. Cadmus is not the chariot maker.

HESPERUS

1. We have been winning very few chariot races lately.
2. Agenor is the wine maker.
3. Cadmus is the tax collector.
4. I am the fishnet weaver.

PHILEMON

1. I am the tax collector.
2. Callisto is the musician.
3. Hesperus' statements are all true.
4. Cadmus is the olive grower.

WHICH HYPERBOREAN IS THE SOROREAN, WHICH ARE THE NOROREANS, WHICH ARE THE MIDROREANS, WHICH IS THE OUTLIER, AND WHAT IS THE JOB OF EACH?

The World's Most Taxing Chariot Race Winner Puzzle

The winners of chariot races were among the heroes of the Hyperboreans. Five such honored ones were discussing the number of chariot races they had won. Each has had more than three wins; no two have had the same number of wins; and each chariot racer's number of wins is divisible by three. The one with the most wins is the Grand Champion. Of the five chariot race winners, little is known except that exactly one of them is an Outlier.

From their statements below, what is the standard of veracity of each, how many chariot races did each win, and which one was the Grand Champion?

AGATHON

1. Lysis is the Grand Champion.
2. Protagoras has had 15 wins.
3. Lysis is a Sororean.
4. Phaedrus is not the Outlier.

LYSIS

1. Sosias is the Outlier.
2. Phaedrus is a Sororean.
3. I am not the Grand Champion.
4. Agathon is not the Grand Champion.

PHAEDRUS

1. I have had 18 wins.
2. Agathon is the Grand Champion.
3. Lysis is the third highest in the number of wins.
4. Protagoras is the Outlier.

PROTAGORAS

1. Agathon has had fewer wins than Lysis.
2. Sosias has had 15 wins.
3. Lysis is the Outlier.
4. Agathon has had more wins than I have had.

SOSIAS

1. I have had more than six wins.
2. Agathon has had more wins than Protagoras.
3. Phaedrus is the Outlier.
4. Phaedrus' third statement is false.

The World's Most Taxing Midville Muddlers Puzzle

Among those who particularly enjoy logic puzzles, some prefer more than any other the type of puzzle that contains several statements, each one of which provides a fragment, or a limited amount, of pertinent information. In total, the statements afford enough, but just enough, to enable the solution to be found.

The puzzles in this section represent several of this type, with one exception: each puzzle contains a false statement, which must be identified before you can arrive at the correct solution.

As in all logic puzzles, men have male-sounding names and women have female-sounding names. There will never be, say, a man named Barbara or a woman named Bob.

The Midville Muddlers baseball team depends on four players to score most of their runs. The positions of the four are the three outfielders (right fielder, center fielder, and left fielder) and the catcher. From the statements that follow, determine the first name (Henry, Ken, Leo, or Stan), surname (one is Dodson), position, and batting average of each player. (Their batting averages are .280, .295, .310, and .325.) One of the following statements is false.

1. Neither Leo nor the catcher has a batting average over .300.

2. Three who are neighbors are Clements, the right fielder, and the player who bats .325.

3. The center fielder bats .295.

4. Stan's batting average is 30 points higher than that of Ken, who does not live near any of the other three.

5. Brooks and Henry, who is not Ashley, both bat over .300 and are in competition to see which will score the most runs this season.

6. Henry, who is neither the right fielder nor the left fielder, has a lower batting average than the catcher.

The World's Most Taxing Fishing Vacation Plans Puzzle

Carl and three of his friends who are avid fishermen decided to visit four of the world's finest sport fishing locations over a period of four years. Each friend had a different favorite location, so they chose the order in which they would take the trips by drawing the place names from a hat. Based on the statements below, what is the first name (Andy, Bill, Carl, or Dennis) and surname (one is Cole) of each friend, what was the favorite fishing location of each, and what was the order in which the trips were to be taken? One of the statements below is false.

1. Andy and Barrott work for the same company; Bill is self-employed.
2. The Iceland trip was planned for the year before the Alaska trip, which was not Andy's favorite destination.
3. Carl and Barrott and their wives frequently play bridge together.
4. Whelan's favorite fishing location was the third trip, which was neither Patagonia nor New Zealand.
5. Whelan and Cole are married; the other two are not.
6. Dennis was disappointed that his favorite destination, New Zealand, was not to be the first; Crowley's favorite destination was planned for the last trip, so he was unsympathetic.
7. Barrott's favorite destination was the first.

The World's Most Taxing White-Water Rafting Puzzle

Eight friends decided to try white-water rafting on a nearby river. They rented four two-person rafts; one was yellow, one was green, one was red, and one was blue. They selected partners for the four rafts and agreed on a destination at the end of a white-water run. Based on the following statements, one of which is false, what is the first name (Alan, Don, Frank, Henry, LeRoy, Paul, Phil, or Walt) and surname (Cook, Gladstone, Hawley, Hughes, O'Brien, Sands, Smith, or Wilson) of each of the friends; which were partners on the four rafts; and what color raft was used by each?

1. Phil and Cook, who were in the same raft, arrived at the destination without incident, but they were not the ones who finished first.

2. The red raft capsized and did not finish; the green raft was first to finish the white-water run.

3. O'Brien and LeRoy were not on the same raft.

4. Paul and Wilson finished last on their raft.

5. Fortunately, Henry is a good swimmer, and he helped his partner, Hughes (whose first name is not Walt), get to shore. They were able to recover their capsized raft, but declined to finish the white-water run.

(continued)

6. Frank was the first to select a raft, and he picked the yellow one. He and Hawley were on the second raft to finish the white-water run.

7. Alan and Hughes were on the same raft; they were the first to finish the white-water run.

8. LeRoy and Smith completed the run and were not in last place.

9. After their nearly tragic capsizing experience, Don and his partner, Gladstone, vowed not to set foot in another raft.

10. Alan did not care that he and his partner finished last; he was just glad that they made it.

The World's Most Taxing Spelling Contest Puzzle

There were five finalists in the city schools spelling contest this year. They competed until four of the five misspelled a word, and the fifth one was declared the winner. From the following statements, one of which is false, what is the first name and surname (Jennings, Knudson, North, Olsen, or Salisbury) of each finalist; who missed what word; and what was the order in which they finished the competition?

1. North, who was not the one who misspelled "physiognomy," had not participated in a spelling contest before. He said he had not expected to do well.

2. "Vicissitude" was misspelled immediately after "bivouac" and immediately before "isthmus."

3. Eleanor was happy that her good friend Jennings was one of the two finalists in the contest.

4. Before Eric misspelled his word there were only two contestants left; he and Olsen had studied together in preparation for the contest.

5. Gordie, who lasted longer in the competition than Jennings, was not the winner.

6. Knudson, who is not Helen, was the first to misspell a word.

7. Helen, Jennings, and Olsen are neighbors.

8. Jennings told Lois that she could not sleep the night before the contest.

The World's Most Taxing Audobon Field Trip Puzzle

Four married couples, who are members of the Audubon Society, undertook a bird-watching field trip to identify the varieties of birds to be observed in the local woods. To cover a sufficient area, each couple walked in a different direction. It was agreed that, for birds that were not common in the region, any sightings were to be recorded as to the time of the sighting and the name of the first person to see and identify the bird. At the end of the day, it was found that a different person was the first to sight each of eight uncommon birds.

From the following statements determine the first name and surname (Brinkley, Dwyer, Eng, or Valentine) of each member, and the variety of bird observed by each. One of the following statements is false.

1. Neither James, Curtis, Mr. Brinkley, nor either of theValentines was the first to sight a western tanager.

2. William was the first to sight a golden-crowned kinglet; he and his wife live near the Brinkleys.

3. Both Rosemary and Nancy, neither of whom is Valentine or Dwyer, were attending their first Audubon meeting and field trip, although both their spouses have been active members for several years.

4. Nancy was the second to sight a western tanager.

5. As program chairperson, Curtis' spouse is quite active in the local Audubon Society chapter and arranges and attends all their outings.

6. A lazuli bunting was first sighted by Angela, who only attends an occasional Audubon Society chapter meeting or outing.

7. Nancy was disappointed that her husband, Curtis, sighted an acorn woodpecker before she sighted her bird.

8. A pine siskin, which was sighted early in the day, and a yellow warbler were first sighted by Mr. and Mrs. Dwyer, not necessarily in that order.

9. Harold was first to sight a white-crowned sparrow, at about the same time that Nancy sighted her bird in a different part of the woods; her bird was not a black-headed grosbeak.

10. Curtis was the last to sight his bird.

The World's Most Taxing Car Pool Puzzle

Six business people travel to and from work in a car pool van driven by a seventh person. The six are picked up each workday morning where they live and are returned home each evening. From the statements that follow, determine the first name (one is Milton), surname (one is Altchech), occupation (one is a computer programmer), sequence of pickup in the morning, and sequence of drop-off in the evening. (Due to traffic patterns, the evening drop-off sequence is not necessarily the reverse of the morning pickup sequence.) One of the statements is false.

1. Amarol feels that she is fortunate to be the first one dropped off in the evening.

2. Neither Neal, Florence, Agassi, nor Atwater is the secretary.

3. Paul is the sixth to be picked up in the morning, but Avenal is the first to be dropped off in the evening.

4. The word processing supervisor is the third to be dropped off in the evening; the secretary is the second to be picked up in the morning and the fifth to be dropped off in the evening.

5. Adams, the attorney, dislikes having to be the first to be picked up in the morning and the last to be dropped off in the evening.

6. Gloria is picked up in the morning immediately after Neal and immediately before Paul. In the evening she is dropped off immediately after Avenal and immediately before Amarol, who is dropped off immediately before Evelyn.

7. Avenal, who is not the systems analyst, and Amarol are members of a men's choral group.

8. The personnel manager, who is not Atwater, is not the fourth or fifth to be picked up in the morning.

The World's Most Taxing Summer Student Puzzle

Six students at the university decided to each take one class during the summer session. Each selected a separate subject conducted by a different professor. On the campus there are six buildings in a row, identified consecutively as A to F. Each student attended class in a different one of the six buildings.

Identify each student's first name and surname (Karr, Peterson, Rogers, Sawyer, West, or Williams), class subject (one is economics), professor, and the building in which the class attended was held.

1. Louise, whose surname is not Karr, and Rogers attend classes in adjacent buildings; neither of them is studying English.

2. Carl, who is studying history, attends class in a building that is adjacent to both Sawyer's and Burt's building.

3. Victoria's classroom building is next to that of Peterson.

4. Professor Denton, whose subject is not music, does not teach in a building adjacent to that of Professor Carson.

5. Professors Harrison and White teach in buildings that are at the two ends of the row; neither teaches psychology or music.

6. Building B—which is neither the music building nor the building in which Williams attends his class—is where Professor Landers teaches.

7. Professor Carson's building is not D; his law students this summer are all men.

8. John takes law from Professor White two buildings from where Professor Harrison teaches.

9. Neither Fran, Williams, nor Peterson have their class in a building at either end of the row.

10. Rogers feels fortunate to have Professor Landers as an instructor; John feels the same way about his professor, whose building is next to that of Professor Harrison.

11. Sawyer is one of Professor Bradford's best students.

The World's Most Taxing Chess Player Puzzle

Each of six members of the City Chess Club has his or her preferred series of opening moves and no two prefer the same opening. Three of the preferred openings are king's pawn openings and three are queen's pawn openings. The three king's pawn openings are the Bishop's Opening, the King's Gambit, and the Ruy Lopez. The three queen's pawn openings are the Stonewall System, the Colle System and the Queen's Gambit. Each player also has a preferred defense against king's pawn openings and a preferred defense against queen's pawn openings. No two prefer the same defense.

From the following statements, one of which is false, determine each member's first name (Dan, Edith, Fred, George, Harry, or Jeff), surname (one is Davis), preferred opening, and preferred defense (one defense against queen's pawn openings is the Benoni Defense).

1. George and Gruber are two of four members who are evenly matched and enjoy competing against each other; the other two are the one who prefers the King's Gambit opening and the one who prefers the Sicilian Defense against king's pawn openings and the Tarrasch Defense against queen's pawn openings.

2. Draper always opens with the Stonewall System when he has the white pieces; he dislikes the French Defense against king's pawn openings, and rarely uses the Cambridge Springs Defense against queen's pawn openings.

3. Duvall and Fred, neither of whom uses the French Defense or the Caro-Kann Defense against king's pawn openings, usually win when they play any of the other four.

4. The one who prefers the Bishop's Opening prefers the Pirc Defense against king's pawn openings and the Meran Defense against queen's pawn openings, except when playing Harry, who is by far the strongest player among the six members.

5. Campbell, whose first name is not Edith, likes the King's Gambit because of the number of possible variations; Jeff prefers the Ruy Lopez.

6. Edith always opens with a king's pawn.

7. The second-strongest player is Evans, who does not open his games with the Queen's Gambit; when defending against queen's pawn openings, he does not use the Nimzo-Indian Defense.

(continued)

8. The player who prefers to open with the Colle System does not use Petroff's Defense when defending against king's pawn openings.

9. The player who usually opens with the Stonewall System believes that it gives her the best chance to be competitive.

10. The player who favors the Two Knights Defense against king's pawn openings does not use the Cambridge Springs Defense against queen's pawn openings; one of the players who favors a king's pawn opening favors the King's Indian Defense against queen's pawn openings.

THE WORLD'S
MOST MYSTIFYING
LOGIC PUZZLES

The World's Most Mystifying Educational Accomplishment Puzzle

The adventures of Prince Tal take place in a faraway kingdom at a distant time. Prince Tal encounters the ferocious beasts, giants, and enchantresses that abound in that land. The puzzles in this section contain assumptions, only some of which will lead you to the correct solutions. The challenge is to determine which assumptions are valid and which are invalid.

Even though noblemen of the kingdom spent considerable time seeking adventures, education was not neglected. Prince Tal excelled in one area of his education and did especially well in another. From the following statements, determine in which subject Prince Tal excelled and in which second subject he did especially well.

1. If Prince Tal excelled in chivalry, he did especially well in horsemanship.
2. If Prince Tal excelled in horsemanship, he did especially well in fencing.
3. If Prince Tal did especially well in horsemanship, he excelled in fencing.
4. If Prince Tal excelled in fencing, he did especially well in chivalry.
5. If Prince Tal did especially well in chivalry, he excelled in horsemanship.

The World's Most Mystifying Dragon Battle Puzzle

For noblemen to do battle with dragons was considered the ultimate adventure. Sir Aard, Sir Bolbo, and Sir Delfo have each had a successful encounter with one or two dragons. Among the three noblemen, they encountered a total of five dragons: Biter, Black Heart, Dante, Flame Thrower, and Old Smoky. No dragon was encountered by more than one nobleman. Consider the following statements:

1. If Sir Aard encountered Dante, then Sir Delfo did not encounter Flame Thrower.
2. If Sir Aard did not encounter both Biter and Black Heart, then Sir Bolbo encountered Flame Thrower and Sir Delfo encountered Old Smoky.
3. If Sir Delfo encountered Black Heart, then Sir Aard encountered Dante.
4. If Sir Bolbo did not encounter both Dante and Biter, then Sir Delfo encountered Flame Thrower and Sir Aard encountered Black Heart.
5. Flame Thrower and Dante were not encountered by the same nobleman.
6. If Sir Delfo did not encounter both Black Heart and Flame Thrower, then Sir Aard encountered Biter and Sir Bolbo encountered Old Smoky.

WHICH NOBLEMEN ENCOUNTERED WHICH DRAGONS?

The World's Most Mystifying Tilting Puzzle

It was the custom for noblemen to practice tilting when there were no pressing adventures. One afternoon, Sir Aard, Sir Bolbo, Sir Delfo, Sir Gath, Sir Keln, and Prince Tal paired off for this exercise into three matches. Consider the following statements:

1. If either Prince Tal or Sir Aard tilted with Sir Keln, then Sir Bolbo tilted with Sir Gath.
2. If Sir Gath tilted with Prince Tal, then Sir Keln tilted with Sir Delfo.
3. If Prince Tal tilted with Sir Delfo, Sir Keln tilted with Sir Gath.
4. If Sir Gath tilted with Sir Bolbo, Sir Delfo tilted with Prince Tal.
5. If Prince Tal tilted with Sir Aard, then Sir Bolbo tilted with Sir Gath.
6. If Sir Gath tilted with Sir Keln, then Prince Tal tilted with Sir Aard.
7. If Prince Tal tilted with Sir Bolbo, then Sir Keln tilted with Sir Aard.

WHO TILTED WITH WHOM?

The World's Most Mystifying Fearsome Beast Encounter Puzzle

The Fearsome Beast, whose head was like that of a lion and whose hair was black and shaggy, was said to be as big as an elephant and faster than a deer. Few had ever seen it, but the beast reportedly had been observed in a remote area of the kingdom. Prince Tal and his three comrades, Sir Aard, Sir Bolbo, and Sir Delfo, were determined to confront the elusive monster. To this end, they set out in the search.

They encountered the monster, but at the first sight of the beast, their horses reared, threw two of the riders, and bolted for distant parts. One of the two thrown noblemen quickly climbed a tree, while the other was left prostrate on the ground, momentarily stunned. The Fearsome Beast jumped over the fallen nobleman and quickly departed.

From the following statements determine which nobleman was prostrate on the ground, which one climbed a tree, and which two were not unhorsed.

1. If Sir Bolbo climbed a tree, then Sir Delfo and Prince Tal were not thrown.
2. If Sir Delfo climbed a tree, then Sir Aard and Prince Tal were not thrown.
3. If Sir Aard was prostrate on the ground, then Prince Tal and Sir Bolbo were not thrown.
4. If Sir Aard was not thrown, then Sir Bolbo was not thrown, and Sir Delfo was prostrate on the ground.
5. If Prince Tal did not climb a tree, then either Sir Bolbo or Sir Delfo climbed a tree.
6. If Sir Bolbo was prostrate on the ground, then Prince Tal and Sir Delfo were not thrown.

The World's Most Mystifying Strange Creature Puzzle

Strange creatures are occasionally seen in the kingdom and different kinds have been seen by different inhabitants. Given the following statements, can you determine which of Prince Tal and his four fellow noblemen saw which kind of creature? (No two saw the same kind of creature.)

1. If Sir Bolbo saw a monoceros, then Sir Delfo saw a satyr.
2. If Sir Bolbo saw a bonnacon, then Prince Tal saw a monoceros.
3. If Sir Keln did not see a leucrota, then Sir Aard saw a satyr.
4. If either Sir Bolbo or Sir Aard saw a basilisk, then Sir Delfo did not see a monoceros.
5. If Prince Tal saw a bonnacon, then Sir Aard saw a basilisk.
6. If Prince Tal saw a monoceros, then Sir Delfo saw a leucrota.
7. If Sir Delfo did not see a basilisk, then he saw a monoceros.
8. If Sir Delfo did not see a satyr, then Sir Bolbo did not see a leucrota.

The World's Most Mystifying Enchantress Puzzle

As a knight-errant, Prince Tal traveled the kingdom in search of adventure. He frequently relied on hospitality in the castles, abbeys, and hermitages along his way. One evening he was invited into a strange castle that, unbeknownst to Prince Tal, was inhabited by an enchantress who cast a sleeping spell on him. When Prince Tal awoke, he found himself in the castle dungeon, where he was held for ransom.

After he was ultimately released, Prince Tal, still suffering some aftereffects of the sleep-inducing spell, had difficulty recalling how long he had been imprisoned, or how he had been freed. He could not remember whether his fellow noblemen had stormed the castle and released him, whether he had broken the dungeon door and escaped, whether the dungeon keeper (who was a loyal subject of the king) had left the dungeon door open for him, or whether the ransom had been paid.

Based on the following statements, can you clarify the outcome of Prince Tal's misadventure?

1. If the noblemen stormed the castle or the dungeon keeper left the door open, then Prince Tal was imprisoned for one day or three days.

2. If Prince Tal's imprisonment was for one day or one week, then he broke the dungeon door or the noblemen stormed the castle.

3. If Prince Tal's imprisonment was neither for three days nor for one week, then the dungeon keeper didn't leave the door open nor was the ransom paid.

4. If he broke the dungeon door or the ransom was paid, then Prince Tal was imprisoned for one week or two weeks.

5. If he did not break the door and the ransom was not paid, then Prince Tal was imprisoned for three days or the dungeon keeper left the door open.

6. If Prince Tal's imprisonment was not for one day or two weeks, then he did not break the dungeon door and the castle was not stormed.

7. If Prince Tal's imprisonment was for three days or two weeks, then the dungeon keeper left the door open or the ransom was paid.

The World's Most Mystifying Rescue Puzzle

Rescuing fair damsels in distress was an important responsibility of Prince Tal and his fellow noblemen. A total of six maidens were rescued by five noblemen. Based on the following statements, determine which damsels were rescued by which noblemen.

1. If Sir Keln rescued either Maid Marion or Maid Mary, then Sir Aard rescued either Maid Muriel or Maid Marie.
2. If Prince Tal rescued either Maid Matilda or Maid Marie, then Sir Bolbo rescued either Maid Mary or Maid Marion.
3. If Prince Tal rescued either Maid Mary or Maid Morgana, then Sir Bolbo rescued either Maid Matilda or Maid Marion.
4. If Sir Bolbo rescued either Maid Mary or Maid Marie, then Sir Keln rescued either Maid Matilda or Maid Morgana.
5. If Sir Aard rescued either Maid Muriel or Maid Marie, then Prince Tal rescued either Maid Mary or Maid Morgana.
6. If Sir Keln did not rescue either Maid Marion or Maid Mary, then Sir Aard rescued Maid Marion, unless he rescued Maid Muriel.
7. If Sir Bolbo rescued either Maid Marion or Maid Matilda, then Sir Delfo rescued both Maid Muriel and Maid Marie.
8. If Sir Aard did not rescue Maid Marie, then Prince Tal rescued Maid Marion, unless he rescued both Maid Matilda and Maid Muriel.

The World's Most Mystifying
Four Dragon Encounter Puzzle

Among the dragons that Prince Tal has encountered, four were especially ferocious and challenging: Dante breathed plumes of flame 50 feet long (or so it seemed), Quicksilver could fly as fast as sound (or so it seemed), Vesuvius was as large as a mountain (or so it appeared), and Meduso was capable of turning to stone anyone who looked him directly in the eye (Prince Tal fought this dragon using his peripheral vision).

None of the confrontations with these four dragons was conclusive. In one case, Prince Tal's fellow noblemen arrived in time to save him. In another case, just before being overwhelmed, Prince Tal feigned death until the dragon departed. At another time, the dragon quit after developing an uncontrollable coughing fit from inhaling too much smoke (a common affliction among dragons). In another case, Prince Tal forgot his shield and had to leave without actually fighting.

From the following statements, determine the order in which Prince Tal encountered the four dragons, and what the outcome was in each case.

(Continued)

1. If Vesuvius was not the second or third dragon encountered, then Prince Tal's fellow noblemen arrived in time to save him during this confrontation.

2. If the first encounter was with the dragon Dante, then the fourth encounter was with the dragon Meduso.

3. If Prince Tal did not feign death during the fourth encounter, then the fourth confrontation was not with the dragon Dante.

4. If Prince Tal's fellow noblemen arrived in time to save him during the first encounter, then the first encounter was with the dragon Quicksilver.

5. If the second encounter was with the dragon Dante, then Prince Tal's fellow noblemen arrived in time to save him.

6. If Prince Tal feigned death in his confrontation with the dragon Meduso, then it happened during the third encounter.

7. If Prince Tal's second confrontation was with Quicksilver or Vesuvius, then the dragon suffered a coughing fit during this encounter.

8. Prince Tal did not forget his shield during the first and third encounters, unless he feigned death during the second encounter.

The World's Most Mystifying One-Dragon Puzzle

There are few dragons in the kingdom of Lidd, and they have been put on the endangered species list.

Dragons are of two types. Some have reasoned that devouring domestic animals and their owners is, in the long run, not healthy for dragons. They are known as rationals. Some dragons, on the other hand, are reluctant to give up their traditional ways, nor do they fear humans. They are known as predators. The King has decreed that rational dragons shall be protected. Knights caught slaying a rational dragon are dealt with severely.

In addition to being rationals or predators, dragons in Lidd are of two different colors related to their veracity. Gray rational dragons always tell the truth; red rationals always lie. Red predators always tell the truth; gray predators always lie.

There is something appealing to a dragon about being in a land in which knights are not constantly trying to build their reputations by slaying them. It was not surprising, therefore, that the blue dragons from the adjacent land of Wonk began appearing in the kingdom of Lidd. Blue dragons are rationals or predators, but they all lie.

To tell if a dragon is protected, it would help to know its color. However, there is an affliction endemic to humans in Lidd: they are color blind. To them, all dragons look gray.

A dragon is approached by a knight looking for adventure. The dragon, asked his color and type, responds as follows:

DRAGON: I am either blue or gray.

WHAT TYPE IS THE DRAGON?

The World's Most Mystifying Two-Dragon Puzzle

Two armed knights confront two dragons, each of which is asked his color and type. Their answers follow:

A. 1. I am from Wonk.

2. B and I are both predators.

B. 1. A is not from Wonk, but I am.

2. I am a rational.

WHAT COLOR AND TYPE ARE EACH DRAGON?

The World's Most Mystifying Three-Dragon Puzzle

A knight in armor cautiously approaches three dragons, who offer the following information:

A. 1. C is from Wonk.

   2. I am not a red predator.

B. 1. A is from Wonk.

   2. A and C are both rationals.

C. 1. B is from Wonk.

   2. B is a predator.

WHAT ARE THE COLOR AND TYPE OF EACH DRAGON?

The World's Most Mystifying Dragons from Wonk Puzzle

A knight confronts three dragons, exactly two of which are known to be blue dragons from Wonk, and asks each his color and type. Their answers follow:

A. 1. B is from Wonk.
   2. I am a rational.

B. 1. C is from Wonk.
   2. I am a rational.

C. 1. I am a rational.

WHAT COLOR AND TYPE ARE EACH DRAGON?

The World's Most Mystifying Colorful Dragons from Wonk Puzzle

Three dragons, exactly one of which is blue, provide the following information:

A. 1. C is a gray rational.
   2. I am a gray rational.

B. 1. A is a predator.
   2. A is blue.
   3. I am a rational.

C. 1. A is not gray.
   2. B is from Wonk.

WHAT COLOR AND TYPE ARE EACH DRAGON?

The World's Most Mystifying
At-Least-One from Wonk Puzzle

The knights of Lidd are seeing more blue dragons than usual. Four knights encounter four dragons, at least one of which is blue, and ask about their colors and types. The dragons' statements follow:

A. 1. I am either a gray predator or a red rational.
    2. B is red.

B. 1. A and I are both rationals.
    2. C is a red predator.
    3. I am gray.

C. 1. I am not gray.
    2. I am a rational.
    3. B is a predator.

D. 1. C and I are both predators.
    2. I am red.
    3. A and B are both blue.

WHAT ARE THE COLOR AND TYPE OF EACH DRAGON?

The World's Most Mystifying Three Dragons Puzzle, Again

A lone knight nervously approaches three dragons, at least one of which is from Wonk. They volunteer the following information:

- A. 1. I am either red or gray.
  2. C and I are the same color.

- B. 1. A is not red.
  2. C is blue.

- C. 1. A's statements are false.
  2. B is not a rational.

WHAT COLOR AND TYPE ARE EACH DRAGON?

The World's Most Mystifying Protection Puzzle

A knight looking for a dragon to slay confronts three. He asks each about his color and type. Their answers follow:

- A. 1. I am gray.
    2. We three are protected by the King's decree.
    3. C is red.

- B. 1. I am not protected by the King's decree.
    2. C is gray.

- C. 1. A and I are not the same type.
    2. A is red.
    3. B is a rational.

WHAT COLOR AND TYPE ARE EACH DRAGON?

The World's Most Mystifying Dragon Coloring Puzzle

Three dragons respond to a very wary knight as follows:

A. 1. If asked, B would claim that C is a predator.
    2. I am gray.
    3. B is a rational.

B. 1. If asked, C would claim that A is a rational.
    2. C is red.

C. 1. If asked, A would claim that B is red.
    2. A is gray.

WHAT COLOR AND TYPE ARE EACH DRAGON?

The World's Most Mystifying Puzzle from the Addled Arithmetician, 1

Letters and numbers—to the Addled Arithmetician they are much the same thing. At least it appears so, as he has them reversed.

In this section you will find addition, subtraction, and multiplication problems that he has prepared. Your challenge is to replace the letters with the correct digit. (A zero never appears as the leftmost digit of a number.)

As if mixing digits with letters was not confusing enough, the Addled Arithmetician has forgotten that each letter should represent the same digit wherever it occurs in a puzzle.

In these puzzles, each letter represents the same digit wherever it occurs in a given mathematical problem (above the line). Wherever a letter appears in the answer to the problem (below the line) it represents a digit that is one more than or one less than the digit represented by the same letter above the line. For example, if B equals 4 above the line, all B's below the line will be equal to either 3 or 5.

Each letter above the line represents a digit that has a difference of one from the digit represented by the same letter below the line. The digits are 0, 1, 2, 3, 4, and 5.

	A	F	C	E
+	A	D	D	B
	B	F	B	F

WHAT DIGIT OR DIGITS ARE REPRESENTED BY EACH LETTER?

The World's Most Mystifying Puzzle from the Addled Arithmetician, II

Each letter above the line represents a digit that has a difference of one from the digit represented by the same letter below the line.
The digits are 0, 1, 2, 3, 4, and 5.

	F	B	A	C	B
−	D	A	F	E	B
	C	F	D	E

WHAT DIGIT OR DIGITS ARE REPRESENTED BY EACH LETTER?

The World's Most Mystifying Puzzle
from the Addled Arithmetician, III

Each letter above the line in this puzzle represents a digit that has a difference of one from the digit represented by the same letter below the line.

The digits are 0, 1, 2, 3, 4, 5, and 6.

	D	G	A	E	C
+	E	F	B	A	C
C	F	G	D	G	F

WHAT DIGIT OR DIGITS DOES EACH LETTER REPRESENT?

The World's Most Mystifying Puzzle from the Addled Arithmetician, IV

Each letter above the line represents a digit that has a difference of one from the digit represented by the same letter below the line.

The digits are: 0, 1, 2, 3, 4, 8, and 9.

	E	D	B	D	D
	E	D	B	D	D
+	E	D	B	D	D
C	F	A	B	D	E

WHAT DIGIT OR DIGITS ARE REPRESENTED BY EACH LETTER?

The World's Most Mystifying Puzzle from the Addled Arithmetician, V

Each letter in the multiplication problem (above the top line) represents a digit that has a difference of one from the digit represented by the same letter in the answer to the problem (below the top line).

The digits are 0, 1, 2, 3, 4, and 5.

		C	A	E
x		E	C	E
		E	C	A
	D	F	B	
E	C	A		
E	B	B	B	A

WHAT DIGIT OR DIGITS ARE REPRESENTED BY EACH LETTER?

316

The World's Most Mystifying Puzzle from the Addled Arithmetician, VI

Each letter above the line represents a digit that has a difference of one from the digit represented by the same letter below the line.

The digits are 0, 1, 2, 3, 4, 5, and 6.

	B	D	C	A	B	F	B
−	E	E	B	G	E	A	E
		G	E	E	F	C	F

WHAT DIGIT OR DIGITS DOES EACH LETTER REPRESENT?

The World's Most Mystifying Puzzle
from the Addled Arithmetician, VII

Each letter above the line represents a digit that has a difference of one from the digit represented by the same letter below the line.

The digits are 0, 1, 2, 3, 4, 5, and 6.

				F	C	C
			F	A	C	C
		B	A	E	C	A
+	A	D	C	F	A	A
	A	C	B	A	C	A

WHAT DIGIT OR DIGITS ARE REPRESENTED BY EACH LETTER?

The World's Most Mystifying Puzzle from the Addled Arithmetician, VIII

··

Each letter in the problem (above the top line) represents a digit that has a difference of one from the digit represented by the same letter in the answer (below the top line).

The digits are 0, 2, 3, 5, 6, 8, and 9.

		D	E	B
x			D	G
		E	E	E
B		F	G	
A		E	C	E

WHAT DIGIT OR DIGITS ARE REPRESENTED BY EACH LETTER?

The World's Most Mystifying Four Horse Puzzle

Alice, Danielle, Harriet, and Mary each own a horse and enjoy riding together. One day they decided to trade horses for the afternoon. Each woman rode a horse owned by one of the others, and no two women traded horses. From the statements below, what is the name of each friend's horse (one is Champ), and what is the name of the horse each rode?

1. Harriet rode the horse owned by Danielle.
2. Mary's horse was ridden by the owner of the horse named Charger.
3. The horse named El Cid was ridden by the owner of the horse ridden by Alice.
4. The horse named Charger was ridden by the owner of the horse ridden by Harriet.
5. The horse named Silver was ridden by the owner of the horse named El Cid.

The World's Most Mystifying Five Thespians Puzzle

Five local actors presented a murder mystery play in the Midville Theater. The five actors were Raymond, Rodney, Roland, Ronald, and Rupert. The five characters in the play were, interestingly enough, all namesakes of the actors, although no actor performed the role of his namesake. The parts in the play were magistrate, murderer, sheriff, victim, and witness. Based on the following, what was each actor's part and what was the name of the character he played?

1. The character played by Raymond was the namesake of the actor who played the murderer.

2. The namesake of the actor who played the magistrate was the character that was the murderer.

3. The character that was the sheriff was played by the actor whose namesake was the character played by Rupert.

4. The character played by Roland was the namesake of the actor who played the witness.

5. Roland did not play the victim, murderer, or sheriff.

6. The character played by Ronald was the namesake of the actor who played the magistrate.

7. The character that was the victim was played by the actor whose namesake was the character played by Rodney.

8. The namesake of the actor who played the murderer was the character that was the victim.

The World's Most Mystifying Five Author Puzzle

Authors James Blackledge, Sarah Hastings, John Montague, Milton Quincy, and Florence Williams met at a convention. In a casual conversation, they were surprised to discover that each writes using a pseudonym that is the surname of one of the others. Further, no two writers use the same pseudonym. Based on the following statements, what pseudonym does each use and what is the category of book that each authors?

1. The one who writes historical novels, who is not Sarah, uses as a pseudonym the surname of the author of mystery novels.

2. John's surname is used as the pseudonym of the author of mystery novels.

3. The one who writes mystery novels had one of his books on a bestseller list.

4. Milton, who writes general fiction, uses the surname of the author of biographies as his pseudonym.

5. Blackledge is the pseudonym of the writer whose surname is used as the pseudonym of the author of travel books.

6. The surname of the author of historical novels is used as the pseudonym of the author of travel books, who considers that the research involved is his favorite recreation.

The World's Most Mystifying St. Bernard and Dalmation Puzzle

Four friends, Sam, Sidney, Simon, and Smitty, enjoy dogs, and each has a St. Bernard and a Dalmatian. Each friend has named his two dogs after two of the other three friends. There are no duplicate names among the four St. Bernards and no duplicate names among the four Dalmatians.

Based on the following statements, what is the name of each owner's dog?

1. Simon's St. Bernard is the namesake of the owner of the Dalmatian named Sidney.

2. Smitty's Dalmatian is the namesake of the owner of which Sam's St. Bernard is the namesake.

3. The Dalmatian named Sam is owned by the owner of which Smitty's St. Bernard is the namesake.

4. Sam's Dalmatian is the namesake of the owner of the St. Bernard named Simon.

5. Sidney's Dalmatian is the namesake of the owner of the St. Bernard named Smitty.

The World's Most Mystifying Islanders' Boat Puzzle

Of four friends, O'Boyle, O'Brien, O'Bradovich, and O'Byrne, each has one daughter, spends considerable time on the water, and has both a sailboat and a fishing boat. Each friend has named his two boats after two different daughters of the other three friends. There are no duplicate names among the four sailboats and no duplicate names among the four fishing boats. Based on the following statements, who is the daughter of each of the four friends (one daughter is named Odette), and what are the names of each owner's boats?

1. O'Byrne's fishing boat is named after the owner's daughter after which O'Boyle's sailboat is named.

2. Neither Olivia O'Boyle nor Ophelia O'Byrne enjoys boating.

3. O'Byrne's sailboat is named for the daughter of the owner of the fishing boat named Olivia.

4. O'Brien's fishing boat, which is not named Olga, is named after the daughter of the owner of the sailboat named Ophelia.

5. O'Bradovich's fishing boat is not named Ophelia, nor is his sailboat named Olivia.

The World's Most Mystifying Classic Book Writer Puzzle

....

Six couples, the Brontës, the Conrads, the Dickenses, the Forsters, the Kafkas, and the Tolstoys, belong to a classics book club. Recently, they exchanged gifts of books. Each couple gave a book to one of the other couples. Each couple is the namesake of the author of one of the books given; no two couples gave a book by the same author; and no couple gave or received a book by an author of which they were the namesakes. The following statements apply:

1. The Conrads did not give or receive a book by Brontë, Forster, or Tolstoy.

2. The namesakes of the author of the book given by the Dickenses gave a book by Dickens to the Tolstoys.

3. The book by Forster was received by the namesakes of the author of the book that was given to the couple who gave the book by Dickens to the namesakes of the author of the book received by the Forsters.

4. The Brontës received a book by Conrad from the namesakes of the author of the book given by the Conrads.

5. The namesakes of the author of the book received by the Dickenses gave a book by Forster to the namesakes of the author of the book given by the namesakes of the author of the book given by the Kafkas.

WHICH COUPLES GAVE BOOKS BY WHICH AUTHORS, AND WHO RECEIVED THEM?

The World's Most Mystifying Two Inhabitant Puzzle

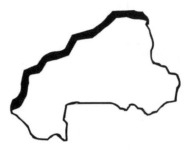

In the Land of the Liars, there are those who speak the truth only in the morning and lie in the afternoon. They are called Amtrus. There are also those who speak the truth only in the afternoon and lie in the morning. They are known as Pemtrus. If it were only that simple. You will also find some do not fit the traditional Land of Liars veracity patterns. More on them later.

Two inhabitants make the statements below. One is an Amtru and one is a Pemtru.

A. It is afternoon.
B. I am a Pemtru.

IS IT MORNING OR AFTERNOON, WHICH IS THE AMTRU, AND WHICH IS THE PEMTRU?

The World's Most Mystifying True Statement Puzzle

Of the three who make the following statements, two are Pemtrus and one is an Amtru.

    A. B is a Pemtru.
    B. A's statement is true.
    C. A's statement is false.

IS IT MORNING OR AFTERNOON, AND TO WHICH GROUP DOES EACH INHABITANT BELONG?

The World's Most Mystifying Three Inhabitant Puzzle

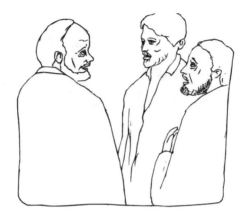

Two Pemtrus and an Amtru make the statements below:

A. B is a Pemtru.
B. C is a Pemtru.
C. A is the Amtru.

IS IT MORNING OR AFTERNOON, WHICH IS THE AMTRU, AND WHICH ARE THE PEMTRUS?

The World's Most Mystifying Four Inhabitant Puzzle

Four inhabitants make the following statements. They are two Amtrus and two Pemtrus.

    A. B is an Amtru.
    B. C is a Pemtru.
    C. A and D are from different groups.
    D. A and B are from the same group.

IS IT MORNING OR AFTERNOON, AND TO WHICH GROUP DOES EACH OF THE FOUR INHABITANTS BELONG?

The World's Most Mystifying
Five Inhabitant Puzzle

Five inhabitants are asked to which group each belongs. They are three Amtrus and two Pemtrus. They respond:

    A. I am a Pemtru or it is morning.

    B. I am an Amtru or it is afternoon.

    C. D and E belong to the same group.

    D. A is an Amtru.

    E. B is a Pemtru.

IS IT MORNING OR AFTERNOON, WHICH ONES ARE AMTRUS, AND WHICH ONES ARE PEMTRUS?

The World's Most Mystifying Four Valley Inhabitant Puzzle

In the Land of Liars, there is a valley in which the inhabitants have their own lying patterns. The Amtrus speak the truth in the morning and lie in the afternoon, except that in statements in which they directly refer to another indivudal in the same group by name (letter designation), they lie in the morning and speak the truth in the afternoon. The Pemtrus speak the truth in the afternoon and lie in the morning, except that in statements in which they directly refer to another in the same group by name, they lie in the afternoon and speak the truth in the morning.

Four valley inhabitants, who are represented equally by both groups, are asked to which group each belongs. They make the statements below, although the fourth valley inhabitant, D, chooses to remain silent.

    A. D and I belong to the same group.
    B. A and I belong to the same group.
    C. B is a Pemtru.

IS IT MORNING OR AFTERNOON, AND WHICH GROUP IS REPRESENTED BY EACH OF THE FOUR INHABITANTS?

The World's Most Mystifying Three Valley Inhabitant Puzzle

Asked their groups, three valley inhabitants respond as follows:

A. C and I are both Pemtrus.

B. C and I are not both Amtrus.

C. If you were to ask A about this guy [pointing to B] and A used this guy's name, A would say that this guy is an Amtru.

IS IT MORNING OR AFTERNOON, AND WHICH GROUP IS REPRESENTED BY EACH OF THE THREE SPEAKERS?

The World's Most Mystifying Liar on the Hill Puzzle

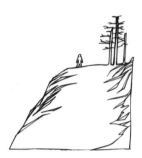

On a small isolated hill in the Land of Liars live a few who are obstinate and who pride themselves on being different. They are neither Amtrus nor Pemtrus. In making statements when in the company of other inhabitants of the Land of Liars, a hill inhabitant will speak the truth only if none of the others speak the truth, and will lie if any of the others speak the truth.

It is afternoon. Of the four speakers, exactly one is a hill inhabitant. C claims he is the one. Their statements follow:

    A. B is an Amtru.
    B. C is a Pemtru.
    C. I live on the hill.
    D. A is a Pemtru.

WHICH SPEAKER IS THE HILL INHABITANT AND WHAT ARE THE OTHER THREE?

The World's Most Mystifying One from the Hill Puzzle

Four from the Land of Liars, including exactly one hill inhabitant, make the following statements:

A. Either D is an Amtru or he lives on the hill.

B. C is either an Amtru or a Pemtru.

C. I live on the hill or B lives on the hill.

D. C's statement is true or C is a Pemtru.

IS IT MORNING OR AFTERNOON, WHICH ONE IS THE HILL INHABITANT, AND WHAT ARE THE OTHER THREE SPEAKERS?

THE WORLD'S MOST DAUNTING MATH PUZZLES

The World's Most Daunting Fishing Puzzle

Four men went fishing. They caught six fish altogether. One man caught three, another caught two, one caught one, and one didn't catch anything. Which man caught how many fish? What did each of the fishermen use for bait?

1. The one who caught two fish wasn't Sammy nor the one who used worms.

2. The one who used the flatfish didn't catch as many as Fred.

3. Dry flies were the best lure of the day, catching three fish.

4. Torkel used eggs.

5. Sammy didn't use the flatfish.

The World's Most Daunting Jump Rope Puzzle

Some kids were jumping rope (double Dutch) at the school break. They counted how many times each one jumped before missing (9, 12, 17, 20, and 25). See if you can figure out how many jumps each kid made.

1. Gary jumped eight fewer times than Arnie.

2. Combined, Danielle, and Ruth jumped 37 times.

3. Jan jumped 8 more jumps than Danielle.

4. Gary and Danielle are separated by just three jumps.

5. Arnie's jumps number 5 more than Danielle.

The World's Most Daunting Pocket Change Puzzle

Five boys went to the store to buy some treats. One boy had $4. One boy had $3. Two boys had $2, and one boy had $1. Using the following clues, determine how much money each boy started with and how much each had when he left the store (95¢, 70¢, 40¢, and 10¢).

THE CLUES ARE:

1. Alex started with more than Jim.

2. Scott spent 15¢ more than Dan.

3. Duane started with more money than just one other person.

4. Alex spent the most, but he did not end with the least.

5. Dan started with 66% as much as Scott.

6. Jim spent the least and ended with more than Alex or Dan.

7. Duane spent 35¢.

The World's Most Daunting Temperature Puzzle

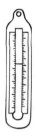

A sixth-grade class project involved keeping track of the average temperature of the classroom over a two-week period in January. The results of the study showed that, at one particular time of the day, the temperature was always at its lowest point. Try to figure out when, during the day, the temperature was lowest, and the reason for it.

1. The automatic heating system in the school comes on at 6:00 in the morning.
2. No students arrive before 8:30. The first temperature reading takes place at that time.
3. The temperature is taken at half hour intervals from 8:30 until 3:00 in the afternoon, when the students go home.
4. The automatic heating system goes off at 2:00.
5. The highest temperature reading is at 10:00.
6. The 2:30 reading of the temperature shows a cooling off, but not the lowest temperature.
7. Morning recess is from 10:20 to 10:35.
8. Afternoon recess takes place from 1:45 until 2:00.
9. The highest temperature over the two-week period was 74 degrees F (23.3 degrees C).

SO, WHEN *WAS* THE TEMPERATURE AT ITS LOWEST, AND WHY?

The World's Most Daunting Coast to Coast Puzzle

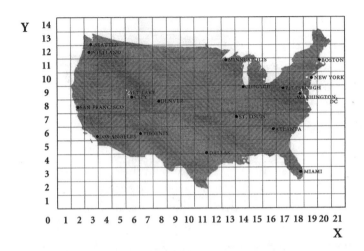

Jacques and Chi Chi rode bikes across the United States. They stopped at several major cities along the way like Seattle, Portland, San Francisco, Salt Lake City, Denver, Los Angeles, Phoenix, St. Louis, Chicago, Minneapolis, Pittsburgh, Atlanta, Washington, D.C., Miami, New York, and Boston. Figure out where they went and the order in which they visited the cities based on the coordinates given in the clues below. (The visited city is the one "closest" to the intersection of the coordinates.)

They started their journey at X6, Y5.5.

Their first stop was at X3, Y5.5; then they rode on to X1.5, Y7.5.

Then they stopped off in the city at X2.5, Y11.5.

From there they rode to X5.5, Y8, and then to X7.5, Y8.

They stayed a few days at X11, Y4, and three days at X13, Y6.5.

From there they rode to X13.5, Y9, then to X16.5, Y9.

Finally, tired but happy, they ended their journey at X18, Y8.5.

START TO FINISH, WHAT ARE THE ELEVEN AMERICAN CITIES VISITED BY JACQUES AND CHI CHI?

The World's Most Daunting Coffee Puzzle

A few friends meet each morning for coffee. For one of them, it is the only cup of coffee all day. For another, it's only the first of eight cups. Zowie!

Your challenge is to figure out how many cups of coffee each person drinks per day (1, 4, 5, 6, or 8), how many sugar lumps they use per cup (1, 2, 4, or 6), and whether or not they put in milk.

1. Jan uses three times as many lumps as the person who drinks four cups.

2. Three people, including the one who uses four lumps, use no milk.

3. The one who drinks 1 cup a day (not Max) drinks his coffee black without sugar.

4. Doris uses both milk and sugar.

5. Max, who uses no milk, uses half as many sugars as the person who drinks twice as many cups as he does.

6. Boris drinks two more cups than Jan, but Jan uses two more sugars than Boris.

The World's Most Daunting
Decimal Ruler Puzzle

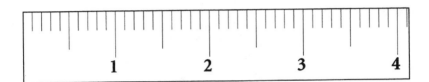

This ruler measures inches but, instead of measuring them in the usual way, in sixteenths, it measures them in *tenths*. In other words, the standard inch is divided into ten (decimal) units, rather than sixteen units.

When we measure something with this decimal ruler, it is expressed as the number of inches plus the tenths. For example, the line just below measures 3.4 inches. Go ahead, check it out (mark the length on a straight piece of paper and then hold it next to the ruler).

Now, using paper and this ruler, measure these other lines.

a _____

b _____

c _____

d _____

e _____

f _____

g _____

CHECK YOUR MEASUREMENTS IN THE SOLUTIONS.

The World's Most Daunting
Destry's Missing Numbers Puzzle

Destry has five boxes, arranged from left-to-right. Each is supposed to have a decimal number in it, but they're all empty! Help Destry find his missing numbers and put them back in their boxes.

Here are some clues to where the numbers should go:

1. One square (the sum of 11.09, 6.21, and 5.04) is to the left of a square with the difference between 13.27 and 1.34.

2. C is not 13.47 but another square is.

3. One square has a number larger than square B by 13.78.

4. The square with a sum of 13.62, 3.98, 7.00, and .57 is between B and E.

5. The smallest number is B; the largest is E.

The World's Most Daunting E.F. Bingo Puzzle

1/4	3/8	1/8
6/7	1/3	2/10
4/5	3/5	4/10

2/5	2/3	1/6
1/7	4/5	3/8
1/2	3/9	2/6

5/8	2/10	2/6
6/7	8/9	3/7
1/3	1/4	9/11

1/2	5/8	3/10
1/4	1/3	2/12
2/6	4/10	2/3

Four girls—Lorraine, Michelle, Wanda, and Sheila—are in a serious game of E.F. Bingo (E.F. stands for equivalent fractions). Their cards appear above in the order their names are listed. The first one to fill in a line on her card (up-and-down, across, or diagonally) wins. To solve this puzzle, figure out which girl wins and gets to yell "Bingo!"

The fractions come up and are called in this order:

1. "Four twentieths"
2. "Eighteen twenty-seconds"
3. "Four tenths"
4. "Six tenths"
5. "Two eighths"
6. "Ten sixteenths"
7. "Twelve fourteenths"
8. "Four twenty-eighths"
9. "Six sixteenths"
10. "Six twentieths"
11. "Eight twelfths"
12. "Sixteen eighteenths"
13. "Four twelfths"

The World's Most Daunting Famous Person Puzzle

There's a famous person's name spelled out in twelve boxes arranged from left-to-right. Using the coding provided, figure out the letters of the name and solve this puzzle.

A=1	E=5	I=9	M=13	Q=17	V=22
B=2	F=6	J=10	N=14	R=18	W=23
C=3	G=7	K=11	O=15	S=19	X=24
D=4	H=8	L=12	P=16	T=20	Y=25
				U=21	Z=26

CLUES:

Boxes 7 and 10 are U – P

Box 2 is C x E

Boxes 4, 8, and 9 are the same letter: F + J – B

Box 6 is Z – Y + J

Box 12 is E^2

Box 1 is O – E

Box 5 is X divided by D

Box 11 is G x C – Q

Box 3 is T + E + D

The World's Most Daunting Flighty Decimals Puzzle

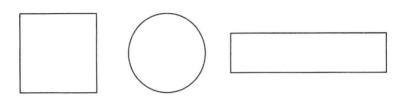

Normally trustworthy and reliable, the decimals below got a little out of hand. They escaped from their geometric shapes and were scattered all over the place! Now the decimals are all lined up in two rows (below) in order from the largest to smallest, but they really need to be put back into their proper geometric places. Your job is to do just that.

5.20	4.39	4.01	3.71	2.60	1.42
1.16	1.01	.72	.30	.07	.03

Here are clues to where the decimals are to go (four decimals in each shape) in the geometric spaces below:

1. 4.39 and 4.01 are supposed to be in the same figure; 5.20 (the ringleader) is supposed to be in a different one.
2. Decimals 3.71 and 1.01 are together in the rectangle.
3. The total in the circle, where .07 is supposed to be, is 6.46.
4. The smallest total comes from the rectangle, where .30 is supposed to be.
5. The difference between the totals of the square and the circle is 5.96.
6. Decimal 1.16 is supposed to be in the circle.

ADD THE DECIMALS ASSIGNED TO EACH SHAPE AND CHECK YOUR TOTALS AGAINST THE SOLUTION.

The World's Most Daunting Heather's Garden Puzzle

Heather's garden is out of control! She planted it just so, and then went to surfing at a beach. When she got back from her trip, she found the turnips mixing with the cabbages, the pole beans mixing with the carrots, and the rows jumbled all over the place. Plus, field mice have gotten in and some of the garden is missing!

Heather had made a map so she would remember how much she planted where, but the mice got that too! See if you can reconstruct the garden's contents for her.

1. The most rows are neither spinach nor cabbages.
2. There are two more rows of carrots than turnips and two more rows of spinach than carrots.
3. There are four more rows of spinach than turnips.
4. There aren't as many rows of pole beans as "cukes" (cucumbers in garden talk).
5. There is one less cabbage row than spinach.
6. Heather doesn't like turnips so much, so she planted just one row (mostly to sacrifice to the mice, but they don't care all that much for turnips, either!).

The World's Most Daunting Mathathon Puzzle

Several girls were trying to work some math problems. Several boys said they could help them find the solutions. The girls said, "Fat chance!" So there was a contest between the girls and the boys to see who was best at solving the problems. Check it out and see who won.

Each problem is worth 10 points if the answer is correct; -5 points if it is wrong.

Problem 1 9 x .3 = The girls said 2.7, the boys said 2.7.
Problem 2 1.06 + .089 + 11.2 + 6.34 =
   The girls said 18.689, the boys said 18.768.
Problem 3 1/2 + 3/4 = The girls said 1 1/4, the boys said 1.25.
Problem 4 13.88 – 6.96 = The girls said 6.92, the boys said 7.92.
Problem 5 4.003 x 99 =
   The girls said 396.297, the boys said 386.297.
Problem 6 2 1/3 x 1/2 = The girls said 1.166, the boys said 1.1.
Problem 7 .33 divided by 3 = The girls said .11, the boys said 1.1.
Problem 8 6.66 + 3.75 + 9.07 =
   The girls said 19.48, the boys said 19.38.

SO, WHO WAS BEST AT DOING MATH—OR AT LEAST AT WORKING THESE PARTICULAR PROBLEMS?

The World's Most Daunting Mountain Climb Puzzle

Dacon and his friends all went mountain climbing this summer, but not together. They climbed different mountains. Using the clues, see if you can figure out who climbed which mountain, and the heights they climbed (9,000; 8,000; 7,5000; 11,000; or4,500.)

1. Dacon climbed higher than 4500 feet, but not on Goat.

2. Jake climbed higher than both Macom and the one who climbed Sleepy.

3. The mountain which is 9000 feet is not Old Baldy or Goat.

4. The shortest mountain was not climbed by Bacon.

5. Mirre is shorter than the mountain climbed by Macom, but higher than the one climbed by Drakon.

6. Sleepy is not the tallest, but taller than Goat.

7. Raleigh is taller than Goat, which is taller than the ones climbed by Drakon and Dacon.

The World's Most Daunting Mountain Race Puzzle

Five people will race to the tops of mountains of different heights (Mt. Stewart, 8,989; Mt. Morgan, 8,124; Mt. Waring, 7,876; and Mt. Picard, 9,125 ft.). Their first names are Andy, Gerald, Dale, Paul and Jim. Their last names are Anderson, Brown, Dorsey, McGee, and Stiller. To have a fair race, each person will carry a weight (50, 40, 30, 20 or 10 lbs.); the person climbing the lowest mountain, the heaviest backpack weight, etc.

Using the clues, figure out each person's full name, the mountain each will climb, and the weight to be carried in each backpack.

1. Paul's pack weighs 30 lbs.
2. Andy's mountain is 865 ft. higher than the one Brown is climbing.
3. Gerald's pack weighs the same as Dale's minus McGee's.
4. Stiller's pack is half as heavy as the person's climbing Mt. Morgan.
5. Jim's and Dorsey's packs combined weigh 60 lbs.
6. Anderson's pack is 20 pounds lighter than Dale's.

The World's Most Daunting Ned's Newspaper Route Puzzle

Ned delivers papers in his neighborhood. In January he had 43 customers. He wanted to make a little more money, so he went door to door, and by April he had found five new customers. One new customer gets just a daily paper, two get just a Sunday paper, and two get both. What you need to do is figure out which of his new customers gets what, and the color of their houses (grey, green, white, yellow, or blue).

1. The Simpsons get both papers; their house is not white.

2. The Browns' house is neither grey nor the color of one of the houses that gets just the Sunday paper.

3. The customer's name who subscribes to just the daily paper begins with J.

4. The customer in the green house does not get a Sunday paper.

5. Mr. Johnson lives in the blue house.

The World's Most Daunting Wild Numbers Puzzle

¼   ½   ¾   1

A group of untamed, wild numbers has been terrorizing the neighborhood lately. The math police are in need of help rounding them up and placing them in their correct places. Can you help? *Please, before it's too late!*

Here are the culprits. They look orderly because they are lined up in three columns, but they really need to be connected up with the correct shapes—six to each shape. Hurry!

.5	100%	75%
$^6/_8$	$^3/_{12}$	$^7/_{14}$
.75	three-fourths	$^5/_{20}$
50%	.250	whole
$^4/_{16}$	$1.00	75¢
$^4/_8$	$^6/_{24}$	$^{10}/_{10}$
one-fourth	half a dollar	$^3/_6$
$^5/_5$	$^9/_{12}$	$^4/_4$

The World's Most Daunting Zox Puzzle

The nation of Zox consists of five islands: Zog, Zod, Zob, Zop, and Zoz. The total population of all five islands is 750 Zoxians.

Figure out how many Zoxians live on each island. Below are some clues to help you.

1. The smallest island has $^1/_{10}$ as many Zoxians as all of Zox.
2. The largest island is Zod. The smallest island is not Zoz.
3. One island has $^1/_5$ of the total population of Zox. Another island has $^1/_3$.
4. Zob is one and a half times larger than one of the other islands.
5. Zop has 100 more people than the smallest island.

The World's Most Daunting Auction Puzzle

The Clydesdale County Fair held its annual fund-raising auction last week. Five of the people who bought items are listed here.

Your challenge is to match the last names (Green, White, Black, Brown, and Grey) of the purchases with their first names(Irene, Denise, Duane, Dan, and Elroy), identify which items each one bought, and figure out how much each one paid (the lowest amount that anyone paid was $3.50).

Here are a few clues:

1. Elroy is not Grey.
2. The man who bought the coffee paid the highest price, twice that of the fruit.
3. The cheese sold for $2.00 less than the coffee and was purchased by Black.
4. Ms. Green bought the pie for ²/₃ the cost of the cake.
5. White and Daune shared their cake and coffee.
6. The pie cost $0.50 more than the fruit.
7. Dan paid $6.00 for his item.
8. Neither Elroy, Denise, nor Black paid over $5.00.

The World's Most Daunting Biology Class Puzzle

Kristi and five of her friends (Kate, Kristen, Kurt, Kyle and Kevin) have each adopted an animal (a bat, hamster, mole, rat, fly, or ladybug that is 1, 1.3, 11, 14, 18, or 23 cm) in biology class. See if you can figure out which animal (the W's) belongs to which student (the K's).

1. Walter can fly; Willy can't.
2. Kristi's animal is 14 cm (6 in) long.
3. The ladybug is not a lady, nor the smallest.
4. Willy is 5 cm (2 in) shorter than the largest animal.
5. Kyle's animal is neither a fly nor a ladybug.
6. Walter is 10 cm (4 in) shorter than the bat, who's 3 cm (about 1 in) shorter than Wendy.
7. Wanda is the largest.
8. Kurt's animal is the smallest.
9. The hamster belongs to Kevin.
10. Willy is neither the rat nor the hamster.
11. Weldon, who is able to fly, belongs to Kristen.
12. Kate's adoption measures 18 cm (7 in).

The World's Most Daunting Caleb's Checkbook Puzzle

Five people were discussing their checking accounts. Caleb, who is a spend-thrift, is almost broke. But Ms. Wilson still has good bit of her earnings left. Can you figure our how much money each of the five people start with in their checking accounts($2,050; $1,987; $1,940; $1,004; or $1,699), what their current balances are($1,004; $970; $423; $68; or -$45), and what are their full names(Caleb, Barbara, Sam, Joyce, or Millard; and Brown, Jones, Smith, Wilson, and Jackson) ?Here are a few clues:

1. Joyce is not Jones.
2. Caleb's bills amounted to $1919.00 for the month.
3. Millard, who started with more than Jackson or Brown, ended with less than either Caleb or Wilson.
4. Joyce's balance was exactly half of what she started with.
5. Sam's and Jackson's balances, when added together, were $1427.00.
6. Millard's bills were: rent $850.00, telephone $95.00, utilities $220.00, insurance $400.00, car payment $290.00, food $240.00.
7. Brown spent the least amount on bills—$695.00. Smith spent the most.
8. Barbara's bills totaled $1326.00.

SO, WHO IS WHO AND HOW MUCH MONEY DID THEY EACH START OUT AND END UP WITH?

The World's Most Daunting Chicken Mountain Puzzle

At the top of Chicken Mountain live five chicken farmers. Each farmer thinks his chickens are the best. Farmer McSanders says his chickens are best because they lay the most eggs. Farmer Saffola says his chickens make the best fryers. (On each farm there are 392, 441, 500, 552, or 598 chickens; each bird lays 4.2, 2.8, 4.0, 4.6, or 4.8 eggs; and each egg costs .73, .84, .94, .64 or .71.)

See if you can figure out which farmer does have the best chickens, based on the following facts plus the formula provided to grade the chickens.

1. The chickens with the best feathers live on the McCombe farm. They sell for $0.73.
2. The chickens which sell for $0.64 produce 105 eggs per day. It's not the Poularde farm.
3. Farmer Saffola has 500 chickens.
4. The farm which produces 115 eggs per day sells its chickens for $0.71.
5. The smartest chickens live on the McPlume farm.
6. The best fryers get the most money.
7. Farmers McSanders and McPlume have 833 chickens between them.
8. The smallest farm produces the most eggs and the second-best price.
9. The biggest chickens produce 4.8 eggs per chicken on the Poularde farm.

BEST CHICKENS ON CHICKEN MOUNTAIN GRADING FORMULA:
A divided by B x C + D

The World's Most Daunting Chocolate Chip Cookies Puzzle

Five of the world's foremost chocolate chip cookie bakers arrived for the annual Cookie Fiesta. While the bakers all agreed on most of the ingredients that go into their famous chocolate chip cookies, they did not agree at all on the right number of chips per cookie or the amount of time they should be baked to come out perfect. Determine the full names of the five cookie bakers(Effie, Ruby, Thelma Georgia, or Miriam; Spicer, Applestreet, Strudel, Bundt, or Honeydew), the number of chips each puts in her cookies (5, 7, 8, 9, or 10) and how long they leave them to bake (16 m/9s, 16m/17s, 17m, 17m/7s, 17m/8s).

Here are a few clues:

1. Ms. Strudel bakes her cookies for 17 minutes 7 seconds.
2. Effie uses 2 chips fewer than Ruby does.
3. Ms. Applestreet bakes her cookies 51 seconds longer than Thelma does.
4. Ms. Spicer uses one less chip than Ms. Applestreet puts in her cookies.
5. Ms. Honeydew uses more chips than Ms. Spicer does.
6. Ruby isn't Ms. Honeydew.
7. Ms. Spicer bakes for less time than do either Miriam or Georgia.
8. The woman who bakes her cookies for 17 minutes 7 seconds uses 7 chips.
9. Georgia bakes hers for 17 minutes 8 seconds, 1 second longer than Ruby does.
10. The person using 5 chips isn't Ms. Spicer.

The World's Most Daunting Dessert Puzzle

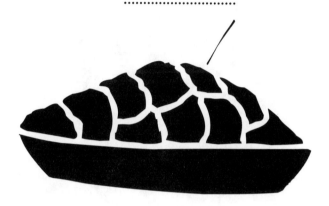

Four friends (Jane, Pete, Tom, or Sarah; Smith, Brown, Grey or Jones) went out to a new restaurant to try their desserts(fig cookie, apple pie, custard, and chocolate cake). Although some were very hungry, others weren't so they didn't eat the full portions they were served ($^1/_6$, $^3/_4$, $^2/_3$, or $^1/_8$.)

Using the clues, determine the full names of the four friends, the kind of dessert each had, and the amount eaten.

1. Ms. Jones' dessert had been cut into eight pieces.
2. Jane ate her dessert with a spoon. It was served in a measuring cup that was divided into three equal-size portions. She ate the dessert down to the bottom line.
3. The one who ate the fig cookie was neither Smith nor Jane.
4. The apple pie was cut into six pieces.
5. Pete and Grey play basketball together.
6. Brown and Tom paid for the meal.
7. Pete's dessert wasn't divided into thirds.
8. Grey didn't eat any dessert beginning with the letter C.
9. The fig cookie was sliced into quarters. The person who ate it left one of the pieces.
10. The apple pie wasn't eaten by Grey or Sarah.
11. No one has a first and last name that begin with the same letter.

The World's Most Daunting Dog Apartments Puzzle

There are six dogs (MacTavish, Chico, Ivan, Wilfred, Taz, and Spunky). Each dog lives on a different floor (in apartments 103, 221, 341, 408, 512, and 609), eats a different amount of dog food (2, 4, 6, 8, 10, or 12 lbs.) each week, and takes a different number of baths (2, 3, 4, 6, 9, or 12) each month. Figure out which floor each dog lives on, the amount of food each one eats, and the number of baths each one takes.

1. The dog in 221 eats twice as much as the one who takes 1 bath a week.
2. MacTavish eats four pounds less than Spunky, but takes five more baths.
3. The dog that eats 32 pounds a month takes 3 baths a week.
4. Wilfred lives two floors above Spunky. Spunky lives two floors above Chico.
5. Taz and the dog on the 6th floor eat a combined weight of 80 pounds in a month.
6. The dog in 341 eats 24 pounds a month and bathes once a week.
7. The dog in 408 eats fewer pounds in a month than he takes baths.
8. The dog on the 5th floor eats 16 pounds a month and takes one less bath than Chico.

The World's Most Daunting Field Trip Puzzle

Duloc and his pals held bake sales and earned enough money to take a field trip with their teacher, Mr. Oonla. In fact, they made enough to go all the way to the planet Earth!

When they arrived at the third planet in the Sol system, they discovered the gravitational pull was very different from what they were used to back on Nolu Si. Mr. Oonla was curious about the difference in weight, how much his students weighed in Earth ounces. An Earth ounce is equivalent to 11 Nolu Si ounces, except that on Nolu Si the measurement isn't called ounces but qinae.

According to the following clues, how much in Earth ounces do each of these five students weigh? How much do they weigh back on Nolu Si?

1. Sio weights 50.6 qinae. He outweighs everyone except Phren, who weighs 13.2 qinae more.
2. Ontrus, the lightest, weighs 27.5 qinae less than Duloc.
3. Jorn weighs 5.5 qinae less than Sio, and 2.2 qinae more than Duloc.

The World's Most Daunting
Flea Market Leftovers Puzzle

There were a few unsold items, listed below, left over from the flea market. Bernie told some friends who had helped her with the sale to each take one of the items home. Can you figure out who took which item?

ITEM	MEASUREMENT
Nut	diameter 1.25 in
Pencil	end to end 17.2 cm
Compass	height 16.5 cm
Pencil sharpener	height 5 $^1/_2$ in
Bolt	length 4.5 cm

1. Dan took one item which was shorter than the item Sandy took by 1.3 centimeters.
2. The item taken by Bob was one and one-quarter inches taller than the item taken by Irene.
3. Doris' item was 7 centimeters less than Bob's.
4. Sandy's item was 12 centimeters less than Doris'.

The World's Most Daunting
Four Cups Puzzle

Four cups, A to D, are arranged side by side. Each contains a certain amount of liquid measured in ounces(3, 5, 8, or 11). One cup contains water, another oil, one holds vinegar, and the other apple juice. Which cup has which liquid and how much is in each?

Here are some clues:

1. The cup with oil is between the cups containing 3 oz. and 5 oz.
2. The vinegar isn't in cup C.
3. There's more apple juice in the cups than water, but more oil than apple juice.
4. The water is between the juice and the oil.
5. The difference in ounces between the vinegar and the juice is 3.
6. Cup D doesn't contain oil, and doesn't have the least amount of liquid in it.
7. Cup C has more liquid than does cup A.
8. The cup with 11 oz. isn't vinegar.

The World's Most Daunting Fractions Prom Puzzle

The annual Fractions Prom was held last week. Six couples went to the dance together (Two Thirds, One Sixth, Three Fifths, One Fourth, Three Eighths, One Tenth, One Third, Five Sixths, One Eighth, One Fifth, Seven Eighths, and Two Fifths). They sat at three tables. Because One Third and Three Fifths were still angry at each other over an argument about which of them was more important, they refused to sit together. Otherwise, everybody got along quite well.

From the following clues, see if you can figure out which fractions went to the prom with which other fractions, and which of the three tables they shared.

1. One Eighth and his date shared a table with One Fourth and her date, but it was not table 3.
2. The sum of One Tenth and her date was $^1/_2$. The sum of everyone at that table was $1\ ^3/_{10}$.
3. One Sixth and Three Eighths didn't share a table.
4. One Third and his date totaled 1.
5. Seven Eighths and Three Eighths shared table 2. Their dates totaled 3/8.
6. One Fifth's date is not Two Thirds.

The World's Most Daunting Fund-Raiser Puzzle

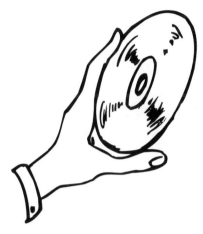

Three eighth-grade classes (125, 208, 214) at a large school competed in a fund-raising event by reading books. The person who read the most books (9, 12, 13, 18, 21, 23, 24, 27, 28, 32, 34, 36, or 42) won a CD player. The class that read the most books won a field trip to an amusement park. No two students read the same number of books.

From the following clues, which student won the player (Nancy, Bill, Jerry, Sam, Tinzen, Julia, Harry, Eric, Jennifer, Teresa, Danny, Joan, or Dennis), and which class got to go to the amusement park?

1. Sam, in room 125, read half as many books as Eric, who read half as many as Danny.
2. Nancy read twice as many books as Harry, who is in room 125.
3. Room 125 includes the students who read 24 books and 34 books.
4. Teresa read three times as many as Sam.
5. Bill is in room 208, which totaled 113 books.
6. Jennifer read half as many books as Tinzen.
7. There are just three students in room 214, including Jennifer, Jerry, and the winning student.
8. Dennis read ten more books than Nancy.
9. Bill read just one more book than Harry.
10. No one in room 214 read fewer than 21 books.
11. The winning room included the person who read the fewest books.
12. The total number of books read in room 214 was 91.
13. Joan read fewer books than Julia, who read more books than Jerry.

The World's Most Daunting Golf Puzzle

Hole	1	2	3	4	5	6	7	8	9	Total
Par	4	5	3	4	4	5	4	4	3	36
Jim	5	5	4	4	6		5	3		
Jan		7	3	4	5	5	5		3	
Jon	6	5	4	5	5		4	5		
Jed	5	6		4	5	6		6	4	

Four friends played golf. The scorekeeper wasn't alert and missed recording a few scores. Find the correct missing scores and figure out everyone's total. All four players had different scores.

Oh yes, and who was the lazy scorekeeper?

1. Jan had the lowest scores on holes #1 and #6.
2. The total scored for hole #3 was 14.
3. Jed's total score was higher than Jan's.
4. The total score for all four players was 169.
5. Just one player shot a birdie (1 under par)—Jim, 3 on #8.
6. The scorekeeper's total score was 44—the highest.
7. Jon shot par on one of his missing scores. He shot one over par on the other.
8. The total scored for hole #6 was 23.
9. Jim's total score was higher than Jan's, but not as high as Jon's.

The World's Most Daunting Grade Book Puzzle

Test	1	2	3	4	5	6	7	8	9
Alban	45	56	84	36	78	34	46		98
Astrid	49	60		50	86	45	36	20	87
Amos	38	70	90		100	48	38	20	97
Angus	39		94	50	94	49	45	19	100
Avril	44	68	88	50	89		39	20	100

A math teacher gives a test once a week. All the students took all the tests. Unfortunately, the teacher forgot to record some of the scores. Find each student's missing test score, then total their scores and find the students' averages and final grades.

AVERAGE	GRADE
62–70	A
57–61	B
52–56	C
49–51	D

1. Astrid's missing test score is the same as the average of the student with the A.
2. Amos got a perfect score on test 2. Angus missed it by 2 points.
3. The total of all five students' total scores is 2628.
4. The missing score on test 8 is 18. On test 6 it's 33.

HINT: Start with clue 2.

The World's Most Daunting Hot Dogs Puzzle

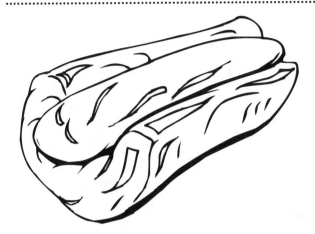

One student from each fifth-grade class in McDonald Elementary School (Gerald, Isabella, Germaine, Tony, or Ginger) decided to try to set a new school record for the most hot dogs eaten during one lunch period.

From the following clues, see if you can tell how many hot dogs each student ate (12, 16, 20, 22, or 24), the students' last names (Smith, Jones, Green, Brown or White), and their room numbers (201, 202, 203, 204, or 205).

1. Isabella, whose last name is not Green, ate three-fourths as many hot dogs as Tony.
2. Ginger is in room 203.
3. Brown ate four more hot dogs than Gerald, and two more than White.
4. Green's room is between Gerald's and Ginger's rooms.
5. Germaine ate more hot dogs than Gerald, who ate more than Green.
6. The student from room 204 ate 8 fewer hot dogs than the student in room 201.
7. Smith's classroom is 202.

The World's Most Daunting Longest Drive Puzzle

Six golfers (Desmond, Simon, Lyle, Lester, Henry, and Jake) had a contest to see who could hit the ball farthest. The golfers used four different-size clubs (3-wood, 2-iron, driver, and 5-wood).

When they tried to compare the distances, they discovered that some has been measured in yards and some in meters. Confusing?

Determine who the golfers are (Baring, Bates, Jenkins, Pym, Reed, or Rivers), how many yards or meters each one hit the ball (257 m, 283 m, 263 m, 244 m, 261 m, or 282 m), and the club size each one used. (If needed, refer to the simple yards/meters conversion formulas at the bottom of this page.)

1. Henry did not use his driver when he hit his booming 282-meter drive. Two of the guys did, including Baring.
2. The longest drive was hit with a driver, but not by Reed or Simon.
3. The shortest drive, 244 meters, was hit with a 5-wood, but not by Bates or Jake.
4. Desmond's drive went 257 meters, 4 yards shorter than Pym's.
5. The 2-iron drive went 263 meters, 20 fewer than Lester's.
6. Lyle used the 5-wood.
7. Henry and Rivers each used their 3-woods. Henry's went 23 yards farther.

CONVERSION FORMULAS:
Metres x .92 = yards
Yards x 1.09 = meters

The World's Most Daunting Multiplication Jeopardy Puzzle

For a change, Dale and some friends studying for a multiplication test (Sue, June, Neil and Tina) gave each other the problem answers (products) and tried to figure out the two numbers in the problem. From the clues, figure out each student's full name (James, Jones, Jensen, Johns or Johnson), the product each was given, and the correct multiplier (5, 7, 8, 9, or 11) and multiplicand (13, 14, 15, 16 or 18). One of the products (where multiplicand and multiplier intersect) is 144.

1. Dale's multiplicand is 14.
2. Tina's last name is not Johns.
3. June's multiplier is 9.
4. Neil is neither James nor Jones.
5. Miss Jensen's product is 120.
6. The person whose multiplicand is 13 is not James, Jensen, or Mr. Johnson.
7. Tina's product is 143.
8. Neil's multiplicand is 18. His product is 126.
9. Johns' multiplier is 7.

The World's Most Daunting Old House Puzzle

Six different families (Barnes, Carpenter, Lewis, Parker, Smith, and Warner) have lived a total of 88 years in an old house. The original owners lived there half the total number of years. A second family lived there a quarter of the years. The third family lived in the house half that. Then a family lived there five years. The fifth family lived there two years. And the sixth family still lives there.

Each family painted the house a different color (blue, brown, green, yellow, and red). Right now, it is white. How long did each family live in the old house? What color did each family paint it?

1. The Smiths lived there eleven times longer than the Parkers.
2. The house was yellow for two years.
3. In all, the house was painted three different colors—blue, yellow, and white—for 11 years.
4. The color was changed from green to brown after the Carpenters moved.
5. The house was either brown or red for 33 years.
6. The Barneses lived there longer than the number of years the house was blue and white.
7. The house was yellow when the Warners moved in.

The World's Most Daunting Play Ball Puzzle

Toddy and some of her friends (Teddie, Teresa, Tanya, Tom, and Tillie) had to bring a ball, representing their favorite sport, to class. Toddy brought the ball weighing the least.

Determine who brought which ball (ping-pong, tenns, golf, soccer, basketball, or football) how much each ball weighed (1.5, .8, 15, 22, 2, or 16 oz.), and what color it was (orange, white, green, red, brown, or yellow).

1. The golf ball weighed less than the ball that Tanya brought, and also less than the brown ball.
2. Tom's ball weighed more than the red one.
3. The soccer ball, which was 14.5 ounces heavier than Teresa's ball, was not orange.
4. The person who brought the orange ball was not Teddie, whose ball weighed 15.2 ounces more than the Ping-Pong ball.
5. The ball that weighed more than all of them except for one was white.
6. The heaviest was the basketball, and the lightest was yellow.
7. The 2-ounce ball was green, and smaller than the red one and the ball brought by Teddie.
8. The ball brought by Tillie was ten times heavier than the golf ball.

The World's Most Daunting Potato Chips Puzzle

Everyone in Mr. Glitzwhizzle's classroom (Gazelda, Gerald, Hubert, Sally, Amos, and Elmo) agreed that no one could eat just one potato chip, but decided to have a contest to see who could eat the most in three minutes. Five students, and Mr. Glitzwhizzle himself, entered the race. From the clues below, figure out the last names of the students (Kettledrummel, Grugenminer, Crackenberry, Witteyspooner and or Jones) and Mr. Glitzwhizzle's first name, and how many bags of chips (3, 6, 9, 12, 18, or 24) each one ate.

1. Witteyspooner and Gazelda together didn't eat as many bags as Elmo or Jones did.
2. Hubert ate twice as many bags as Grugenminer.
3. Sally's last name does not start with G.
4. Kettledrummel ate one-fourth as many bags as Hubert did.
5. Mr. Glitzwhizzle ate 18 bags. Gerald could eat only half that many.
6. Hubert ate as many bags as Elmo and Gazelda combined.

The World's Most Daunting Queen Rachel's Bridge Toll Puzzle

When the new Queen Rachel Bridge was built, Queen Rachel decided to charge a toll. Each person who crosses the bridge is charged .05 of the value of their shoes ($2.80, $3.60, $4.80, $7.20, and $7.60) So, if a person's shoes are worth $1.00, that person has to pay 5¢ in toll. Figure out how much each person (Chiquita, Cindy, Kurt, Taber, and Caleb) has to pay to cross the Queen's bridge, and the color of their shoes (red, green, blue, white or black).

1. Kurt's shoes are not green, nor is green the color of the shoes worth $3.60.
2. The person with the blue shoes must pay 36¢ toll.
3. Taber pays a higher toll than Cindy. Neither of them wears black shoes.
4. The person whose shoes are worth $3.60 is not Caleb.
5. One person, whose shoes are not green or red, pays an 18¢ toll.
6. The person with the red shoes pays 14¢ toll.
7. Caleb pays 24¢.
8. The person with the white shoes pays 38¢ toll.
9. Cindy's shoes are blue.

The World's Most Daunting Rhoda Tiller Puzzle

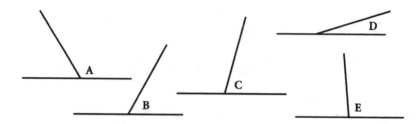

Someone has given these five figures actual names (Val, Ruta, Asper, Rhoda, and Ed). Can you believe it? Using your protractor, measure the angles above, then use the clues, giving interior or exterior angles, to figure out who is who (Tiller, Gus, Baggy, Able, or Veda).

1. Ms. Veda measures 105 on the outside.
2. Mr. Able's exterior angle is 122.
3. The 61-angle figure is not Asper or Rhoda.
4. Tiller has the 163 outside measurement.
5. The figure with the 95 angle is not Ed, Val, or Ruta.
6. Gus' interior angle is 85. Baggy's is not 58.
7. Rhoda's outside angle measures 163.
8. Neither Mr. Able nor Ruta is the 75er.

The World's Most Daunting Sand Puzzle

Six men (Mr. Logan, Mr. Driver, Mr. Thomas, Mr. Lang, Mr. Antonelli, and Mr. Waters) divided 120 pounds of sand to be used for concrete projects they were building into these percentages, 12.5, 6.25, 18.75, 21.875, 3.125, and 37.5. Mr. Thomas' project was a good bit smaller than Mr. Logan's project, so Mr. Thomas needed less sand.

Using the percentages, clues provided, and your ability to convert the percentages into weight in pounds, figure out how much sand each man took.

1. Mr. Logan took just a little over 26 pounds, which was not the most taken.
2. Mr. Driver took the least amount.
3. Mr. Antonelli took 30 fewer pounds than Mr. Lang.
4. Mr. Waters took twice as much sand as Mr. Driver and Mr. Thomas combined.

The World's Most Daunting Shapes Puzzle

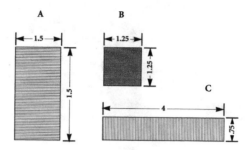

The shapes on this page are measured in decimal units. Your job is to create a new shape (which will not be a square or a rectangle) using the lines described in the clues. Your shape must show the decimal units.

1. The top line of your shape is half as long as the combined distance of the top of B and the side of C.
2. The bottom line of your shape is the same length as the top of C less the top of A multiplied by 1.5.
3. The left side of your shape is twice as long as two sides of B less one side of C. This side is perpendicular to the top line.
4. The right side of your shape is the same length as the top of C less one half the top of A.

The World's Most Daunting Skateboard Contest Puzzle

Five kids (Jimmy, Sally, Lenny, Roger, and Kenny) in the finals of the Fossil Street skateboard contest ride their boards from home to the site for the event. From the clues provided, figure out the kids' full names (Linden, Lyle, Mander, Cooper, or Chapman), the number of blocks each has to ride to the contest (1, 3, 7, 8, or 11), and the street on which they live (Elm, Main, Chestnut, Acorn, or 11th).

1. Chestnut Avenue is 4 blocks farther away than where Roger lives.
2. Ms. Mander lives on Main Street, 8 blocks away from Lenny.
3. Cooper lives 4 blocks from Linden and 7 blocks from Kenny.
4. Chapman lives six blocks farther away than 11th Street.
5. Kenny, whose last name starts with "L", lives closer than Sally.
6. Jimmy lives on Elm Street.

The World's Most Daunting Slug Crawl Puzzle

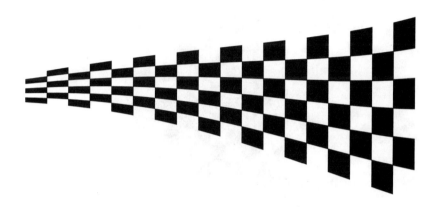

Several prominent slugs entered the annual crawling contest . Last year's winner, Slippo, is favored to win again. A newcomer, Slig, is considered a "dark slug."

Work out the clues and deduce each slug's crawl distance (.6, 1.2, 1.5, 1.8, 2.1, or 2.3 cm), the color of his leash (purple, green, white, blue, red, or yellow), and the name of his owner (Gerald, Walter, Jack, Bob, Harry, or Bill).

1. The purple-leashed slug crawled 2.1.
2. Bob is not the owner of Oozey.
3. Slimball wore green.
4. The slug who went .6 belongs to Bill.
5. Slig wore red.
6. The winner wore blue.
7. Woozey was not last.
8. Walter's slug did not wear green or blue.
9. Slimeball went half as far as Woozey.
10. Jack's slug was the winner.
11. Gooey crawled .2 less than Slippo.
12. The yellow-leashed slug crawled 1.8.
13. Gerald's slug, who crawled 1.5, wore red.
14. Harry owns Gooey.

The World's Most Daunting Square Count Puzzle

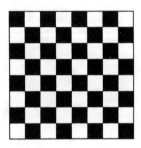

In a checkerboard there are over 200 squares. Using the checkerboard shown above, see if you can find all the squares in each of the following rows and columns. Note that the largest squares are comprised of nine.

1. Columns A & B, rows 1-8
2. Columns A, B, & C, rows 1-3
3. Columns B, C, & D, rows 1-4
4. Columns A, B, C, & D, rows 2-4
5. Columns C, D, & E, rows 1-5
6. Columns A, B, & C, rows 1-6
7. Columns A-D, rows 1-4

The World's Most Daunting Taber's Birdhouse Puzzle

Taber, who is building a birdhouse, is making a scale drawing of the project. The areas of each piece are: 6.4, 2.8, 4.0, 3.25, and 5.5 cm. See if you can match them with the parts.

1. The length of the side is 3.2 centimeters.
2. The width of the top is 1.25.
3. The narrowest piece is the back, with a width of just .8 centimeters.
4. The bottom is 2.75 centimeters long and 2.0 wide.
5. One piece is 2.5 by 1.6.
6. Two pieces have the same dimension: 2.0. the side is one of them.
7. The top is a long, thin rectangle.

The World's Most Daunting Time Zone Puzzle

Nick, who lives in Boston, decided to phone seven of his friends (Lori, Deb, Jan, Duke, Cary, Alex, and Gene) for a conference call. It was 7:00 A.M. there when he began making the calls. Using the clues below, try to determine where the seven friends are located (Boston, London, Wellington, Honolulu, Nairobi, Perth, Mazatlan, or Cape Town).

1. Lori was awakened by the phone ringing at 5:00 A.M.
2. Duke was having a noon meal.
3. Cary was 5 hours later than Deb.
4. Gene just finished lunch and was sitting down for a 1 o'clock meeting when the phone rang.
5. Jan was watching a late-night TV news show, which started at midnight.
6. Alex was 10 hours earlier than where Duke was.

The World's Most Daunting Turkeys in the Road Puzzle

Farmer McLynden just spilled crates of turkeys—all over Highway #246!

When those birds were on the truck they were in six crates, 50 to each crate, merrily on their way to market to meet the happy-turkey butcher. (Sshhh, turkeys don't know what a butcher is or they wouldn't be so happy!) But when that tire blew! Wow-e-e-e-ee! Now the turkeys are out of the crates and running all over the place, and farmer McLynden is having a hard time gathering them up and getting them back into the crates.

Finally, when all the chickens he can find are re-crated, McLynden's turkey-head count tells him that some of the gobblers got away (maybe they were helped, because we all know turkeys just aren't that smart). Anyway, there are no longer fifty birds in each of the crates.

Using the clues above, figure out how many turkeys are not in each of the six crates.

1. There are 233 turkeys left.
2. One end crate has the most turkeys in it; the other end has the fewest, a difference of 13 turkeys.
3. Crate #3 has 6 more turkeys than #2.
4. Crate #5 has 2 fewer turkeys than #1.
5. Crate #4 has 35 turkeys, three more than the crate with the fewest.

The World's Most Daunting Vegetable Soup Contest Puzzle

Five people (Benny, Lily, T-Bone, and Slim) each bought 15 cans of vegetables for a soup contest. No one bought the same number of any one kind (corn, peas, carrots, asparagus, and beans), but 5 of one kind, 4 of another, 3 of another, and so on. Also, no vegetable was bought in the same quantity by any two people. Given all that, can you figure out how many cans of each vegetable each person bought and how much the purchases cost? Also, who won the contest for the tastiest soup?

1. The person who spent $6.43 bought 5 cans of asparagus and 3 cans of beans.
2. Lily spent the least amount of money, $1.66 less than T-bone. She bought 3 cans of carrots, 5 of peas, and 1 of corn.
3. Benny spent $1.20 on asparagus and $1.55 for corn and peas.
4. Joshua bought 2 cans of peas and spent $4.52 for his corn and carrots combined.
5. The person who won the contest bought 1 can of carrots and spent $7.42 total, 99¢ more than Benny.
6. T-bone spent the most. He bought 5 cans of corn, 4 of beans, and 1 of asparagus.

SHOPPING LIST

corn 58¢

peas 39¢

carrots 44¢

asparagus 24¢

beans 64¢

The World's Most Daunting Boxes Puzzle

....

	1	2	3	4
A	11	6	15	3
B	5	8	12	10
C	16	1	14	7
D	9	2	13	4

Sixteen boxes are each worth the number inside. Their names are intersections of rows (letters) and columns (numbers), i.e., the lower left corner box is D-1 or 1-D. It is worth 9 points.

Four boys (Bryce, Jeremy, Boyd, and Kevin) playing a game are trying the make the most points by trading boxes. Everyone must have four boxes at all times. From the clues, how many points does each boy have at game's end?

1. Jeremy didn't own any of the boxes in the A row.
2. Boyd's highest number is A-3.
3. B-2 and C-1 belong to the same boy, who isn't Bryce.
4. Bryce doesn't own any boxes in the 1 column.
5. On the last play of the game, Jeremy traded his 4-B for B-1.
6. D-2, A-2, and D-3 all belong to the same player.
7. C-1, B-3, and 4-D all belong to the same player.
8. Kevin's score was 4 higher than Boyd's.
9. Three of Boyd's boxes are in the A row.
10. Jeremy has just one box in the B row, which is B-1.

The World's Most Daunting Elevator Puzzle

Ives and Newell are in charge of counting the people who get on and off the elevator in a hotel. They take turns riding to the top floor and back down, counting as they go. After two such trips each morning, two around noon, and two in the evening, there is an average taken.

The hotel manager wants to know today's average.

1. On Newell's noon trip there were 32 fewer people than in his morning count.
2. Ives counted a total of 122 in the morning and noon counts, just one higher than his evening count, but 24 more than Newell's evening count.
3. Ives' morning count is the same as Newell's average.
4. Ives' evening count was 37 more than Newell's morning count.

HINT: Clue 2 gives most of the information needed to get started.

The World's Most Daunting Figs Puzzle

Brandon is a fig counter. The figs are kept in five boxes. Using the following clues, see if you can figure out how many figs are in the boxes today. (There are no fractions of figs; whole figs only!)

While you're at it, figure out the average number of figs in all five boxes.

1. The total number of figs in box C is 1/3 of half the total of those in box E.
2. Box B has twice as many figs as C and E combined.
3. There are 120 figs in one of the boxes.
4. Box A has half as many figs as E, which is also 10 fewer than D.
5. D has 1/4 as many as B.

The World's Most Daunting Foul Shots Puzzle

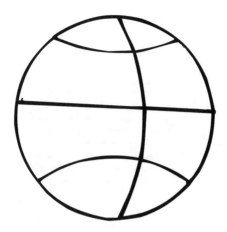

Sometimes they make 'em, sometimes they don't! Using your excellent understanding of percentage, see if you can figure out the foul-shooting percentage for each of these six players (#12, #18, #22, #27, #34, #49) this season. The highest is 83%. The lowest is 57%. For reference, the attempt numbers are 176, 98, 113, 134, 184, and 45; the successful shot numbers are 94, 36, 102, 58, 89, and 132.

1. Player #34 had 102 successful shots, 30 fewer than the player who shot 71%.
2. The player with 57% (not #49 or #22) attempted 176 shots.
3. The player with 98 attempts shot 59%.
4. Player #27 shot 66%.
5. Player #12 had the fewest attempts and shot 80%.
6. The player with the highest percentage (not #18) made 38 fewer shots than #49.

The World's Most Daunting Garage Sale Puzzle

Mr. Pazzini, Mr. Schmidt, Ms. Cullen, Ms. Higgins, and Mr. Havill found sweaters, dresses, dressers, telephones, tires, and bicycles. Ms. Gaskin liked a clothing item. A man bought an old dresser. Who bought what? What were the original ($2, $15, $3, $20, $9, or $12) and purchase ($8, $6, $12, $10, $0.75, or $0.50) prices?

1. The bicycle was bought at 50% off. The buyer's name starts with H.

2. Ms. Cullen bought the item priced at $15.00 for 4/5th that amount.

3. The tires sold for $1.00 less than the asking price.

4. The item that sold for $0.50 was an article of clothing.

5. Mr. Pazzini spent $4.00 less than Ms. Cullen.

6. Ms. Higgins paid for her dress with a $20.00 bill and received $19.25 in change.

7. Ms. Gaskin spent less for her item than Mr. Schmidt, who spent less than Mr. Pazzini.

8. The item originally priced the highest didn't sell for the highest price, nor did the lowest-price item sell for the lowest amount.

The World's Most Daunting Great Pencil Sale Puzzle

Four sixth-grade classes decided to sell pencils to raise money to go to a concert. Each class bought 500 pencils for $0.03 each (this cost must be deducted before any profit is made). They agreed that the class that made the most money (each class was allowed to charge any amount for their pencils) could sit in the front row at the concert.

Using the clues below, figure out how much profit each class made(219, 375, 413, or 500 pencils at 5/$.40, 10/$.75, $.10, or $.15), and which class got to sit in the front row(Mr. Pendip's, Ms. Glenwhip's, Ms. Rimdip's, or Mr. Slimhip's).

1. The least amount of profit was $11.30 less than the winning amount.
2. Mr. Pendip's class made $3.80 more in profit than the class that sold its pencils at 10 for 75¢.
3. The class that sold 219 pencils was not Mr. Pendip's.
4. Ms. Rimdrip's class sold its pencils for 7¢ more per pencil than Mr. Slimhip's class.

The World's Most Daunting Hidden Grades Puzzle

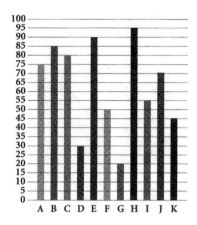

Ms. Stonebelt told four of her best math students that their grades were hidden in the charts below. Using all the clues, see if you can figure out the grade each one received.

1. Dan's percentage is B + K – 1/2C.
2. Bernard's grade is based on G + I + D – Dan's percentage plus sixty-five.
3. Jason earned a grade higher than Bernard. He scored 2E divided by 3 + (1/2J) – 2.
4. Dexter's grade, the only one of the four without a plus or a minus, was derived from:
(A + C – [1/2F]) x 1/5G divided by 10 + 1/2J

GRADING SYSTEM

96–100	A	81–83	B-	69–71	C-
92–95	A-	77–80	C+	62–68	D
89–91	B+	72–76	C	0–61	F
84–88	B				

The World's Most Daunting High Rent Puzzle

A group of six people (Adrienne, Peter, Danielle, Farah, Sarah, and Jacob), who live in the same apartment building, got together one day for lunch. As they ate and talked, they discovered that each one lived on a different floor (12, 14, 17, 21, 24, and 25) and that no one paid the same amount of rent. In fact, they learned that the higher the floor, the higher the rent, and that one person's rent is $525.

Your task is to figure out from the following clues the full names of the six renters (Adams, Price, Drake, Jordan, Stuart, and Falk), and the floor on which each lives, and the amount of rent they pay.

1. Ms. Jordan lives between Danielle and Adams.
2. the highest rent is not paid by Flak, Stuart, or Peter. It is $175 more than the 17th floor.
3. Floor 21 is rented at $75 more than where Adams lives and $50 less than what Adrienne pays.
4. Sarah pays $475, $175 less than Ms. Drake.
5. Price's rent is $50 higher than Adrienne's and $100 more than Jacob's.
6. The rent at the 12th floor is $450. No one with the initial P or A lives there.
7. Stuart's rent is lower than Jordan's.

The World's Most Daunting Hundred-Miler Puzzle

In a 100-mile bicycle race, Chet and his friends (Dave, Bob, Kurt and Rick) finished within 31 minutes of each other! From the clues, find each rider's last name (Day, Johns, Seig, Brown or White), the bike color (tan, grey, red, blue or green), the time each finished (6:32, 6:40, 6:09, 6:21, or 6:39 hours and minutes), and his average speed (15.65, 15.82, 15.62, 16.42, or 16.10).

1. Both Dave and Seig rode over 6 ¹/₂ hours. Dave's bike is grey.
2. Day's bike, which beat Seig's green one, is blue.
3. The rider who rode for 6:32 hours was on a red bike.
4. Rick and the rider of the red bike both averaged under 16 mph.
5. The tan bike averaged 16.42.
6. The blue bike's rider is not Kurt, nor the one who took 6:40 hrs.
7. Brown, who rode in 6:09, is not Kurt or Bob.
8. Kurt's average beat Johns, who beat the green bike rider.

The World's Most Daunting Motorcycle Puzzle

Old Mrs. Frizzle needed a new motorcycle because her old one was worn out from so many trips to town. She summoned her five sons—Luke, Jake, Swizzle, Jeremiah, and Malcolm—and told them, "Boys, I need a new motorcycle. It must be purple and it must have one extra tire. Also, I must have a new helmet, a new leather outfit, and new goggles. The one who finds me the best deal shall earn a handsome prize."

The sons met secretly and agreed that each would buy one of the five items and they would split the prize as follows: the one who bought the motorcycle would get 50% of the prize, the one who bought the tire would get 20%, the ones buying the outfit and the helmet would each get 12%, and the one buying the goggles would get 6%.

See if you can deduce which son bought which of the five items and how much Mrs. Frizzle gave as a prize.

1. Swizzle Frizzle did not buy the helmet.
2. Malcolm earned 60¢ less than Jake.
3. Luke earned more than Jeremiah but less than Swizzle.
4. The one who bought the helmet—not Malcolm—earned 90¢.

The World's Most Daunting Party Time Puzzle

Aunt Hildy is having another wild tea party—on Sunday at 3 P.M. sharp! Aunt Hildy does not like guests to arrive early or late! (A nephew was cut out of her will for being seven seconds late to a dinner honoring her cat, Fred.) Now Aunt Hildy has put you in charge of making sure that everyone arrives *precisely* on time.

Since you know how far everyone lives from Aunt Hildy (the total mileage is 1131 miles for all five), you want to send letters to them specifying the average speed they must travel and the time they must leave in order to arrive exactly at 3:00 P.M. Using the clues, work out the correct information to send and keep handy.

1. Cousin Ansel will leave half an hour before Niece Gwendolyn.
2. Great Aunt Lucille will average 64 mph (no tickets, please!).
3. Nephew Fredrick needs to leave at 11:00 A.M.
4. Gwendolyn lives 319 miles away, 111 more than Great Aunt Lucille.
5. Ansel will travel a steady 58 miles per hour.
6. Uncle Jed lives 60 miles away and needs to leave at 1:30 P.M.
7. The one who leaves at 11:45 lives 12 miles farther than the one who lives 4 hours away.

The World's Most Daunting Roommates Puzzle

Twelve people (Greg, Dawn, Terry, April, Diane, Gary, Sandra, Tina, Duke, Jason, Sue, and Kris) share six college rooms (1, 2, 3, 4, 5, and 6). Match each with their roommates, room numbers, and the color of their rooms (blue, green, yellow, beige, pink, or white).

1. Kris and Terry share a room.
2. Diane's roommate is not Sandra.
3. Duke does not live in #6, which is yellow.
4. Neither #5 nor #4 is blue or beige.
5. The pink room has an odd number, but it is not #3.
6. April lives in #5 with Sandra.
7. Dawn's roommate is not Tina.
8. The blue room is even numbered.
9. Jason lives in the green room; Sandra in the white one.
10. Sue is not in #3.
11. Gary's room is blue.

HINT: Strangely, the girls' rooms are odd numbered and the boys have even-numbered rooms.

396

The World's Most Daunting Runners Puzzle

After Sandy, Peter, Wendy, Kerry, Todd, Bob, Darlene, and Lynn finished practice, they compared how far each had run and how many minutes it had taken them. Using the clues given below, determine how many kilometers each of the runners ran (18, 12, 11, 10, 9, 8, 5, or 4) and their average speed per kilometer (7, 7.5, 8, 8.5, 9, 9.5, 10.5, or 11).

1. Darlene spent 99 minutes running 1.86 miles farther than Kerry.
2. Todd ran 3.72 miles fewer than Wendy.
3. Peter, who ran 3.1 miles in 35 minutes, ran farther than Bob, who ran for 30 minutes.
4. Wendy's total time was 3 hours, 18 minutes.
5. Sandy ran .62 miles farther than Lynn.
6. Lynn ran an average of 2 minutes per kilometer slower than Sandy.
7. For one runner, the average minutes per kilometer and the number of kilometers run were the same number.

CONVERSION CHART

miles kilometers

miles	kilometers	miles	kilometers	miles	kilometers	miles	kilometers
.62	1	2.48	4	4.34	7	5.58	9
1.24	2	3.10	5	4.96	8	6.20	10
1.86	3	3.72	6				

The World's Most Daunting
Stephanie's Investments Puzzles

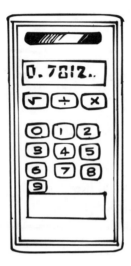

Stephanie invested some of her money into five companies (Smith and Co., Alaco, Dowin Products, Corbett & Sons, and Cortell). Figure out what product each company sold (paper, aluminum, soft drinks, or siding), how much Stephanie invested in each ($200, $100, $500, $300, or $800), and her loss or profit (10% profit, 20% loss, 30% profit, 5% loss, or 15% profit).

1. Dowin Products showed a 30% profit, Stephanie's profit for that product was $40.
2. Stephanie made the most money from the paint company, which was not Corbett or Cortell.
3. Aluminum was Stephanie's worst investment, costing her $160.
4. Alaco makes siding. Cortell does not produce soft drinks.
5. Corbett & Sons showed a 20% loss.
6. Stephanie invested $300 into Cortell.
7. Her $200 investment cost her 5%.
8. Smith and Co. returned $50 to Stephanie.

The World's Most Daunting Tallest Puzzle

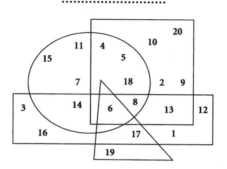

Six friends decided to turn out for basketball. One of the things their coach did first was to measure their heights. Using the clues, and the shapes with numbers (in inches) below, figure out how tall each boy is.

S = the sum of the numbers inside the square
C = the sum of the numbers inside the circle
T = the sum of the numbers inside the triangle
R = the sum of the numbers inside the rectangle

1. Brad's height is 2T - 15.
2. Kevin's height is T divided by the only number found in all four shapes, times ten, + 3.
3. Monte's height is S - R, times the only number in just the triangle and the rectangle, minus the only number in just the square and the rectangle.
4. Duane's height is C divided by 4, plus 3, times 3.
5. Kris' height is T + C, divided by the next to the lowest number in the circle, times the next to the lowest number in the rectangle, minus seven.
6. Tom's height is S - 1 divided by the largest number in the triangle, times the largest number in the square, minus the three numbers that lie in the circle only, plus seven.

THE WORLD'S
GREATEST CRITICAL
THINKING PUZZLES

The World's Greatest Brain Net Puzzle

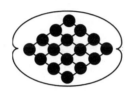

Your brain is an incredible piece of machinery. About the size of a squished softball, it contains billions of brain cells. These cells make more connections than all the phones in the world. It's this huge network that produces your brain power! Want to feel the "brain net" in action?

Take a look at the drawing above. Your job is to figure out how many different paths can get you across from start to finish.

You can only move to the right. You can't go back. When you arrive at a "fork," take either the top or bottom route. Start counting.

The World's Greatest Predicting Path Puzzle

One of your brain's most powerful capabilities is the ability to think visually. When we think in this way, we construct a mind's eye image of a shape, scene, or concept. This image can be rotated, changed, moved, and analyzed. How good are you at visual thinking? Here's your first chance to find out.

Suppose we roll the wheel along the flat surface. Draw the shape that would be traced by the point within the wheel.

Now let's put the small wheel along the inner rim of a larger circle. What shape path would a point on the smaller wheel trace?

The World's Greatest Who's That? Puzzle

Look into a mirror and who do you see? You? Perhaps, but it's not the same you that everyone else sees. Its a right-left reversed image. The ear that appears on your left side is seen by others on your right side.

SUPPOSE YOU WANT TO SEE YOURSELF EXACTLY AS OTHERS SEE YOU. HOW CAN YOU SET UP TWO SMALL MIRRORS SO THAT YOUR REFLECTION ISN'T REVERSED?

The World's Greatest Leftovers Again Puzzle

Your brain is divided into two halves. The left half is more number-oriented, rational, and concrete. Your right half is more creative, playful, and artistic. To solve this next puzzle, you'll have to borrow a little from both sides of your brain.

In an art class, students are taught how to shape a 1 ounce bag of clay into a small statue. During this process, some clay remains unused (actually, it falls to the floor). For every five statues that are made, there is enough extra clay to make one more statue. Suppose a student is presented with 25 ounces of clay. What is the maximum number of statues he can sculpt?

The World's Greatest Brownie Cut Puzzle

Now that art class is over, it's time for cooking class.

A chocolate brownie emerges from the oven. Karen cuts the square brownie in half. She then divides one of the halves into two smaller but equal parts.

Before she can eat the larger piece, two of her friends unexpectedly arrive. Karen wants everyone to have the same amount of dessert. In the fewest number of cuts, how can she produce three equal portions?

The World's Greatest Balancing Gold Puzzle

A gold bar balances with $^9/_{10}$ of 1 pound and $^9/_{10}$ of a similar gold bar. How much does each gold bar weigh?

The World's Greatest Thrifty Technique Puzzle

Don't put that balance away! You'll need it along with a few pounds of brain cells to help solve this next problem.

By the way, did you know that Albert Einstein's brain was "normal" in weight? For the most part, it resembled an ordinary brain. There was, however, a slight difference. He had extra "cleanup" cells (called neuroglial cells). These cells move around the brain to get rid of dead or injured nerve cells. Perhaps his "well swept" brain super-charged his intelligence?

You have nine gold coins. One of the coins is counterfeit and is filled with a lighter-than-gold substance. Using a balance, what strategy can you use to uncover the counterfeit coin?

To make things a little more difficult, you must identify the fake coin with only two uses of the balance.

The World's Greatest Tricky Tide Puzzle

In the Bay of Fundy, the tides can vary in height by almost 50 feet. The bay in our puzzle has a tidal range of only 6 feet. A boat moors in the middle of this bay. A ladder hangs down from the deck of the boat and touches the flat sea surface. The rungs are 1 foot apart.

At low tide, ten rungs of the ladder are exposed. At high tide, the water level rises 6 feet. How many of the rungs will remain exposed?

The World's Greatest Breaking Up Is Hard to Do Puzzle

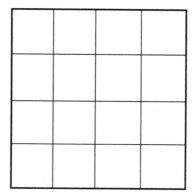

How fast can you think? Faster than a speeding bullet? Faster than electricity? For most of us, thoughts race around our brains between 3 and 300 mph. Who knows, this puzzle may break your brain's speed record.

The square encloses a 4 x 4 grid. There are five different ways this grid can be divided into identical quarters. Each way uses a different shape. Can you uncover the layout of all five patterns?

The World's Greatest Disorder Puzzle

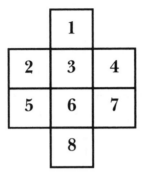

Buildings crumble. Living things decompose. It's a scientific principle that things tend to go from order to disorder. The fancy name for this principle is entropy. There are, however, a few things that appear to go against this tendency. Crystals grow and become more complex. Living things take simple chemicals and build complex tissues.

This puzzle, however, uses entropy. Notice how neat and orderly the arrangement of numbers is. Now, let's play the entropy game and rearrange the numbers so that no two consecutive numbers touch each other. They cannot align side by side, up and down, or diagonally.

The World's Greatest True or False Puzzle

··

Here's a totally different type of problem. This one is based on logic. Two cultures of aliens live on the planet Trekia, the carpals and the tarsals. The carpals always lie. The tarsals always tell the truth.

A space traveler arrives on Trekia and meets a party of three aliens. She asks the aliens to which culture they belong. The first one murmurs something that is too soft to hear. The second replies, "It said it was a carpal." The third says to the second, "You are a liar!" From this information, figure out what culture the third alien belongs to.

The World's Greatest Pack Up Your Trouble Puzzle

A fragile item is to be shipped in a cardboard box. In order to prevent the item from hitting against the walls of the box, plastic foam cubes are used as "bumpers." There are ten of these cubes. How can you position them along the inner walls of the box so that there is an equal number of cubes along each wall?

The World's Greatest
Don't Come Back This Way Again! Puzzle

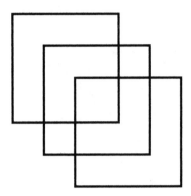

The pitcher plant is a carnivorous plant that eats insects. An unfortunate insect walks into the pitcher plant's flower. When it tries to reverse direction, it can't. Tiny spines on the petals' surface face downward, which forces the insect to move in one direction—down.

Here's your chance not to go back. The shape above is made with one continuous line. Starting anywhere, can you complete the shape without lifting your pencil from the page? As you probably guessed, your path cannot cross over itself.

The World's Greatest Meet Me on the Edge Puzzle

Did you know that an ant can lift about fifty times its body weight? If you had that power, you'd be able to lift over 2 tons!

Suppose we position one of those powerful ants on a corner of a sugar cube. On the opposite corner, we position a fly. Suppose the two insects begin walking toward each other. If they can only walk along the edges of the cube (and never go backwards), what is the probability that their paths will cross?

The World's Greatest Only the Shadow Knows Puzzle

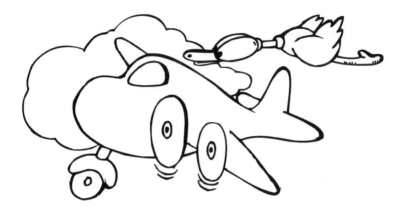

A medium-size jet has a wingspan of 120 feet. An albatross is a bird with a wingspan of about 12 feet. At what altitude would each object have to fly in order to cast shadows of equal size?

The World's Greatest More Shadow Stuff Puzzle

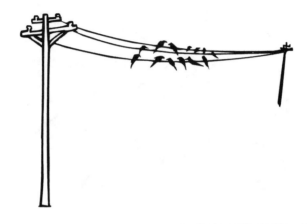

At a certain time of day, a 25-foot telephone pole casts a 10-foot shadow. At that same time, how high would a tree have to be in order to cast a 25-foot shadow?

The World's Greatest Trip Time Puzzle

Did you know that the speed record for cars is over 700 miles per hour? To attain this supersonic speed, the cars use rocket engines. They move so quickly that if the car body had wings, the vehicle would fly!

The car in our problem is much slower. In 1 hour, traveling at 30 mph, it climbs to the top of the hill. When the car reaches the top, the driver remembers that she left her field guide to mountain life back home. She immediately turns around and drives downhill at 60 mph. Assuming that she spent no time at the top, what was her average speed?

The World's Greatest Average Puzzle

How fast can you ride a bicycle? To get into the *Guinness Book of Records* for human-powered cycling, you'd need to ride faster than 60 mph.

An ordinary cyclist travels up and down a hill. Going up, she maintains a constant speed of 10 mph. It takes her 1 hour to get to the top. Assuming that the hill is symmetric, what speed must she maintain on the way going down if she wishes to average 20 mph? Before you bask in victory, the answer is not 30 mph.

The World's Greatest Palindrome Puzzle

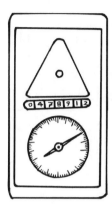

A palindrome is a word or number that reads the same backward as it does forward. Numbers such as 606 and 4,334 are palindromes.

While driving his car, Bob (so much of a palindrome lover that he changed his name from John to Bob) observes that the odometer reading forms a palindrome. It displays the mileage 13,931.
Bob keeps driving. Two hours later, he looks at the odometer again and, to his surprise, it displays a different palindrome!

WHAT IS THE MOST LIKELY SPEED THAT BOB IS TRAVELING?

The World's Greatest Stacking Up Puzzle

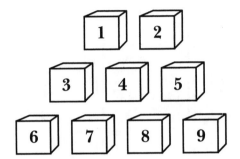

Can you arrange these numbered blocks into three equal stacks so that the sum of the numbers displayed in each stack must be equal to any other stack?

The World's Greatest Star Birth Puzzle

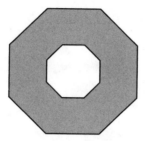

Trace this octagon pattern onto a separate sheet of paper. Then decide how to divide this shape into eight identical triangles that can be arranged into a star. The star will have eight points and an octagon-shaped hole in its center. When you think you've come up with an answer, trace the pattern onto the octagon. Cut out the separate parts and reassemble them into a star.

The World's Greatest Flip Flop Puzzle

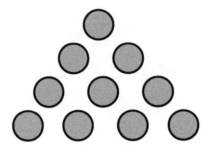

Did you know that the ancient Egyptians believed that triangles had sacred qualities? This may have led to the superstition about walking under a ladder. When a ladder is placed against a wall, it forms a triangle. To walk through the triangle might provoke the wrath of the gods.

The triangle above is made up of ten disks. Can you move three of the disks to make the triangle point in the opposite direction?

The World's Greatest Crossing Hand Puzzle

Picture in your mind a clock with a face and hands. Between the hours of 5 A.M. and 5 P.M., how many times will the hour and minute hands cross each other?

The World's Greatest What's Next? Puzzle

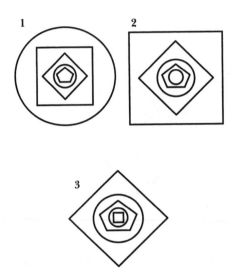

EXAMINE THE FIGURES ABOVE. CAN YOU SEE WHAT THE PATTERN IS AND FIND OUT WHAT THE FOURTH FIGURE IN THIS SERIES SHOULD LOOK LIKE?

The World's Greatest Trying Triangle Puzzle

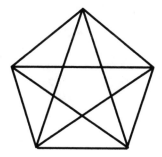

HOW MANY TRIANGLES CAN BE FOUND IN THIS FIGURE?

The World's Greatest Flipping Pair Puzzle

Place three coins with their indicated side facing up as shown. In three moves, arrange the coins so that all three have the same side facing up. A move consists of flipping two coins over to their opposite side.

NOTE: Flipping the pair of outer coins three times doesn't count!

The World's Greatest Missing Block Puzzle

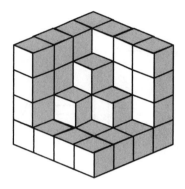

Examine the figure of blocks above. Let's assume that the hidden blocks are all in place. How many additional blocks are needed to fill in the empty region to complete this cube?

Once you've made your guess, look at the pattern again. Assume that the hidden blocks are all in place. Now let's suppose that all the blocks you can see are vaporized. How many blocks would be left behind?

The World's Greatest Matchstick Memory Puzzle

$$| - ||| = ||$$

$$\times - | = |$$

$$||| - || = |\vee$$

Years ago, matchsticks were made from small sections of wood. These common and inexpensive objects were perfect props for after-dinner or parlor room activities. Nowadays, toothpicks offer the same advantages. So get your picks together and arrange them in the three patterns shown above.

As you can see, each line of toothpicks forms an incorrect equation. The challenge is to make each one correct by changing the position of only one of the toothpicks in each row.

The World's Greatest Sum Circle Puzzle

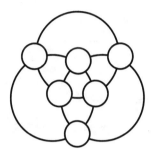

Place the numbers one through six within the six smaller circles shown above. Each number must be used only once. The numbers must be placed so that the sum of the four numbers that fall on a circle's circumference is equal to the sum of the numbers on any other circle's circumference.

Think it's easy? Give it a try.

The World's Greatest Many Rivers to Cross Puzzle

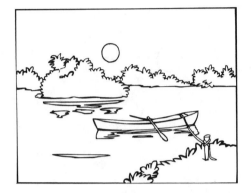

Let's take a break from puzzles and go on a rowboat ride across the river. There are four adults who want to cross it. They come upon a boy and a girl playing in a rowboat. The boat can hold either two children or one adult. Can the adults succeed in crossing the river? If so, how?

The World's Greatest Train Travel Puzzle

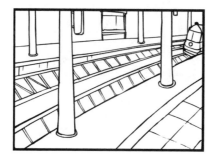

A train travels at a constant rate of speed. It reaches a stretch of track that has fifteen poles. The poles are placed at an equal distance to each other. It takes the train 10 minutes to travel from the first pole to the tenth pole. How long will it take the train to reach the fifteenth pole?

The World's Greatest Miles Apart Puzzle

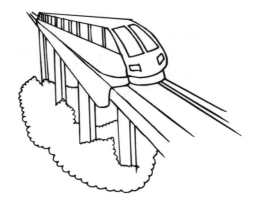

The distance from New York to Boston is 220 miles. Suppose a train leaves Boston for New York and travels at 65 mph. One hour later, a train leaves New York for Boston and travels at 55 mph. If we assume the tracks are straight paths and the trains maintain a constant speed, how far apart are the trains 1 hour before they meet?

The World's Greatest Passing Train Puzzle

Coming from opposite directions, a freight train and a passenger train pass each other on parallel tracks. The passenger train travels at 60 mph. The freight train travels at 30 mph. A passenger observes that it takes 6 seconds to pass the freight train. How many feet long is the freight train?

The World's Greatest Souped-Up Survey Puzzle

A survey agency reported their results in the local newspaper. The report states that exactly 100 local lawyers were interviewed. Of the 100, seventy-five lawyers own BMWs, ninety-five lawyers own Volvos, and fifty lawyers own both a BMW and a Volvo.

Within a short time after the report, several lawyers argue that the survey results are incorrect. How can they tell?

The World's Greatest Toasty Puzzle

In order to make French toast, Ricardo must fry both sides of a bread slice for 30 seconds. His frying pan can only hold two slices of bread at once. How can he make three slices of French toast in only $1\frac{1}{2}$ minutes instead of 2 minutes?

The World's Greatest Circle Game Puzzle

Examine the pattern of circles above. Can you place the numbers 1 through 9 in these circles so that the sum of the three circles connected vertically, horizontally, or diagonally is equal to 15?

The World's Greatest Fare Split Puzzle

Michelle rents a car to take her to the airport in the morning and return her home that evening. Halfway to the airport, she picks up a friend who accompanies her to the airport. That night, she and her friend return back to Michelle's home. The total cost is $20.00. If the amount to be paid is to be split fairly, how much money should Michelle pay?

The World's Greatest Pentagon Part Puzzle

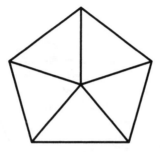

The pentagon above is divided into five equal parts. Suppose you color one or more parts gray. How many different and distinguishable patterns can you form? Each pattern must be unique and not be duplicated by simply rotating the pentagon.

The World's Greatest Bagel for Five Puzzle

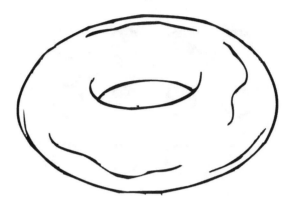

You and four friends have decided to split a bagel for breakfast. The five of you are not fussy about the size of the piece each will receive. In other words, all the pieces don't have to be the same size.

USING TWO PERFECTLY STRAIGHT CUTS, IS IT POSSIBLE TO DIVIDE THIS BAGEL INTO FIVE PIECES?

The World's Greatest Coin Move Puzzle

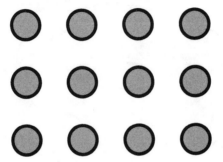

Place twelve coins in the pattern shown above. Notice how they form the corners of six equal-size squares.

CAN YOU REMOVE THREE OF THE COINS TO HAVE ONLY THREE EQUAL-SIZE SQUARES REMAINING?

The World's Greatest Trapezoid Trap Puzzle

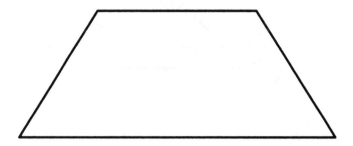

DIVIDE THE TRAPEZOID ABOVE INTO FOUR IDENTICAL PARTS.

The World's Greatest A+ Test Puzzle

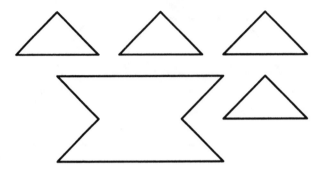

Here's a math challenge of a different sort. Trace these five shapes onto a sheet of stiff paper. Use a pair of scissors to carefully cut them out. Then assemble the shapes into a "plus" sign.

The World's Greatest Mismarked Music Puzzle

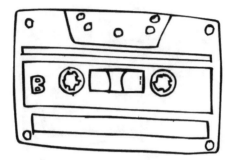

There are three boxes filled with audiocassette tapes. One box contains rap tapes, another contains jazz tapes, while the third contains both rap and jazz tapes. All three boxes have labels identifying the type of tapes within. The only problem is that all the boxes are mislabeled. By selecting only one box and listening to only one tape, how can you label all three boxes correctly?

The World's Greatest Measuring Mug Puzzle

Without the aid of any measuring device, how can you use a transparent 16-ounce mug to measure a volume of water that is exactly 8 ounces?

The World's Greatest Coin Roll Puzzle

Two identical coins are positioned side by side. In your mind's eye, roll the coin on the left (Coin A) over the other coin (Coin B). When Coin A reaches the opposite side of Coin B, stop. In which direction will Coin A's head be facing?

NOW, LET'S SUPPOSE THAT COIN A ROLLS COMPLETELY AROUND COIN B. IF SO, HOW MANY ROTATIONS DOES COIN A MAKE AROUND ITS OWN CENTER?

The World's Greatest Painting on the Side Puzzle

You are presented with several white cubes and a bucket of red paint. To make each of them different, you decide to paint one or more sides of each cube red. How many distinguishable cubes can you make with this painting method? Remember that any painted side must be painted completely to make it distinguishable from any other painted side.

The World's Greatest Magic Triangle Puzzle

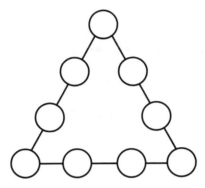

Here's a magic triangle whose sides are formed by sets of four numbers. To solve the puzzle, place the numbers one through nine each in one of the circles. When you are finished, the sums of all three sides must be equal.

THERE ARE THREE DIFFERENT SUMS THAT CAN BE USED TO REACH THE SOLUTION. CAN YOU FIND ALL THREE?

The World's Greatest Pattern Puzzle

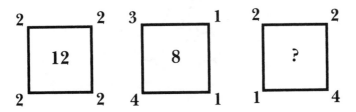

The arrangement of numbers above represents a pattern. This pattern is a mathematical relationship among the numbers in each square, so don't look for things like spelling, days of the week, cryptograms, or codes. Can you uncover the pattern and fill in the question mark in the last square?

The World's Greatest Frog Jump Puzzle

A frog falls into a well that is 18 feet deep. Every day the frog jumps up a total distance of 6 feet. At night, as the frog grips the slimy well walls, it slips back down 2 feet. At this rate, how many days will it take the frog to jump to the rim of the well?

The World's Greatest Army Ant Puzzle

Two small armies of ants meet head-on along a jungle path. Both armies would prefer to pass each other rather than fight. There is a small space along the side of the path. It is only large enough to hold one ant at a time. Is it possible for the armies to pass each other? If so, how?

The World's Greatest No Sweat Puzzle

There are six players on a coed volleyball team. After an exhausting game, each girl drinks 4 cups of water. Each boy drinks 7 cups of water. The coach drinks 9 cups.

A TOTAL OF 43 CUPS OF WATER IS CONSUMED BY EVERYONE. HOW MANY BOYS AND HOW MANY GIRLS ARE ON THE TEAM?

The World's Greatest Go Figure! Puzzle

On a distant planet, there are four forms of life beings: zadohs, pug-wigs, kahoots, and zingzags. All zadohs are pugwigs. Some pugwigs are kahoots. All kahoots are zingzags.

Which of the following statement(s) must then be true?

1. Some zadohs are zingzags.
2. Some kahoots are zadohs.
3. All kahoots are pugwigs.
4. Some zingzags are pugwigs.
5. All zingzags are zadohs.
6. Some zadohs are kahoots.

The World's Greatest Square Pattern Puzzle

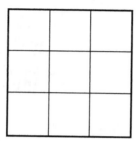

Suppose you have to paint all nine squares in the grid above using one of three colors: red, blue, or green. How many different patterns can you paint if each color must be represented in every row and every column? Each pattern must be unique. In other words, a new pattern can't be made by simply rotating the grid.

The World's Greatest Bouncing Ball Puzzle

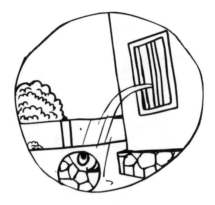

Did you know that when a ball strikes the ground, its shape distorts? This distortion stores the energy that powers its rebound. The more its shape changes, the higher the ball will bounce.

The ball in this puzzle rebounds to half the height from which it is dropped. Suppose it is dropped from a 1 meter height. What distance would the ball travel before it comes to rest?

The World's Greatest Complete the Pattern Puzzle

....

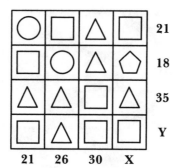

Use the pattern above to determine the value for X and Y.

The World's Greatest Checkerboard Puzzle

A full-size checkerboard has eight rows and eight columns that make up its sixty-four squares. By combining the patterns of these squares, you can put together another 140 squares. The pattern below is one-fourth the area of a full-size checkerboard. What is the total number of squares that are found in this smaller pattern?

The World's Greatest Cutting Edge Puzzle

Kristin wants to remodel her home. To save money, she decides to move a carpet from one hallway to another. The carpet currently fills a passage that is 3 x 12 feet. She wishes to cut the carpet into two sections that can be joined together to fit a long and narrow hallway that is 2 x 18 feet.

WHAT DOES HER CUT LOOK LIKE?

The World's Greatest Die Is Cast Puzzle

Which die is unlike the other three?

The World's Greatest Playing with Matches Puzzle

Thirty-two soccer teams enter a statewide competition. The teams are paired randomly in each round. The winning team advances to the next round. Losers are eliminated. How many matches must be played in order to crown one winner?

The World's Greatest Competing Click Puzzle

Let the Mouse Click Competition Begin!

Emily can click a mouse ten times in 10 seconds. Buzzy can click a mouse twenty times in 20 seconds. Anthony can click a mouse five times in 5 seconds. Assume that the timing period begins with the first mouse click and ends with the final click. Which one of these computer users would be the first to complete forty clicks?

The World's Greatest Another Pattern Puzzle

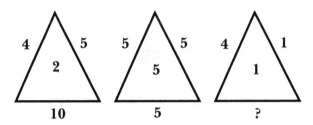

Here is another mathematical pattern that relates the four numbers of each triangle. Can you uncover the pattern and use it to complete the third triangle?

The World's Greatest Vive le Flag Puzzle

The French tricolor flag is made up of three vertical stripes (the one above has horizontal stripes): red, white, and blue. Suppose you are given four different colors of fabric and asked to create a different flag using the same tricolor design. If no two adjacent stripes can be the same color, how many different combinations of color patterns are there?

HINT: Don't forget that the flag pattern can be flipped over!

The World's Greatest Pizza Cut Puzzle

Five people want to share a square pizza, unlike the round one above. The first person (who is really hungry) removes a quarter of the pie. When the others find out, they are annoyed and try to divide the remaining three-fourths into four equal and identically shaped slices. The cuts must be straight.

HOW MUST THEY CUT THE REMAINING PIZZA IN ORDER TO PRODUCE FOUR IDENTICAL SLICES?

The World's Greatest Slip Sliding Puzzle

For this challenge, you'll need to get seven coins and duplicate the star above. Place a coin on any of the star's eight points. Then slide the coin along one of the straight lines to its endpoint. Place a second coin on another point. Slide this one down to its endpoint. Continue in this manner until all seven coins have been placed.

NOTE: It can be done—but you'll need to develop a strategy.

The World's Greatest A, B, See? Puzzle

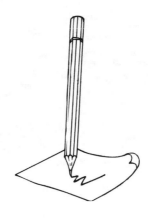

$$
\begin{array}{r}
AB \\
\times AB \\
\hline
ABB
\end{array}
\qquad
\begin{array}{r}
AA \\
+AA \\
\hline
BBC
\end{array}
\qquad
\begin{array}{r}
ABA \\
+BAB \\
\hline
BBBC
\end{array}
\qquad
\begin{array}{r}
ABA \\
+BAA \\
\hline
CDDD
\end{array}
$$

EACH LETTER STANDS FOR A DIFFERENT DIGIT IN EACH EQUATION. CAN YOU DECODE EACH ONE?

The World's Greatest Spare Change Puzzle

Jonathan has a pocket full of coins. Yet he doesn't have the right combination of coins to make change for a nickel, dime, quarter, half dollar, or dollar.

WHAT IS THE LARGEST VALUE OF COINS JONATHAN CAN HAVE IN HIS POCKET?

The World's Greatest Puzzling Price Puzzle

A puzzle book costs $5.00 plus one-half of its price. How much does the puzzle book cost?

The World's Greatest Gum Drop Puzzle

In preparation for a party, Heather fills a large jar with gum drops. Before the party begins, Michael sees the gum drop jar. He (hoping that no one will realize) takes one-third of the drops. Soon after, Tanya takes one-third of the gum drops (she too hopes that no one will notice). Finally, Britt appears and, like the others, she takes one-third of the gum drops.

IF FORTY GUM DROPS ARE LEFT IN THE JAR, HOW MANY DID IT ORIGINALLY CONTAIN?

The World's Greatest Go-Cart Crossing Puzzle

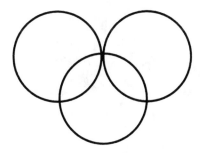

Three go-cart tracks are built as shown. Each track forms a separate one-third of a mile loop. Three go-carts begin riding at the same time from the central point where all three tracks cross. One go-cart travels at 6 mph, another at 12 mph, and the third at 15 mph.

HOW LONG WILL IT TAKE FOR ALL THREE GO-CARTS TO CROSS PATHS FOR THE FIFTH TIME?

The World's Greatest Table Manners Puzzle

Four couples enter a restaurant. How many ways can they be seated at a round table so that the men and women alternate and no husband and wife sit next to each other?

The World's Greatest Winning Slip Puzzle

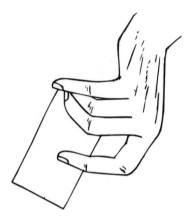

A contest is fixed. Everyone knows it, including the contestants. One of the contestants, however, makes it to the final playoff level.

The master of ceremonies presents the following challenge: "This box contains two slips of paper. One slip has the word 'winner' printed on it, the other has the word 'loser.' Your task is to select the winning slip—without looking of course."

The contestant knows that this challenge is fixed. He realizes that both slips have the word 'loser.' How can he select one slip and win the challenge? By the way, the contestant can't declare this contest is a fraud or he'd lose his current winnings.

The World's Greatest Ancient Man Puzzle

An Ancient Greek was said to have lived one-fourth of his life as a boy, one-fifth as a youth, one-third as a man, and spent the last 13 years as an elderly gent. How old was he when he died?

The World's Greatest Lights Out! Puzzle

The total output of electrical energy from your brain is only about 20 watts. That's not an avalanche of power (especially when you consider that most household light bulbs use five times that amount). Now try powering up with this problem.

Imagine that you can't sleep because you are kept awake by the flashing neon lights that shine through a square store window. The window measures 10 x 10 feet.

A friend assures you that he can cover up half the area of the window but still leave a square section that is 10 x 10 feet. This will then satisfy both you and the storekeeper. You think your friend has lost it. Has he?

The World's Greatest Pencil Puzzle

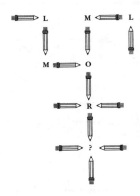

CAN YOU UNCOVER THE LOGIC USED TO CREATE THIS LAYOUT? IF SO, USE THAT SAME LOGIC TO DETERMINE THE LETTER FOR THE QUESTION MARK.

The World's Greatest Sounds Logical Puzzle

It's the weekend! Saturdays and Sundays are the days that Sheila, Ramon, and Niko shop together for music. The CDs they purchase are either rock 'n' roll or jazz. When they visit the music store, each person will purchase one and only one CD. Here are the rules that govern their selections.

1. Either Sheila or Ramon will pick rock 'n' roll, but not both of them.
2. If Sheila picks rock 'n' roll, Niko picks jazz.
3. Niko and Ramon do not both pick jazz.

WHICH ONE OF THE THREE PURCHASED A JAZZ CD ON SATURDAY AND A ROCK 'N' ROLL CD ON SUNDAY?

The World's Greatest Triangular Tower Puzzle

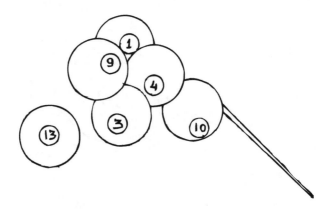

Suppose ten billiard balls are placed in the standard triangular rack. If additional billiard balls are placed on top of this pattern, some balls will roll into the gullies to form a smaller, stable triangle (forget about the balls which roll off the stack). If you add more layers, you'll eventually build a billiard ball pyramid. How many billiard balls and levels would the pyramid contain?

The World's Greatest Criss-Crossed Puzzle

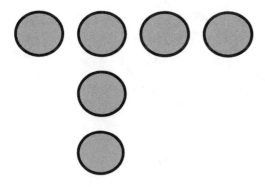

Place six coins in the layout as shown above. Notice that this arrangement forms two columns. The horizontal column has four coins. The vertical column has three coins. Can you move only one coin to form two columns with each containing four coins?

The World's Greatest Crystal Building Puzzle

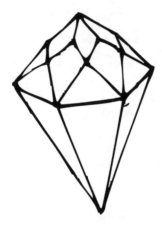

Have you ever looked closely at a crystal? If so, you may have noticed that the crystal has flat sides and uniform angles. That's because a crystal is a repeating arrangement of tiny particles of matter. Often, a central particle is surrounded on all sides by other particles. Here's a puzzle that will help you visualize a crystal pattern.

SUPPOSE YOU COAT A TENNIS BALL WITH GLUE. WHAT IS THE MAXIMUM NUMBER OF TENNIS BALLS THAT CAN ATTACH DIRECTLY TO THIS STICKY SURFACE?

The World's Greatest Testy Target Puzzle

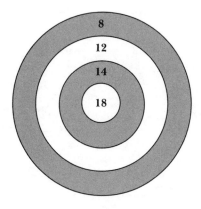

Ten arrows are shot at the target above. One of them misses the target completely. The others all strike it. If the total sum of points is 100, in which part of the target did each arrow strike?

The World's Greatest Eighth Century Enigma Puzzle

Here's a puzzle that can be traced back to the eighth century. A man has a goat, a wolf, and a head of cabbage. He comes to a river and must bring these three things across to the other side. The boat can only take the man plus either the goat, wolf, or cabbage. There is another problem. If the cabbage is left with the goat, the goat will eat the cabbage. If the wolf is left with the goat, the goat will be devoured. How can he transport the wolf, goat, and cabbage to the other side?

The World's Greatest Planet Rotation Puzzle

Our planet spins counterclockwise on its axis. It also has a counter-clockwise revolution around the sun. Suppose both motions now go clockwise. How would this affect the apparent direction of sunrise and sunset?

The World's Greatest Shuffle Puzzle

Pretend you have five cards: a ten, a jack, a queen, a king, and an ace. In your mind's eye, shuffle these five cards together and put the pile face down. If you were to select four cards, returning each card and reshuffling the deck after each pick, what kind of hand would you more likely draw: four Aces or a straight picked in sequence? Can you explain why?

The World's Greatest Some Exchange! Puzzle

The first written puzzles appeared in ancient Egypt about 1650 B.C. These puzzles were part of an 18 1/2-foot scroll called the Rhind Papyrus. Times have changed since then, but many puzzles haven't. Just try these next ones.

Examine the two stacks of number blocks. If you exchange one block from one column with one block from the other, the number of their sums will be equal. Which blocks need to be exchanged?

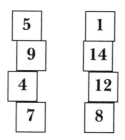

Now that you know how to balance two columns, you're ready to move up to three columns! By exchanging one block from each column, each of the three blocks' sums will be equal. Remember that all three columns must undergo only one exchange.

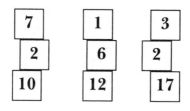

THE WORLD'S MOST
MIND-BOGGLING
WORD PUZZLES

The World's Most Mind-Boggling William's Preference Puzzle

William likes apples better than oranges, and vanilla ice cream better than chocolate. He would rather watch a baseball or football game on TV than hockey, enjoys summer and fall more than spring and winter, thinks *Newsweek* a better magazine than *Time*, and is convinced that *High Noon* is a greater Western movie than *Destry Rides Again*.

CAN YOU EXPLAIN WHY WILLIAM HAS THESE PREFERENCES?

The World's Most Mind-Boggling IDK Band Puzzle

Six college students, all musicians, decided to form a rock band that they named the IDKers. The group consisted of five men and a lead singer named Matilda, who was tall and had red hair. The men were all from New Jersey, but Matilda came to the college from New York. When members of the band were asked what IDK stood for, they agreed that they would always answer, "I don't know."

CAN YOU GUESS WHY THEY SAID THIS?

The World's Most Mind-Boggling Snowball Puzzle

"A snowball sentence," said Mr. Jones to his daughter, "is one in which each word is one letter longer than the preceding word. Do you think you can construct such a sentence?"

The daughter thought for several minutes before she said, "I am not that smart, father."

PROVE THAT THE DAUGHTER WAS SMARTER THAN SHE SAID SHE WAS.

The World's Most Mind-Boggling
Name the Month Puzzle

WHAT MONTH IS INDICATED BY THESE STRANGE SYMBOLS?

The World's Most Mind-Boggling Wrong Caption Puzzle

Professor Letterman, who teaches English at Wordsmith College, has just hired Miss Jones, his new assistant.

THE CAPTION SEEMS NOT TO FIT THE PICTURE. YOU CAN MAKE IT FIT BY CHANGING ONE LETTER.

The World's Most Mind-Boggling Tennis Player Puzzle

WHAT IS THIS TENNIS PLAYER SAYING?

The World's Most Mind-Boggling Four Suit Puzzle

I _____ my dog.
I _____ my cat.
I carry a _____ .
I would love to own a _____ mine.

**IF YOU WERE TO INSERT IN THE BLANKS A SYMBOL FOR
EACH OF THE FOUR PLAYING-CARD SUITS, EACH LINE
WOULD MAKE SENSE.**

The World's Most Mind-Boggling Name the Student Puzzle

I DID THIS SUM

2856104
4454913
——————
73N017

WHAT IS
MY NAME?

THE SUM ON THE BLACKBOARD IS CORRECT. CAN YOU FIND IN THE PICTURE THE FIRST NAME OF THE STUDENT?

The World's Most Mind-Boggling
What Letter? Puzzle

·······································

Lιι

THIS IS A PICTURE OF A LETTER. CAN YOU DECIDE WHAT LETTER IT IS?

The World's Most Mind-Boggling Sad King Puzzle

KING ARE YOU SORRY YOU ARE KING?

WHAT'S SO REMARKABLE ABOUT THE CAPTION BELOW THE PICTURE?

The World's Most Mind-Boggling Short Teaser Puzzle

THERE IS A FAMILIAR WORD OF FIVE LETTERS THAT BECOMES SHORTER IF YOU ADD TWO LETTERS TO IT. WHAT'S THE WORD?

The World's Most Mind-Boggling
Name the Book Puzzle

IN WHAT BOOK ARE THE MONTHS LISTED WITH APRIL APPEARING FIRST AND SEPTEMBER APPEARING LAST?

The World's Most Mind-Boggling Where? Puzzle

....

THERE IS A FAMILIAR SAYING THAT LISTS ALL THE MONTHS, WITH SEPTEMBER COMING FIRST AND FEBRUARY LAST. WHAT SAYING IS IT?

The World's Most Mind-Boggling Two Door Puzzle

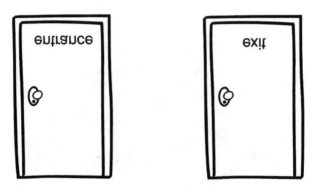

The words on the two doors seem to be written in a strange script. See if you can translate them into English without adding any words to the page. There is a ridiculously easy way to read the two words.

The World's Most Mind-Boggling Family Talk Puzzle

Here you see a drawing based on a photograph of Blake de Kalb, his wife the former Norah Sharon, their three children, and their young dog, Otto.

Your task is to identify each person and the pet with a three-letter word that is a palindrome — a word that spells the same in both directions, like the name of the parents and the dog. For example, the three-letter palindrome for the dog would be PUP.

What kind of car does the family own?

AND AT WHAT TIME OF DAY WAS THE PICTURE TAKEN?

The World's Most Mind-Boggling Name the Girl Puzzle

Mary's father has three daughters. The oldest is named April. The second oldest is named May. What's the first name of the youngest daughter?

The World's Most Mind-Boggling Three Sister Puzzle

There are three blond sisters named Dinah, Betty, and Marilyn. Of the three, only Dinah might dye her hair red.

Concealed in the two previous sentences is something that could explode. Can you find it?

The World's Most Mind-Boggling How Many Cookies? Puzzle

······································

JIM 81, JOAN 812

Jim and his sister Joan discovered a jar of cookies in a kitchen cupboard.

1. Can you interpret the picture's caption?
2. If the jar contained 10 cookies, and Jim and Joan ate all but three, how many cookies would be left in the jar?

The World's Most Mind-Boggling Stop and Snap Puzzle

Mrs. Rendrag and her son Nitram had finished washing and drying the dinner dishes.

"Now that the dishes are done," said Mrs. Rendrag, "let's do the STOP AND SNAP."

The words STOP AND SNAP don't make sense. Do you see how a simple change of their letters will let you know what Mrs. Rendrag actually said to her son?

After you have solved this puzzle, you should have no difficulty learning the real names of Mrs. Rendrag and Nitram.

The World's Most Mind-Boggling
Tommy's Tumble Puzzle

Little Tommy fell off his tricycle and bumped his head so hard that he was knocked unconscious. When he came to, he spoke perfect French. How come?

The World's Most Mind-Boggling How Many Peaches? Puzzle

Joy's father brought a paper sack home from the supermarket. It contained a certain number of peaches. Joy took no peaches from the sack, and she left no peaches in the sack.

HOW MANY PEACHES WERE INSIDE THE SACK?

The World's Most Mind-Boggling Baby Crossword Puzzle

···

1	2	3
2		
3		

ACROSS	DOWN	
1. Uncle	1. Health	
2. Cherry	2. Fresh	
3. Fine	3. Have we	?

If you solve this easy 3 x 3 crossword puzzle, you'll find that in addition to the horizontal and vertical words, each diagonal provides two other words. It is not known whether such a word square, with eight different common English words, can be made without duplicating at least one letter.

The World's Most Mind-Boggling What's the Question? Puzzle

The clerk in the railroad station is responding to the lady's question. Can you guess what she has just asked him?

The World's Most Mind-Boggling Crazy Word Puzzle

ZO–ZO OON

ZOOZ ZCZ

ZO–N ZO–ZC

X–Z

Professor Letterman is holding a sheet on which he lettered what he claims are seven common English words.

IT'S EASY TO FIND OUT WHAT THE WORDS ARE IF YOU PERFORM A SIMPLE OPERATION. WHAT MUST YOU DO?

The World's Most Mind-Boggling Day's End Puzzle

IS IT TRUE THAT DAY BEGINS WITH D AND ENDS WITH E?

The World's Most Mind-Boggling Lisping Verse Puzzle

"You can't," says Tom to lisping Bill,
"Find any rhyme for month."
"You are wrong," was Bill's reply.
"I'll find a rhyme at _____."

The World's Most Mind-Boggling In the Middle Puzzle

PROFESSOR LETTERMAN CLAIMS THAT P IS THE MIDDLE LETTER OF THE ALPHABET. HOW CAN HE BE RIGHT?

The World's Most Mind-Boggling
Missing Letter Puzzle

**AN ELECTRIC SIGN IN THE WINDOW OF MOM'S
RESTAURANT IS MISSING A LETTER. WHAT LETTER IS IT?**

The World's Most Mind-Boggling Missing Word Puzzle

In each of the eight sentences below, there is a word missing. Professor Letterman says it's the same word in all eight places.

Can you supply the one word that makes sense of each sentence?

____ I hit him in the eye yesterday.
I ____ hit him in the eye yesterday.
I hit ____ him in the eye yesterday.
I hit him ____ in the eye yesterday.
I hit him in ____ the eye yesterday.
I hit him in the ____ eye yesterday.
I hit him in the eye ____ yesterday.
I hit him in the eye yesterday ____.

The World's Most Mind-Boggling
Puzzling Door Puzzle

WHAT IN THE WORLD DO THESE STRANGE WORDS ON THE DOOR MEAN?

The World's Most Mind-Boggling Correct-the-Spelling Puzzle

I BIND ON SHE HANK IT FORTH TOO IS THY BUST.

IF YOU CHANGE ONE LETTER IN EACH WORD, IT WILL MAKE A SENTENCE THAT IS A WELL-KNOWN PROVERB.

The World's Most Mind-Boggling SHH! Puzzle

IS THERE ANOTHER COMMON ENGLISH WORD, ASIDE FROM SUGAR, IN WHICH S, AS THE FIRST LETTER, IS PRONOUNCED SH? CAN YOU NAME IT?

The World's Most Mind-Boggling Four Arrows Puzzle

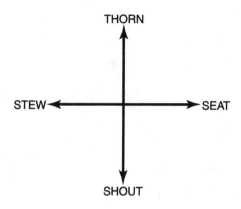

EACH ARROW POINTS TO A WORD. IF YOU REARRANGE
THE LETTERS PROPERLY IN EACH WORD, THE PICTURE
WILL MAKE SENSE.

The World's Most Mind-Boggling
Three-Letter Word Puzzle

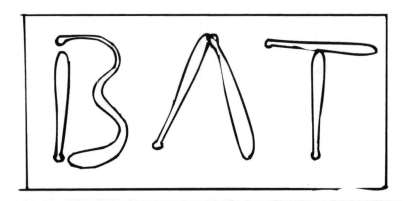

In this sentence there are neither more nor less than ___ words with three letters. What can you put in the blank space to make the sentence correct?

The World's Most Mind-Boggling WYKMIITY and WYLTK Puzzle

When Susan asked Tom what the letters on his T-shirt meant, his reply was, "Will you kiss me if I tell you?" After Susan kissed him, Tom explained the letters. Tom then asked Susan what her letters meant. See if you can figure out what the letters stand for on both T-shirts.

The World's Most Mind-Boggling
ACE GIK MOQ SUWY Puzzle

WHAT IS THE BASIS FOR THE SEQUENCE OF STRANGE THREE-LETTER WORDS PRINTED ABOVE?

The World's Most Mind-Boggling What Is Santa Saying? Puzzle

CAN YOU FIGURE OUT WHAT THIS DEPARTMENT STORE SANTA CLAUS IS SAYING TO THE LITTLE GIRL WHO HAS JUST CLIMBED ONTO HIS LAP?

The World's Most Mind-Boggling Yuletide Rebus Puzzle

THE PICTURE REPRESENTS A LINE FROM A WELL-KNOWN CHRISTMAS SONG. CAN YOU GUESS THE LINE?

The World's Most Mind-Boggling Three Student Puzzle

At a party at Wordsmith College, three students were asked to pin their first names on their clothes. Instead of names, it looks as if these three wrote down numbers instead.

CAN YOU GUESS THEIR FIRST NAMES?

The World's Most Mind-Boggling Ruth's Cipher Puzzle

Ruth numbered the letters of the alphabet as follows:

A = 1
B = 2
C = 3

and so on to Z = 26

She sent the following code message to her friend:

91215225251521

CAN YOU DECODE IT?

The World's Most Mind-Boggling Monkey Talk Puzzle

1. This clever monkey has been taught how to speak. To learn what she is saying, insert the same letter five times in the letter sequence shown.

2. After you have solved this puzzle, see if you can insert the same letter four times in LBM to learn where the monkey is living in a zoo,

3. And insert the same letter three times in BRBR to learn the monkey's name.

The World's Most Mind-Boggling Concealed Creature Puzzle

DOES THE PIGEON WANT TO CATCH THE BUTTERFLY?

The word "pig" is hidden inside the word "pigeon." Can you find the names of four other creatures concealed in the sentence above? Answer on page 87.

The World's Most Mind-Boggling Horse Jingle Puzzle

1 was a racehorse.
2 was 12.
111 race.
2112.

CAN YOU MAKE SENSE OF THIS POEM?

The World's Most Mind-Boggling
Spell the Creature Puzzle

··

Y	Q	U	W	M
T	S	I	F	E
R	H	L	D	N
A	P	O	G	V
B	K	C	X	Z

Put your finger on a letter in the square. By moving the finger left, right, up, or down — but never diagonally — from one square to one next to it, see if you can spell a familiar eight-letter word that stands for a living creature.

The World's Most Mind-Boggling Nagging Question Puzzle

CAN YOU THINK OF AN ANIMAL WHOSE NAME BEGINS WITH N?

The World's Most Mind-Boggling Freezing Frog Puzzle

This poor frog is freezing on a cold winter day. The words FROG and COLD are closely related by the positions of their letters in the alphabet. Can you determine how they are related?

The World's Most Mind-Boggling Three Bunny Puzzle

WHY ARE THESE THREE RABBITS CALLED THE THREE
MUSKETEERS?

The World's Most Mind-Boggling Old Mother Hubbard Puzzle

Old Mother Hubbard
Went to the cupboard
To get her poor dog a bone,
But when she got there,
The cupboard was bare,
And so her poor dog had none.

Professor Letterman says that word-play buffs find something very strange about this old nursery rhyme. Can you determine what it is?

The World's Most Mind-Boggling
Name the Poodle Puzzle

···

WHAT'S THE NAME OF MRS. LETTERMAN'S POODLE.

The World's Most Mind-Boggling Where's the Comma? Puzzle

DID YOU SEE THE LION EATING HERMAN?

Actually, Herman was not injured by the lion. See if you can place a comma in the above sentence to make it read properly.

The World's Most Mind-Boggling Who Does What? Puzzle

On the left are the first names of sixteen women. On the right is a list of sixteen professions. Each woman has one of these jobs. For example, Sue is a lawyer.

See if you can match each name on the left with the related profession on the right.

Sue	Chiropractor
Grace	Waitress
Bridget	Upholsterer
Patience	Engineer
Carlotta	Dancer
Robin	Thief
Ophelia	Physician
Wanda	Milliner
Sophie	Minister
Hattie	Singer
Octavia	Magician
Carrie	Gambler
Betty	Musician
Carol	Used car saleswoman
Faith	Jeweler
Pearl	Lawyer

The World's Most Mind-Boggling
Name the Time Puzzle

See if you can guess the correct times for the following situations:

1. A tiger ate a postman. Let P.M. be an abbreviation for a man who delivers mail. What time is it?
2. What time is it when you have a severe toothache?
3. Three cats are chasing a mouse. What time is it?
4. If your antique clock struck thirteen times, what time would it be?

The World's Most Mind-Boggling
Spell a Name Puzzle

The six shapes shown here have been cut from cardboard. Can you rearrange them to spell a girl's name?

The World's Most Mind-Boggling
Ribbon Loop Puzzle

Put a word in the blank space so that the sentence makes sense when
you read it around the loop.

The World's Most Mind-Boggling Puzzling Landscape Puzzle

Somewhere in the above scene there is something with a name that begins with S. What is it?

The World's Most Mind-Boggling Guess the Pseudonym Puzzle

Armand T. Ringer is an anagram of the name of a writer with whom you are familiar. Who is he or she?

The World's Most Mind-Boggling Ode to Apricots Puzzle

Janet bought some stewed apricots on a cold
February morning for her three children,
Mary, Julie, and Junior.
Apricots are delicious when stewed.
Maybe you don't think so?
Junior doesn't like stewed apricots, but
Julie and Mary believe that they
Augment the taste of cereals and ice cream.
Separately, stewed apricots are also tasty.
Octopuses would surely find apricots a
Novel kind of fruit, but they might
Decline to eat an apricot once they tasted it.

**THIS PECULIAR FREE-VERSE POEM BY ARMAND T.
RINGER HAS SOMETHING REMARKABLE ABOUT EACH
LINE. CAN YOU DISCOVER WHAT IT IS?**

The World's Most Mind-Boggling
Fill the Blank Puzzle

....

In this square
there are ____
e's.

WHAT NUMBER WORD FROM 1 TO 10 WOULD MAKE THE STATEMENT IN THE SIGN ACCURATE?

The World's Most Mind-Boggling Do You Deny It? Puzzle

NO EXPERT ON WORD PLAY CAN DENY THAT THERE IS A FAMILIAR ENGLISH WORD OF FOUR LETTERS THAT ENDS IN ENY. WHAT IS IT?

The World's Most Mind-Boggling Where to Draw the Lines? Puzzle

By adding slash marks between the letters of HESITATE like this:

HE/SIT/ATE

you can make three words. Now see if you can add six slashes to INDISCRIMINATION to make seven common words.

The World's Most Mind-Boggling
He! He! Puzzle

....

Can you name a common word that starts and ends with HE?

Can you name a common word that contains the letters ADAC in that order? It may give you a headache to answer both questions!

The World's Most Mind-Boggling Guess the Punchline Puzzle

This is a test of your ability to make jokes. Each opening remark is followed by a funny punchline. Try to supply the missing line before you check the answers.

1. FATHER: The man who marries my daughter will get a prize.
BOYFRIEND:

2. WOMAN (IN RESTAURANT): Is there soup on the menu?
WAITER:

3. TEACHER: Where was the Declaration of Independence signed?
STUDENT:

4. JUDGE: Order! Order in the court!
PRISONER:

5. WOMAN (TO PSYCHIATRIST): I need help. Nobody pays any attention to me. I feel like I'm invisible.
PSYCHIATRIST:

6. PATIENT (AFTER A PHYSICAL EXAMINATION): How do I stand?
DOCTOR:

7. PSYCHIATRIST: Do you have trouble making up your mind?
PATIENT:

The World's Most Mind-Boggling Wrong Word Puzzle

A man who couldn't read English was attending a convention in the United States. He asked a friend to tell him how to distinguish the men's washroom from the women's.

"It's easy," said the friend. "Just go to the room that has the shortest word on its door."

The man did as he was told, but found himself inside a washroom with a bunch of screaming ladies. How come?

The World's Most Mind-Boggling Typewriter Teaser Puzzle

....

Using only the letters on the second line of the typewriter or computer keyboard, see if you can spell a familiar ten-letter word.

The World's Most Mind-Boggling Change 100 to CAT Puzzle

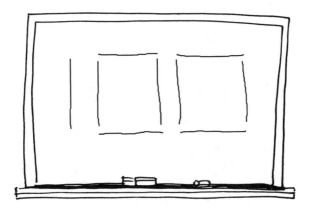

Professor Letterman has drawn nine short lines on the blackboard to represent the number 100. He wants to know who in his class will be the first to see how to change the positions of just two of the lines to make the word CAT.

You can work on the puzzle with toothpicks.

The World's Most Mind-Boggling Marrying Bachelor Puzzle

Tim Rines is a respected bachelor in this hometown, even though he married more than fifty ladies who live there. Rearrange the letters of his name to spell his profession.

Now rearrange the letters of PEPSI-COLA to spell the name that goes in the blank of "The First _____ Church," where you will find Mr. Rines every Sunday morning.

The World's Most Mind-Boggling
HIJKLMNO Puzzle

The letters in the title above, when properly understood, stand for a common liquid. Name it.

The World's Most Mind-Boggling Unusual Word Puzzle

Can you think of a familiar word with three U's in it?

The World's Most Mind-Boggling Clock Conundrum Puzzle

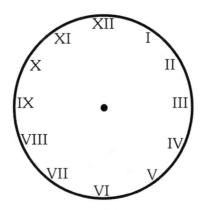

Clocks often use Roman numerals for the hours. When Walter B. Gibson, the writer who created *The Shadow* and wrote many books about magic, was seven, he sent a letter to *St. Nicholas*, a magazine for children. In the letter, which the magazine published, he asked which Roman numeral on a clock suggested the name of a common plant. What did Walter have in mind?

The World's Most Mind-Boggling Ten Body Parts Puzzle

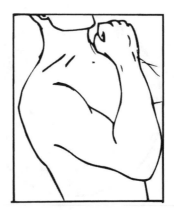

Many parts of the human body have three-letter names, for example, "arm." See if you can think of at least nine others.

The World's Most Mind-Boggling
Opposite Puzzle

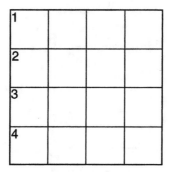

1. shrink
2. green
3. shut
4. came

On this simple crossword puzzle, put words that are the opposite of the definitions given. If you do it correctly, the result will be a word square with the same words vertically as horizontally.

The World's Most Mind-Boggling ERGRO Puzzle

....

Put three letters in front of ERGRO, and the same three letters at the end of ERGRO, to make an 11-letter word that tells you where all the world's oil comes from.

The World's Most Mind-Boggling
One-Letter Caption Puzzle

Under each of the eight pictures, place a single letter that describes the picture. For example, the letter J describes the picture of a Jay. The last picture tells you to look in a mirror.

The World's Most Mind-Boggling Annoyed Sign Painter Puzzle

The owner of the Bell Yacht Company refused to pay the sign painter because he put the words Bell and Yacht too close together.

Late that night the annoyed sign painter returned and changed one letter on the door to indicate how he felt. What letter did he change?

The World's Most Mind-Boggling Fold and Cut Puzzle

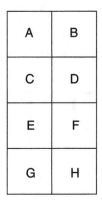

Fold a sheet of paper so that when you open it flat the creases will form eight rectangles. Write in these boxes the first eight letters of the alphabet in order, as shown above.

Now, fold the sheet along the creases in any manner you like to make a packet with the eight rectangles together, like the leaves of a book. With scissors, trim away all four edges of the packet. This will leave you with eight separate paper rectangles.

Spread the eight pieces on the table. Four letters will be faceup and four facedown. Try to form a word with the faceup letters. If you can't make a word, turn the pieces over and try again with the other four letters.

WHAT WORD DID YOU FORM?

The World's Most Mind-Boggling In and Out Puzzle

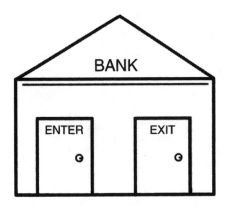

Add a letter to one of the three words in the picture to make a new word that fits the blank space in each of the following three sentences:

1. Do unicorns _____?
2. He had a _____ expression on his face.
3. H is the _____ of nothing.

The World's Most Mind-Boggling From Z to A Puzzle

The alphabet goes from A to Z. What goes from Z to A?

The World's Most Mind-Boggling What Can It Be? Puzzle

Luke had it before. Paul had it behind. Matthew never had it. Girls have it once. Boys can't have it. Mrs. Mulligan had it twice. Mr. Lowell had it once before and twice after.

WHAT IS IT?

The World's Most Mind-Boggling Number Anagram Puzzle

....

Arrange the nine letters of "extension" to spell the names of three numbers, each less than 20.

The World's Most Mind-Boggling ENINYOS Puzzle

....

Can you add the same letter at four different spots in ENINYOS to make an appropriate caption for the illustration?

The World's Most Mind-Boggling
Name the Painting Puzzle

"No hat, a smile," describes a famous painting. If you rearrange the letters, they will spell the name of the painting. What picture is it?

The World's Most Mind-Boggling Locked Safe Puzzle

You see here the three dials of a safe. To open the safe, you must rotate the dials until a familiar six-letter word can be read horizontally, like the letters TUYCNO in the illustration.

WHAT WORD OPENS THE SAFE?

The World's Most Mind-Boggling
Change the Sign Puzzle

A group of children cleverly added punctuation to the sign that allowed them to go swimming. How did they do this?

The World's Most Mind-Boggling
Three B's Puzzle

The words "bubble" and "babble" each contain three B's. Professor Letterman created a hubbub in his classroom when he offered a prize to the first student who could think of a word that had three B's, but which didn't begin with a B. What's the word?

The World's Most Mind-Boggling Horace Spencer Puzzle

Can you complete the second line of what Horace is saying so that it rhymes with the first line?

The World's Most Mind-Boggling What's the Number? Puzzle

The word FORTY is the only number-word with its letters in alphabetical order. What number-word has its letters in reverse alphabetical order?

The World's Most Mind-Boggling NY, PA, AND OZ Puzzle

....

L. Frank Baum, who wrote fourteen Oz books, was born and raised in New York. Ruth Plumly Thompson, who continued the Oz series after Baum died, lived in Pennsylvania.

There are close wordplay associations between the words OZ and NY, and OZ and PA. Do you see how OZ is connected to the two state abbreviations?

The World's Most Mind-Boggling Curious Card Puzzle

Mr. Curio owns an antique shop by the side of the road. When his store is open, he puts four large cards side by side on the window ledge. They bear the letters O-P-E-N.

When he is away, he rearranges the cards to spell a word that tells visitors his store is closed.

HOW DOES HE ALTER THE LETTERS?

The World's Most Mind-Boggling GHGHGH Puzzle

Professor Letterman is explaining to his class how to pronounce the word ghghgh.

"The first gh," he says, "is pronounced the same way as gh in hiccough. The second gh is pronounced like the gh in Edinburgh. And the third gh has the sound of gh in laugh."

If you pronounce all three gh's the way the professor says, what word does it make?

The World's Most Mind-Boggling HAL and IBM Puzzle

....

HAL is the name of a supercomputer on the spaceship featured in the movie version of Arthur Clarke's famous novel, *2001*. IBM is the name of a company that makes computers.

There is a curious relationship between HAL and IBM. Can you discover it?

The World's Most Mind-Boggling Ten Flying Saucers Puzzle

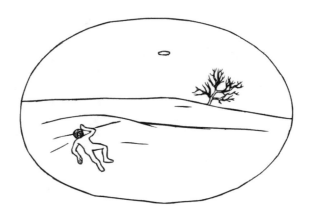

"Have you ever seen a UFO?" I asked Professor Letterman.

"Indeed I have," he replied. "I've seen ten."

Then he added, "I'm only kidding. But here's a word puzzle for you. What operation can you perform on TEN that will change the word to UFO?

The World's Most Mind-Boggling
Kubla Khan Puzzle

In Xanadu did Kubla Khan
A stately pleasure dome decree;
Where Alph, the sacred river, ran
Through caverns measureless to man
Down to a sunless sea.

One of Samuel Taylor Coleridge's most famous poems begins with the five lines quoted above. Do you see what is so remarkable about them?

The World's Most Mind-Boggling Merry Christmas Puzzle

A merry Christmas and a happy new year!
Merry, merry carols you'll have sung us,
Christmas remains Christmas even when you are not here,
And though afar and lonely, you're among us.
A bond is there, a bond at times near broken.
Happy be Christmas then, when happy, clear,
New heart-warm links are forged, new ties betoken
Year ripe with loving giving birth to year.

This poem, by the late British poet J.A. Lindon, has a truly amazing structure. Can you figure out what it is?

The World's Most Mind-Boggling Two Word Puzzle

We __x__ on the __y__ way,
And we __y__ on the __x__ way.

Fill out the two sentences by putting the same five-letter word in the blanks marked x, and a four-letter word in the blanks marked y.

The World's Most Mind-Boggling Blind Bus Driver Puzzle

···

A newspaper headline reads, "Blind Man Is Hired to Drive School Bus."

How can this be true? If you interpret the sentence properly, it will make good sense.

The World's Most Mind-Boggling
Lewis Carroll Puzzle

The first nine letters of the alphabet are A B C D E F G H I. Cross out the H. Can you arrange the remaining eight letters to make two words that accurately describe the clown?

The World's Most Mind-Boggling Curious Sequence Puzzle

What is the next pair of letters in this sequence?
ST ND RD TH __?

The World's Most Mind-Boggling
Name Two Puzzle

....

THREE COMMON ENGLISH WORDS BEGIN WITH DW. CAN YOU NAME AT LEAST TWO?

The World's Most Mind-Boggling Decode a Number Puzzle

··

Each letter in ABCDEFGHIJ, the first ten letters of the alphabet, stands for a different letter in a number that is less than 100. There is only one answer. What's the number?

The World's Most Mind-Boggling Miles and Miles Puzzle

....

NAME FOUR WORDS THAT HAVE A MILE BETWEEN THEIR FIRST AND LAST LETTERS.

The World's Most Mind-Boggling After AB Puzzle

······························

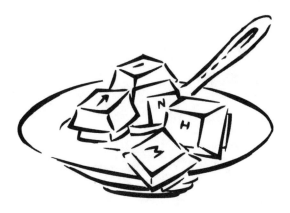

WHAT LETTER IN THE ALPHABET COMES AFTER AB?

The World's Most Mind-Boggling Add a Line Puzzle

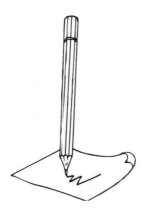

Can you draw a short line on

ABCDE

to turn it into a five-letter word?

The World's Most Mind-Boggling ONE EHT Puzzle

!YAD DOO GAE VAH

SOLUTIONS

THE WORLD'S MOST AMAZING LOGIC PUZZLES

THE WORLD'S MOST AMAZING DUPLGOOSE EGG PUZZLE

CONSIDERATIONS: Assume that D's statement is false. If so, neither A nor C is guilty. This means that either A's statement or that of B must be true. However, without additional information, we cannot determine the guilty one.

Therefore, since it was given that the guilty one can be deduced from the four statements, D's statement must be true. Therefore, the other three statements are false. C did not do it; the guilty one is A.

SUMMARY SOLUTION: A did it.

THE WORLD'S MOST AMAZING HUFFALON THEFT PUZZLE

CONSIDERATIONS: Assume that A is one of the guilty ones and has made a false statement. If so, C is not guilty and has made a true statement. If so, D is not guilty and has made a true statement. If so, B is guilty and has made a false statement. If so, F is guilty and has made a false statement. If so, E is guilty and has made a false statement. Since there are only two guilty ones, the assumption that A is guilty leads to four guilty ones, the assumption is incorrect.

Therefore, A's statement must be truthful. C is one of the two guilty ones and, since C's statement is false, the other culprit must be D.

SUMMARY SOLUTION: C and D are guilty.

THE WORLD'S MOST AMAZING OVERSEER'S THEFT PUZZLE

CONSIDERATIONS: Since the housekeeper and the stable hand each make two false statements, A must be the housekeeper and D must be the stable hand. Otherwise, their first statements would be true. C must be the huffalon groom, whose first statement is true and second statement is false. B is the cook, who has made two true statements.

SUMMARY SOLUTION: A, the housekeeper, is guilty.

THE WORLD'S MOST AMAZING PURLOINED PRICKLY PLUM PIE PUZZLE

CONSIDERATIONS: Assume that A is guilty. If so, all three of his statements are false. Therefore, since the culprit makes one true statement, A must be innocent. Assume that C is guilty. Since all three are known to be lovers of prickly plum pie, C's first statement must be false, as would be statements two and three. C is not guilty. The guilty one is B. His second statement is true and statements one and three are false.

SUMMARY SOLUTION: B stole the prickly plum pie.

THE WORLD'S MOST AMAZING FARM THEFT PUZZLE

CONSIDERATIONS: Assume that Farmhand No. 1 is guilty. If so, Farmhand No. 2's first statement is true and second statement is false. Farmhand No. 4 would also be guilty.

Since it was a given that there was one culprit, it is apparent that Farmhand No. 1 is not guilty. Therefore, Farmhand No. 2's second statement is true: Farmhand No. 4 did not do it. Farmhand No. 4's first statement is true and second statement is false. Farmhand No. 3 is guilty.

SUMMARY SOLUTION: Farmhand No. 3 did it.

THE WORLD'S MOST AMAZING BALLOT BOX STUFFER PUZZLE

CONSIDERATIONS: B's first and third statements contradict each other. One is true and the other is false. Therefore, her second statement must be false. C did not do it.

C's second statement must be true. Therefore, his first and third statements are false. B did not do it. It follows that A is the guilty one by elimination. His second and third statements are false, and his first statement is true.

SUMMARY SOLUTION: A is guilty.

THE WORLD'S MOST AMAZING VILLAGE MARKETPLACE THEFT PUZZLE

CONSIDERATIONS: Assume that B is guilty as indicated by B's second statement. If so, A's first statement is true. Either A's second or third statement, or both, are also true, or C's first and third statements must be true. Therefore, since at least two false statements are made by each suspect, B is not guilty.

Assume that A is guilty. If so, C's second statement is true. Either C's first or third statement, or both, are true, or A's second and third statements are true. Therefore, A is not guilty.

Therefore, C is guilty. A's first and third statements are false, B's first and second statements are false, and C's first and second statements are false.

SUMMARY SOLUTION: C is guilty.

THE WORLD'S MOST AMAZING PRODUCE CART-THEFT PUZZLE

CONSIDERATIONS: Assume that A is guilty. If so, C's second statement must be his false statement. However, all of B's statements would be true. Therefore, since none of the suspects makes all true statements, A did not do it.

Assume C is guilty. If so, all of A's statements would be true. Therefore, C is not guilty. B is the guilty one.

SUMMARY SOLUTION: B is guilty.

THE WORLD'S MOST AMAZING ATTEMPTED-SABOTAGE PUZZLE

CONSIDERATIONS: B's second statement must be false. If true, it would be a contradiction. Therefore, B is not the suspect who makes all false statements. B must be the one whose standard of veracity is unknown.

C's second statement must be false. Therefore, C must be the suspect who always speaks falsely, and A must be the suspect who always speaks truthfully.

C's first statement is false. C did it.

SUMMARY SOLUTION: C is guilty.

THE WORLD'S MOST AMAZING SADDLE THEFT PUZZLE

CONSIDERATIONS: Since no two suspects make the same number of true statements, we can conclude that only one makes three true statements.

All four were on duty during all of the thefts. Therefore, A's second statement is false. C's first and second statements contradict each other; one is true and the other is false. D's second statement is false, since at last one of C's statements is true.

B is the only one without a confirmed false statement. Therefore, all three of B's statements are true, two of C's statements are true, D's first statement is true, and none of A's statements are true.

SUMMARY SOLUTION: As indicated by B's third statement, D is guilty.

THE WORLD'S MOST AMAZING LYING PUZZLE

CONSIDERATIONS: B cannot be the Nororean as claimed, because that would be the truth, and a Nororean cannot speak truthfully. B cannot be the Sororean as the statement would be false, and a Sororean cannot speak falsely. Therefore, B is the Midrorean; A is the Sororean, and C, both of whose statements are false, is the Nororean.

SUMMARY SOLUTION:
  A. Sororean
  B. Midrorean
  C. Nororean

THE WORLD'S MOST AMAZING ONE-TO-ANSWER-FOR-THREE PUZZLE

CONSIDERATIONS: From statement 1, A must be the Midrorean. The statement would be false if made by the Sororean and true if made by the Nororean, neither of which would be possible.

Since statement 1 is truthful, and made by the Midrorean, statement 2 is false; B is the Nororean. Statement 3 is truthful, and C must be the Sororean.

SUMMARY SOLUTION:
  A. Midrorean
  B. Nororean
  C. Sororean

THE WORLD'S MOST AMAZING THREE FISHERMEN PUZZLE

CONSIDERATIONS: Assume that B's third statement is true. If so, then C is the Sororean, as indicated; B is the Midrorean; and A is the Nororean. B's second statement, however, would be false, making A's first statement true.

Therefore, B's third statement is false. C would not truthfully claim to be the Sororean. Therefore, A must be the Sororean, B is the Nororean, since his first and second statements are contradicted by A's statements, and C is the Midrorean.

SUMMARY SOLUTION:
  A. Sororean
  B. Nororean
  C. Midrorean

THE WORLD'S MOST AMAZING ABACUS ABHORRENCE PUZZLE

CONSIDERATIONS: B's second statement is that he is the Midrorean. B is either the Midrorean or the Nororean, and, in either case, his first statement would have to be false.

A's second statement must be true, since it directly contradicts B's false first statement. Therefore, A's third statement, that he is not the Nororean, is true and A must be the Sororean.

Since A's first statement must be true, C's first statement must be false, since it directly contradicts A's statement. Therefore, C's second statement, that he is the Sororean, is false; C is the Nororean and B is the Midrorean.

SUMMARY SOLUTION:
  A. Sororean
  B. Midrorean
  C. Nororean

THE WORLD'S MOST AMAZING CHARIOT RACE WINNER PUZZLE

CONSIDERATIONS: Assume that A was the winner. If so, A's first and third statements are true. However, A's third statement agrees with B's third statement, which means that B's first and third statements are true as well, and B would also be the winner. Therefore, the winner must have been C, whose first and third statements are true.

C's third statement is consistent with A's second statement. Therefore, A is a Midrorean, whose first and third statements are false and second statement is true. B's second statement is inconsistent with our knowledge that the race was strongly contested, with the three finishing close together. Therefore, B, who has made three false statements, is a Nororean.

C's second statement, as with B's second statement, is false. Therefore C, whose first and third statements are true and second statement is false, is a Midrorean.

SUMMARY SOLUTION:
  A. Midrorean
  B. Nororean
  C. The winner, Midrorean

THE WORLD'S MOST AMAZING DISAGREEABLE D PUZZLE

CONSIDERATIONS: A's statement, which implies the existence of four groups, is false, as we know there are three groups.

D's first statement is true, as it disputes A's false statement. Therefore, D is either a Sororean or a Midrorean and, in either case, D's third statement must be true.

Since D's third statement, which is true, disputes C's first statement, which disagrees with B's statement, we can conclude the B's statement is true. Therefore, all four Hyperboreans belong to the same group. Since C's first statement is false and second statement is true, and D's second statement is false, we can conclude that the four are Midroreans.

THE WORLD'S MOST AMAZING TWO-TIMES-FOUR SHEPHERD PUZZLE

CONSIDERATIONS: In the first group of shepherds, the statement "None of us are Sororeans" would have to be false. There was at least one Sororean in the group. Since there was only one statement indicating three Sororeans and one statement indicating two Sororeans, neither statement was truthful. There was one Sororean in the first group.

In the second group of shepherds, the statement "We are all Nororeans" would have to be false. There could be no more than three Nororeans. If the fourth shepherd had chosen to speak, he or she could not have given a truthful response: The statement "One of us is a Nororean" would suggest three Sororeans, but this would require a confirmation from two others. The statement "Three of us are Nororeans" could only be made truthfully by one shepherd (and it was). The statement "Two of us are Nororeans" would require the same statement by one of the other shepherds (it was not). Therefore, there were three Nororeans and one Sororean in the second group.

SUMMARY SOLUTION:
There were two Sororeans in the two groups of shepherds.

THE WORLD'S MOST AMAZING MARS TEMPER PUZZLE

CONSIDERATIONS: A's first statement contains two parts; if either is true, the statement is true. A is not a Nororean, as a Nororean cannot make a true statement. If the statement is true, A is a Sororean; if the statement is false, A is a Midrorean. In either case, A's second statement must be true: B is a Sororean.

B's second statement confirms that A is a Midrorean.

For C's first statement to be true, C would have to be a Sororean, but this is not possible because of C's second statement, which disputes B's first statement and is, therefore, false. Both of C's statements are false; C is a Nororean.

D's first statement is false, as A is not a Nororean. D's second statement, however, which disputes C's second statement, is true: D is a Midrorean.

SUMMARY SOLUTION:
A. Midrorean
B. Sororean
C. Nororean
D. Midrorean

THE WORLD'S MOST AMAZING TRANSFER PUZZLE

CONSIDERATIONS: Assume that B's first statement is truthful. If so, then B's third statement, that A is a Sororean, is also truthful. A's second statement, however, contradicts B's first statement.

Therefore, B's first statement must be false. This means that A's second statement is true, but, from B's third statement, which must be false, we know that A is not a Sororean. A's first and third statements must be false, so A is a Midrorean. Since B's second statement confirms A's first statement, which is false, B is a Nororean.

Since A's first statement is false, C's first statement is true.

D's third statement falsely confirms A's false first statement (as well as B's false second statement). D's second statement agrees with B's false first statement. Therefore, D is a Nororean. Therefore, C's second statement is true: C is a Sororean.

SUMMARY SOLUTION:
A. Midrorean
B. Nororean
C. Sororean
D. Nororean

THE WORLD'S MOST AMAZING OUTLIER PUZZLE

CONSIDERATIONS: A's first statement must be true. It would be false only for a Sororean. Therefore, A is neither a Sororean, since Sororeans always speak truthfully, nor a Nororean, since Nororeans always speak falsely. A could be a Midrorean, but, if so, the first and third statements would be true, and the second and fourth statements would be false. However, as is known to us, A's fourth statement is true. Therefore, A is not a Midrorean; A must be the Outlier.

Assume that D's third statement is truthful. If so, D is the Sororean. However, D's first statement agrees with C's first statement, which also claims all truthful statements. Therefore, since we know that there is only one Sororean, D's third statement is false, as is his first statement and, it follows, C's first statement as well. Therefore, neither D nor C is the Sororean. Therefore, B must be the Sororean.

D's second statement agrees with B's true third statement. Therefore, D is the Midrorean, whose second and fourth statements are true. C is the Nororean, who has made four false statements.

SUMMARY SOLUTION:
A. Outlier
B. Sororean
C. Nororean
D. Midrorean

THE WORLD'S MOST AMAZING HYPERBOREAN HERO PUZZLE

CONSIDERATIONS: Minos' first statement agrees with Actaeon's first statement, which asserts that everything Minos says is false. If Actaeon's first statement was true, Minos could not agree with it. Therefore, it must be false, and, agreeing with it, Minos' first statement is also false. Therefore, neither Actaeon nor Minos is a Sororean. Also, since Actaeon's first statement is false, Minos is not a Nororean. He is either a Midrorean or the Outlier. If Minos is a Midrorean, his third statement would have to be false, but it is true: Actaeon is not a Sororean. Therefore, Minos, whose first statement is false and third statement is true, is the Outlier.

Nisus' first statement is false, since he disputes Minos' third statement, which we know to be true. Therefore, Nisus must be either a Nororean or a Midrorean; in either case, since his first statement is false, his third statement must also be false: Actaeon defeated a griffin. Since Actaeon's second statement denies this, Actaeon is a Nororean.

Pyramus' second and third statements are known to be false, and it follows that the first and fourth statements are also false. Pyramus is a Nororean. From Pyramus' first and fourth statements, which are false, we can determine that Nisus did not defeat the sea serpent and Ceyx did not defeat a chimaera.

From Actaeon's third statement, Ceyx did not defeat a griffin. Therefore, Ceyx must have defeated the sea serpent.

Ceyx's fourth statement, that Actaeon defeated a griffin, is consistent with Actaeon's second statement denying this, which we know to be false. Therefore, Ceyx's second statement is also truthful and Minos must have defeated the second griffin.

Nisus must have defeated a chimaera, and this is confirmed by his second statement. Therefore, Nisus' fourth statement, which asserts that Pyramus defeated the other chimaera, is also true. Nisus is a Midrorean. Ceyx, who defeated the sea serpent, as claimed, is a Sororean.

SUMMARY SOLUTION:

Actaeon:	Nororean	griffin
Ceyx:	Sororean	sea serpent
Minos:	Outlier	griffin
Nisus:	Midrorean	chimaera
Pyramus:	Nororean	chimaera

THE WORLD'S MOST AMAZING MULTIPLE-LEVEL-LIVING PUZZLE

CONSIDERATIONS: From statement 4, E lives above B and below A. From statement 1, A does not live above the third level. Therefore B, E, and A occupy the first, second, and third level respectively.

From statements 2 and 3, C occupies the fourth level, F occupies the fifth level, and D occupies the sixth level.

SUMMARY SOLUTION:

A, 3rd level
B, 1st level
C, 4th level
D, 6th level
E, 2nd level
F, 5th level

THE WORLD'S MOST AMAZING KNOWHEYAN JOB PUZZLE

CONSIDERATIONS: From statement 2, A is the oldest among the four Knowheyans mentioned. Therefore, from statement 1, the Communications Consultant is either A or E, who is not mentioned in statement 2. From statement 4, C (who is the youngest among the four referred to in statement 2) is not the youngest of the five. Therefore, E must be the youngest. Therefore, A is the oldest, and the Communications Consultant.

Also from statement 2, it is apparent that D is the Lunar Energy Engineer.

Statement 3 indicates that of the remaining three, the Airfoil Technician is the oldest and the Synthetic Food Nutritionist is the youngest. Therefore, E is the Synthetic Food Nutritionist. B, who is older than C (from statement 2), is the Airfoil Technician, and C is the Space Planner.

SUMMARY SOLUTION:
A. Communications Consultant
B. Airfoil Technician
C. Space Planner
D. Lunar Energy Engineer
E. Synthetic Food Nutritionist

THE WORLD'S MOST AMAZING KNOWHEYAN ART FAIR PUZZLE

CONSIDERATIONS: From statements 2 and 4, the one who entered the painting was the fourth-place winner. From statement 3, neither A nor C entered the painting, and from statement 4, B was not the fourth-place winner. Therefore, D entered the painting and was the fourth-place winner.

From statements 1 and 6, A did not enter either the holograph or the laser etching, so must have entered the sculpture. From statement 1, A was not the first-place winner, and from statement 5, neither B nor C was the third-place winner. Therefore, A was the third-place winner.

From statement 4, B did not enter the laser etching, and from statement 6, the one who entered the etching was not the second-place winner. Therefore, B entered the holograph and was the second-place winner. C entered the laser etching and was the first-place winner.

SUMMARY SOLUTION:

Entry	Finish Order
A. sculpture	3rd place
B. holography	2nd place
C. etching	1st place
D. painting	4th place

THE WORLD'S MOST AMAZING GULF GAME PUZZLE

CONSIDERATIONS: Statements 1 and 4 indicate that the one with the highest score did not lose one, four, or two balls. Therefore, the one with the highest score lost three balls.

From statements 2 and 3, the one who lost four balls must have been the third-lowest scorer.

From statements 2 and 7, since D was not the one with the second-lowest score or the one with the highest score, and did not lose four balls, D must have been the player with the lowest score. From statement 6, D must have lost two balls. Therefore, from statement 5, B lost three balls and was the one with the highest score.

From statement 7, A was not the one who lost four balls. Therefore, A lost one ball and was the one with the second-lowest score.

Therefore, C was the one with the third-lowest score and lost four balls.

SUMMARY SOLUTION:

Scoring Order	Balls Lost
A. second lowest score	1 ball lost
B. high score	3 balls lost
C. third lowest score	4 balls lost
D. low score	2 balls lost

THE WORLD'S MOST AMAZING LEISURE TIME PUZZLE

CONSIDERATIONS: From statements 1 and 4, neither A, C, nor D plays gulf. Therefore, B is the one who plays gulf. From statements 6 and 7, B does not spend .9 SP or .5 SP in leisure time activities. From statements 2, 3, and 5, the one who enjoys boating must spend .75 SP in leisure time activities. Therefore, B spends .6 SP playing gulf.

Since B is the one who spends .6 SP in leisure-time activities and, from statement 1, neither A nor C spends .75 SP in leisure time activities, D spends .75 SP time in leisure time activities and is the one who enjoys boating.

Since, from statement 3, the one who spends .9 SP in leisure time activities does not enjoy music, this amount of SP must apply to reading. From statement 4, A does not enjoy reading. Therefore, C is the one who enjoys reading and spends .9 SP in leisure time activities.

Therefore, A enjoys music and spends .5 SP in leisure time activities.

SUMMARY SOLUTION:

Activity	Amount of Time
A. music	.5 SP
B. gulf	.6 SP
C. reading	.9 SP
D. boating	.75 SP

THE WORLD'S MOST CHALLENGING LATERAL THINKING PUZZLES

THE WORLD'S MOST CHALLENGING APPLE PUZZLE

The first five girls each took an apple. The sixth girl took the basket as well as the apple in it.

THE WORLD'S MOST CHALLENGING PRESIDENT PUZZLE

They were the same man. Grover Cleveland (1837–1908) served two terms as president of the United States, but the terms were not consecutive. He was president from 1885 to 1889, and from 1893 to 1897.

THE WORLD'S MOST CHALLENGING GAME, SET, AND MATCH PUZZLE

The two men were partners playing doubles.

THE WORLD'S MOST CHALLENGING WONDROUS–WALK PUZZLE

The man did not pass a single pub because he went into every one!

THE WORLD'S MOST CHALLENGING FATHER-AND-SON PUZZLE

Let's say that William's father was sixty, his mother was twenty-five, and his mother's father was forty-five. Because everyone has two grandfathers, it is quite possible for one's maternal grandfather to be younger than one's father.

THE WORLD'S MOST CHALLENGING AMAZING-FALL PUZZLE

The plane was parked on the runway.

THE WORLD'S MOST CHALLENGING GOOD-SHOPPING PUZZLE

The man had neglected to buy a new battery for his hearing aid. The old battery failed just as he was coming in to land and he therefore did not hear his tutor's crucial instructions.

THE WORLD'S MOST CHALLENGING TURN-TO-DRIVE PUZZLE

The brothers were Siamese twins, joined at the side. They lived in Birmingham, Alabama. Because they drove on the right-hand side of the road, the steering wheel was on the left-hand side of the car. The brother who sat on the left always drove. When they were in London, England, the other drove because the steering wheel was on the right-hand side of the car.

THE WORLD'S MOST CHALLENGING SEE-SAW PUZZLE

The deaf man says to the storekeeper, "I would like to buy a saw, please."

THE WORLD'S MOST CHALLENGING LOOKOUT PUZZLE

Although the guards were looking in opposite directions, they were not back-to-back. They were facing each other.

THE WORLD'S MOST CHALLENGING DEADLY DRIVE PUZZLE

The man's expensive designer sunglasses were stolen. He normally wore them while driving. As he came around a bend in the mountain, he was blinded by the evening sun and ran off the road.

THE WORLD'S MOST CHALLENGING MAN-IN-AN-ELEVATOR PUZZLE

Bill was on holiday with his wife and two-year-old son. The boy is a very lively fellow. Bill and his wife found that the best way to tire out the youngster each night was to let him climb five flights of stairs just before his bedtime. He enjoyed doing it, but for Bill it was a chore.

THE WORLD'S MOST CHALLENGING GROWING YOUNGER PUZZLE

Ben was born in the year 2000 B.C., so in 1985 B.C. he was fifteen and in 1980 B.C. he was twenty.

THE WORLD'S MOST CHALLENGING HABITUAL WALKER PUZZLE

On that particular morning all the clocks were due to be moved forward for the summer. Although he had wound all his clocks he had neglected to put them forward one hour. Consequently, when he set out thinking it was 7:45 A.M. it was really 8:45 A.M. He was hit by the 9 o'clock train.

THE WORLD'S MOST CHALLENGING GREENLAND PUZZLE

In about 982 a Norseman, Eric the Red, discovered Greenland. He wanted to encourage people to settle there so he called in Greenland to make it sound attractive. It is a very early example of deliberately misleading labeling!

THE WORLD'S MOST CHALLENGING RADIO PUZZLE

The girl was listening to the radio in her father's car. He drove through a tunnel and the reception was temporarily interrupted.

THE WORLD'S MOST CHALLENGING BOXING MATCH PUZZLE

No man threw a punch because the boxing match was between two women.

THE WORLD'S MOST CHALLENGING NEPHEW PUZZLE

The boy was the woman's son, and therefore he was her brother's nephew.

THE WORLD'S MOST CHALLENGING BARREL TROUBLE PUZZLE

The man filled the barrel with holes! Since there was now less barrel, it weighed less.

THE WORLD'S MOST CHALLENGING RIVAL FAN PUZZLE

The two men were in a restaurant. The Argentinian fan had a fish bone stuck in his throat and was choking. The other man was quick-witted enough to give him a strong blow on the back, thereby dislodging the bone and saving his life.

THE WORLD'S MOST CHALLENGING COMING-UP-FOR-AIR PUZZLE

The girl filled the jar with water at the school. When she reached the appropriate point at the city center, she poured all the water out. What replaced it was a true sample of the surrounding air.

THE WORLD'S MOST CHALLENGING NUTS PUZZLE

The boy suggested that the man take one wheel nut off each of the other three wheels, in order to attach the fourth wheel. Once he had done this, the man could safely drive to the nearest garage with each wheel firmly attached by three nuts.

THE WORLD'S MOST CHALLENGING GOLF PRO PUZZLE

One of the most important tasks for the golf-club professional is giving lessons. Most players are right-handed. They can stand opposite a left-handed teacher and watch and copy him more easily. It is just like looking in a mirror, so it makes learning the correct style of swing easier.

THE WORLD'S MOST CHALLENGING DEDUCTION PUZZLE

He reasoned that she would have called her lover so he simply pressed the redial button on their telephone. When the man answered with his name, the husband told him that he had won a prize draw and asked for the address to which it should be sent.

THE WORLD'S MOST CHALLENGING PENNY BLACK PUZZLE

The postmark used at that time was always black. It was therefore difficult to tell whether a stamp had been franked or not. This led to people reusing used stamps. On a Penny Red, the black postmark was clearly visible.

THE WORLD'S MOST CHALLENGING FLAT TIRE PUZZLE, I

The flat tire was on the man's spare wheel which is kept in the car trunk. The four wheels he drove on all had properly inflated tires.

THE WORLD'S MOST CHALLENGING FLAT TIRE PUZZLE, II

The lecturer separated the four students, so that they were not together in the room, and asked each to write down which of the four wheels of the car had suffered the puncture. Of course they did not all say the same wheel. (The chances of them all picking the same wheel are 1 in 4 x 4 x 4; i.e., 1 in 64.)

THE WORLD'S MOST CHALLENGING BOTTLED FRUIT PUZZLE

The fruit is grown in the bottle. The bottle is tied onto the branch shortly after the fruit starts to form.

THE WORLD'S MOST CHALLENGING COWBOY FATE PUZZLE

The most common cause of death among cowboys was from being dragged along by a galloping horse when the cowboy's foot was caught in a stirrup. This would occur during a fall, or when mounting or dismounting.

THE WORLD'S MOST CHALLENGING VILLAGE IDIOT PUZZLE

The so-called village idiot was smart enough to realize that as long as he kept choosing the fifty-cent piece, people would keep offering him the choice. If he once took the five-dollar bill, the stream of coins would stop rolling in.

THE WORLD'S MOST CHALLENGING ISLAND FIRE PUZZLE

The man should set fire to the ground beneath him and walk toward the main fire. The wind will fan the fire he started, so as to burn out the end of the island toward which the wind is blowing. He can then walk back to a piece of burnt land and stand there safely when the main fire reaches his end of the island.

THE WORLD'S MOST CHALLENGING SLEEPY KINGS PUZZLE

The kings each slept one night only. The calendar changed in France in 1582 and in England in 1752. Previously the Julian calendar had been used, but this had allowed a cumulative error to occur which needed to be corrected. Pope Gregory XIII ordered ten days to be dropped from the year 1582. This order was followed by Catholic countries such as France but not by Protestant ones such as England. England eventually adopted the improved Gregorian calendar in 1752, though by that time the adjustment needed had grown to eleven days.

Incidentally, the thirteen American colonies were under British control so they also changed from the Julian to the Gregorian calendars in 1752. George Washington was born on February 11, 1732, but after 1752 his birthday became February 22, which is when Washington's birthday is now officially observed.

THE WORLD'S MOST CHALLENGING PORTRAIT PUZZLE

The portrait is of the man's daughter.

THE WORLD'S MOST CHALLENGING "WINNING ISN'T EVERYTHING" PUZZLE

One-third of the games finished A, B, C; one-third finished B, C, A; and the other third finished C, A, B. So Alf finished ahead of Bert twice as often as behind him, and the same is true for Bert over Chris, and Chris over Alf.

THE WORLD'S MOST CHALLENGING RELUCTANT DINER PUZZLE

The businessman was a Muslim. He therefore observed the religious fast for the month of Ramadan. During this period Muslims are not allowed to drink, eat, or smoke between sunrise and sunset.

THE WORLD'S MOST CHALLENGING DEATH-IN-A-CAR PUZZLE

The man drove his car to the beach to watch the sunset over the waves. He fell asleep. The tide came in and seeped in around the car doors and windows. He awoke, but with the pressure of the water, he couldn't get out of the car. The water filled the car and drowned him. Later the tide went out and he was found dead in an empty car.

THE WORLD'S MOST CHALLENGING LAST CORD PUZZLE

Incredible as it may seem, some people enjoy leaping off high buildings or bridges with a length of elastic cord fastened to them. This pastime is known as bungee jumping. The poor man in this situation died when he jumped from a high crane in the field and his bungee cord broke.

THE WORLD'S MOST CHALLENGING SATURDAY FLIGHT PUZZLE

Saturday was the name of the man's private plane.

THE WORLD'S MOST CHALLENGING TRAIN PUZZLE

One train went through the tunnel in the early afternoon and the other went through in the late afternoon.

THE WORLD'S MOST CHALLENGING COPYRIGHT PUZZLE

Publishers normally include a nonexistent word or a nonexistent island in a dictionary or atlas, respectively. If it then appears in somebody else's work, they have clear evidence of copying.

THE WORLD'S MOST CHALLENGING RANSOM PUZZLE

This is a true story from Taiwan. When the rich man reached the phone booth, he found a carrier pigeon in a cage. It had a message attached telling the man to put the diamond in a small bag which was around the pigeon's neck and to release the bird. When the man did this, the police were powerless to follow the bird as it returned across the city to its owner.

THE WORLD'S MOST CHALLENGING MOVING PART PUZZLE

The two objects are an hourglass (often used in the kitchen as an egg timer) and a sundial.

THE WORLD'S MOST CHALLENGING EARLY-BURIAL PUZZLE

John Brown lived on a Pacific island close to the International Date Line. When you cross the International Date Line (eastward), your calendar goes back one day. He died on Thursday, December 6, and was flown home that same day for burial. Because the plane flew eastward over the International Date Line it was Wednesday, December 5, when he was buried later that day. (This could happen if the plane flew, for example, from Fiji to Samoa.)

THE WORLD'S MOST CHALLENGING TROUBLE-AND-STRIFE PUZZLE

Mrs. White had been counting her stitches very carefully; the number was well past 300. When Mr. White answered the phone, he told the caller their phone number, 837-9263. Hearing this caused Mrs. White to lose count.

THE WORLD'S MOST CHALLENGING BATH WATER PUZZLE

The water in the pan was already boiling when the butler came in. The longer the maid now heated the water, the less of it there would be (because of the steam) to heat the tub and the water's temperature would not rise any further.

THE WORLD'S MOST CHALLENGING HOLD UP PUZZLE

When the man parked his car outside the bank, he held up twenty-five people who were stuck in traffic behind him. The policeman told him not to park like that again.

THE WORLD'S MOST CHALLENGING WORST SAILOR PUZZLE

The captain would prefer to have ten men like Jim because currently he has fifty men like Jim. He considers almost the entire crew useless, but is stuck with them for the duration of the voyage!

THE WORLD'S MOST CHALLENGING VALUABLE BOOK PUZZLE

The man actually owned two copies of the valuable book. By destroying one copy, he increased the value of the other.

THE WORLD'S MOST CHALLENGING CUDDLY BEAR PUZZLE

The hospital dressed all their teddy bears with bandages. Then they explained to the little children that the poor teddies had to stay at the hospital for their own health and recover. The children reluctantly but sympathetically agreed.

THE WORLD'S MOST CHALLENGING HIGH-SOCIETY DINNER PUZZLE

The man who refused to be searched was an aristocrat who had fallen on very hard times, but was trying to keep up appearances. He was so poor, however, that he could scarcely afford to eat. So, while at the dinner, he secretly lined his pockets with food from the table to keep him going for the next few days. Obviously, if he was searched his secret would be revealed and he would be humiliated.

THE WORLD'S MOST CHALLENGING EIGHT-YEAR-OLD PUZZLE

She was born on February 29, 1896. The year 1900 was not a leap year (only centuries divisible by 400 are leap years), so the next February 29 fell in 1904 when she was eight. She was twelve on her second birthday.

THE WORLD'S MOST CHALLENGING HOLE COVERING PUZZLE

A square or rectangular manhole cover can fall down the hole, while a round manhole cover cannot. The square cover will fit down the diagonal of the hole (unless the rim it sits on is very large) but no matter how you turn a circle it never measures less than its diameter. So, for safety and practicality, all manhole covers should be round.

THE WORLD'S MOST CHALLENGING PROTAGORAS PARADOX PUZZLE

This is a paradox with no clear-cut answer. Both parties have a good case. It would be interesting to see it argued out in court. Whoever lost could claim to have won—the student in losing would still not have won a case, Protagoras in losing would have ensured a first victory for his pupil.

Some believe that the most likely outcome would have been victory for the student. He was after all under no obligation to practise law and up until that point he had not breached the contract. Once Protagoras had lost the first case, however, he could sue a second time on the grounds that the student had now won a case and was in breach of contract. Protagoras would therefore win the second case and recover his fees. Overall, Protagoras would have won.

The student would be smart to choose not to represent himself but to select a good lawyer who could win the first case for him. In that case, since the pupil would still not have won a case, he would have won the contest.

THE WORLD'S MOST CHALLENGING HAND-IN-GLOVE PUZZLE

The manufacturer sent 5,000 right-hand gloves to Miami and 5,000 left-hand gloves to New York. He refused to pay the duty on them so both sets of gloves were impounded. Since nobody claimed them, both lots were subsequently sold off at auction. They went for a very low price (who wants 5,000 left-hand gloves?). Naturally, it was the clever Frenchman who won with a very low bid at each auction.

THE WORLD'S MOST CHALLENGING SCHOOL SUPERINTENDENT PUZZLE

The teacher instructed her pupils always to raise their hands when a question was asked whether they knew the answer or not. If they did not know the answer, they should raise their left hand. If they were sure they knew the answer, they should raise their right hand. The teacher chose a different child each time, but always one who had raised his or her right hand.

THE WORLD'S MOST CHALLENGING TRUMP PUZZLE

It is equally likely that one couple will have all the trumps, as it is that they will have no trumps between them. For if they have all the trumps it must mean that the other pair has none and vice versa.

THE WORLD'S MOST CHALLENGING HOW-TO-BEAT NICK FALDO PUZZLE

The challenger was a blind golfer and he arranged to play the champion at midnight on a dark night. The blind man was at no disadvantage in the dark, but the champion could not see his ball to hit it. (Blind golfers do play matches and tournaments; they rely on others to indicate where their ball and the hole are.)

THE WORLD'S MOST CHALLENGING HOW-TO-BEAT CARL LEWIS PUZZLE

He challenged the Olympic champion to run up a ladder. Since he was the fastest window cleaner in Ireland, he won easily!

THE WORLD'S MOST CHALLENGING MISSING FURNITURE PUZZLE

The man was a circus lion tamer who had unfortunately forgotten his chair when he had to face a bad-tempered lion!

THE WORLD'S MOST CHALLENGING DEAD MAN PUZZLE

The cord around the man's neck was a piece of rawhide which he had soaked in water before entering the room. Once he had tied it tightly around his neck it naturally grew tighter and tighter as it dried.

THE WORLD'S MOST CHALLENGING BUSY HOSPITAL PUZZLE

The wearing of seat belts *was* successful in reducing the number of deaths from road accidents. However, the people who without seat belts would have been killed (and taken to the morgue), *now survived* but with injuries. Consequently, more people were treated for injuries than before.

THE WORLD'S MOST CHALLENGING FALLEN SIGN PUZZLE

The man knew the name of the town he had left that morning. So he replaced the sign so that it correctly named the direction he had come from. It would then be correct for all the other directions.

THE WORLD'S MOST CHALLENGING FALSE FINGERPRINT PUZZLE

The man put his wife's big-toe print on the knife and left it beside the body. He could have used his own toe print but that later could have been traced to him. Once his wife was buried, the "fingerprints" could never be traced.

THE WORLD'S MOST CHALLENGING FOUND, LOST, FOUND PUZZLE

The man fell overboard from a small boat at the seashore. He could not swim well and got into difficulties so he threw away the expensive and heavy binoculars around his neck. He was rescued. He then offered a swimmer a reward to dive down and recover his binoculars. This effort was unsuccessful. Later, however, when the tide went out he was able to pick them up off the sand.

THE WORLD'S MOST CHALLENGING DISABLED CHILD PUZZLE

This is a true story from India. The child was born into a family of beggars in Calcutta. The parents knew that a disabled child would earn more as a beggar than a healthy child would.

THE WORLD'S MOST CHALLENGING INSURANCE PUZZLE

This is a true story from Japan. The man was a keen golfer and his lifelong ambition was to score a hole in one. But this would prove very expensive as the custom at his golf club was that anyone who scored a hole in one had to buy all the other members a drink.

THE WORLD'S MOST CHALLENGING EGG PUZZLE

A spherical or oval egg would roll in a straight line. However, an asymmetrical egg, which is narrower at one end than the other, will tend to roll in a circle. (Try it with a normal hen's egg.) If the eggs are on a cliff edge or other precarious place, the tendency to roll *around* rather than straight is a distinct advantage.

THE WORLD'S MOST CHALLENGING GUARD DOG PUZZLE

The boy brought along with him a female dog in heat. He released this dog into the orchard and the guard dog was thereby distracted.

THE WORLD'S MOST CHALLENGING LAST MESSAGE PUZZLE

The cassette had started at the beginning of the man's utterance. Who could have rewound it?

THE WORLD'S MOST CHALLENGING JAPANESE SPEAKER PUZZLE

The businessman had been taught by a woman and he therefore spoke Japanese like a woman. The speech intonation of men and women is very different in Japan; the masculine approach being more direct and aggressive. To hear a man speaking in a woman's style was unusual and amusing for the Japanese men.

THE WORLD'S MOST CHALLENGING CELLAR DOOR PUZZLE

When the girl opened the cellar door she saw the living room and, through its windows, the garden. She had never seen these before because her parents had kept her all her life in the cellar.

THE WORLD'S MOST CHALLENGING DEADLY SHOT PUZZLE

The man died through suffocation. He was covered by an avalanche of snow which had been started by the sound of his gunshot as he stood at the foot of a snow-covered mountain.

THE WORLD'S MOST CHALLENGING ODD STORY PUZZLE

The first man put one lump of sugar in his coffee. That is an odd number. The second man put one lump in his coffee. That is also an odd number. The third man put ten lumps into his coffee. That is a very odd number of lumps to put into a cup of coffee!

THE WORLD'S MOST CHALLENGING FREE-MAP PUZZLE

The aerial photography enables a much clearer definition of land boundaries, and sizes. A tax on land at that time was based on its estimated area, and these had been largely underestimated. The new maps revealed correct land sizes and the government received more income from the land tax.

THE WORLD'S MOST CHALLENGING FLAT OUT PUZZLE

Who said that the car was on the road? The car was being transported on the train.

THE WORLD'S MOST CHALLENGING SHOCK PUZZLE, I

The man was a prisoner who had been condemned to a very long jail sentence. He paid the prison undertaker to help him escape. The plan was that when the next prisoner died, the man would get into the coffin with the corpse. Later, after the coffin was buried outside the prison walls, the undertaker would dig it up to release the man.

When he heard that a man had died, the prisoner put his plan into action. In the dead of night he climbed into the coffin with the corpse. He fell asleep. He awoke after the burial and lit a match. He then saw that the face of the corpse was that of the undertaker!

THE WORLD'S MOST CHALLENGING SHOCK PUZZLE, II

The man discovered a box containing four glass eyes mounted to a board with a dedication to their previous owners. They had belonged to the four previous husbands of his wife. The men had all died after about a year of marriage. This was the first that he had heard of them. He was recently married and had a glass eye!

THE WORLD'S MOST CHALLENGING DEADLY PARTY PUZZLE

The poison in the punch came from the ice cubes in it. When the man drank from the punch, the ice had just been added and was still solid. Gradually, during the course of the evening, the ice melted, contaminating the punch with the poison.

THE WORLD'S MOST CHALLENGING SPEECHLESS PUZZLE

The two men were both divers. They met one afternoon while scuba diving on the seabed.

THE WORLD'S MOST CHALLENGING HOW-TO-HUG PUZZLE

What the boy had picked up at the library was a volume of an encyclopedia. It was the section covering words beginning with H from "How" to "Hug" and that was what was printed on its cover.

THE WORLD'S MOST CHALLENGING HEALTHY DAIRYMAIDS PUZZLE

Dairymaids caught the disease cowpox (a relatively harmless disease) from cows. This, however, gave them immunity from the related but much more dangerous disease, smallpox. Jenner researched and developed the technique for inoculation with cowpox vaccine which eventually became widespread and overcame the bane of smallpox.

THE WORLD'S MOST CHALLENGING TOOTHACHE PUZZLE

When the man had been very poor he had entered into a contract with a Swedish medical institute. For a certain sum of money he promised them his body after his death for medical research. He later inherited money and asked to buy back this obligation. The institute refused, so he sued them in court. Not only did he lose his case, but the judge ordered him to pay the institute compensation for having had his teeth removed without the permission of their future owners!

THE WORLD'S MOST CHALLENGING LAKE PROBLEM PUZZLE

You pour into the lake a known quantity of a concentrated chemical or vegetable dye. After allowing some time for the harmless chemical to disperse, you take samples of the water in several places. The more diluted the solution, the greater volume of water in the lake. Precise analysis of the concentration of chemicals in the samples would give a good estimate of the water volume of the lake.

THE WORLD'S MOST CHALLENGING REALIZATION PUZZLE

The man had just visited his wife in a hospital. She was on a life-support machine following a car accident. As he was walking down the stairs, all the lights went out. There had been a power cut and the emergency back-up systems had failed. He knew immediately that his wife had died.

THE WORLD'S MOST CHALLENGING DEADLY DISH PUZZLE

The dish that the two men ordered was albatross, to remind themselves of when they had been stranded on a desert island many years earlier. When one of the men tasted it, he realized that he had never tasted albatross before. This meant that the meat he had been given to eat on the island was not albatross, as he had been told, but the flesh of his son who had died when they first reached the island.

THE WORLD'S MOST CHALLENGING MEN-IN-UNIFORM PUZZLE

The angry man was a convicted prisoner. He was being transported in the van and was handcuffed to a prison officer. When a suitable opportunity arose, the prisoner had produced a gun and demanded that the officer release him. The officer had put the key to the handcuffs in his mouth before struggling with the prisoner. The gun went off killing the officer, but not before he had swallowed the key. The prisoner was therefore handcuffed to the body of the man he had just killed.

THE WORLD'S MOST NEARLY IMPOSSIBLE BRAIN BAFFLERS

THE WORLD'S MOST NEARLY IMPOSSIBLE BRAIN BAFFLER, ONE

Red in the face

THE WORLD'S MOST NEARLY IMPOSSIBLE BRAIN BAFFLER, TWO

3,816,547,290

THE WORLD'S MOST NEARLY IMPOSSIBLE BRAIN BAFFLER, THREE

Eleven students passed Exam One only, three passed Exam Two only, and eight passed Exam Three only. Thus ten students passed more than one exam.

THE WORLD'S MOST NEARLY IMPOSSIBLE BRAIN BAFFLER, FOUR

Each match will eliminate one player, so starting with eighty-nine players will require eighty-eight matches to decide the winner.

THE WORLD'S MOST NEARLY IMPOSSIBLE BRAIN BAFFLER, FIVE

Ö.2–2, which shows that two twos can make five!

THE WORLD'S MOST NEARLY IMPOSSIBLE BRAIN BAFFLER, SIX

Square meal

THE WORLD'S MOST NEARLY IMPOSSIBLE BRAIN BAFFLER, SEVEN

For White to win, he has to force one of Black's knights to move. Then, provided White's king is safe from unwanted checks and White has not moved his own knights, White wins with Ne4 mate or Nd5 mate. The actual winning move will depend upon which knight Black eventually moves.

Black can delay moving a knight for fifty-nine moves! His tactic is to shunt the rook at a4 to and fro to a3 whenever he can. Accordingly, and taking the route that avoids unwanted checks, White uses his king to inhibit the shunting rook by timing the arrival of his king at b5 to follow Black's move Ra3.

On the first four occasions White does this, Black keeps his rook out of danger by moving a pawn on the e file. On the fifth occasion, to avoid moving a knight and to save his rook, Black must block his rook in with a5-a4. On his next move Black is compelled to move a knight and expose himself to an instant checkmate. Note that if Black moves his pawns before he has to, then the mate is simply speeded up. With Black's best defense as shown below, White will mate in sixty.

White's first move can be either Ke8 or Kd6. White's king then proceeds d7, c8, b7, b6, b5. By moving to d7 via e8 or d6, the White king arrives at b5 after an even number of moves. Thus, for move six, Black's shunting rook will be at a3 and Black must move a pawn, lose his rook, or be mated. To defer mate as long as possible, Black must play e4-e3.

After Black's move, e4-e3, White moves his king away from b5 and Black can continue with the shunting of his rook. White must now move his king back to b5 in an odd number of moves in order to catch the shunting rook at a3. The shortest route for White to achieve this that avoids unwanted checks is b6, b7, c8, d7, e8, f8, f7, e8, d7, c8, b7, b6, b5, and this he repeats four times. On moves 19, 32, and 45 Black takes a break from shunting his rook and moves a pawn on the e file. On move 58, however, Black can do no better than to block his rook in with a5-a4. White then plays a waiting move, Kb6. If Black moves the knight at b4, then White mates with Nd5, and if Black moves the knight at d2, then White mates with Ne4. This gives White mate in sixty.

THE WORLD'S MOST NEARLY IMPOSSIBLE BRAIN BAFFLER, EIGHT

No U-Turn

THE WORLD'S MOST NEARLY IMPOSSIBLE BRAIN BAFFLER, NINE

2,100,010,006

THE WORLD'S MOST NEARLY IMPOSSIBLE BRAIN BAFFLER, TEN

Ep is greater than pe; to two decimal places, ep = 23.14 and pe = 22.46

THE WORLD'S MOST NEARLY IMPOSSIBLE BRAIN BAFFLER, ELEVEN

A A K A A K K K

THE WORLD'S MOST NEARLY IMPOSSIBLE BRAIN BAFFLER, TWELVE

By changing his mind, B reduced his chance of winning the game.

The only way in which EEE can appear before OEE is if the first three throws of the die are EEE. Otherwise, the sequence EEE must be preceded by an O. The probability of the first three throws being E is $(1/2)3$, so if B chooses OEE when A has chosen EEE, then B wins with probability $7/8$. If B chooses OOO in response to A's choice of EEE, then B's chance of winning is $1/2$.

THE WORLD'S MOST NEARLY IMPOSSIBLE BRAIN BAFFLER, THIRTEEN

Round of drinks on the house

THE WORLD'S MOST NEARLY IMPOSSIBLE BRAIN BAFFLER, FOURTEEN

11, 47, and 71

THE WORLD'S MOST NEARLY IMPOSSIBLE BRAIN BAFFLER, FIFTEEN

TWELVE = 130760, THIRTY = 194215, and NINETY = 848015

THE WORLD'S MOST NEARLY IMPOSSIBLE BRAIN BAFFLER, SIXTEEN

A straight-line route that takes the spider one meter down to the floor, forty meters across the floor, and nine meters up toward the ceiling is fifty meters.

Two quicker straight-line routes, found by drawing straight lines from the spider to the fly on a flattened plan of the warehouse, are shown below. The first of these sees the spider heading up the side wall, crossing the ceiling, and finally approaching the fly from above. The distance of this route is Ö(14² + 46²) = 48.08 meters.

The third straight-line route sees the spider heading diagonally to the floor, then up the side wall, crossing the corner of the ceiling and again at the end approaching the fly from above. The distance of this route is Ö(20² + 42²) = 46.52 meters.

The shortest route is 46.52 meters.

THE WORLD'S MOST NEARLY IMPOSSIBLE BRAIN BAFFLER, SEVENTEEN

Ambiguous

THE WORLD'S MOST NEARLY IMPOSSIBLE BRAIN BAFFLER, EIGHTEEN

Smith served first. One possible proof is as follows:

Whoever served first would have served on twenty of the points played and the other player would have served on seventeen of them. Suppose the first player won x of the points on which he served and y of the points served by his opponent. The total number of points lost by the player who served them is then $20 - x + y$. This must equal thirteen, since we are told that twenty-four of the thirty-seven points were won by the player serving. Thus $x = 7 + y$, and the first server won $(7 + y) + y = 7 + 2y$ points in total. This is an odd number, and only Smith won an odd number of points. Thus Smith served first.

THE WORLD'S MOST NEARLY IMPOSSIBLE BRAIN BAFFLER, NINETEEN

White's key move of 1 Ka5!! seems self-destructive and a sure provocation for Black to play 1 . . . e1(Q)+. White's reply, 2 Kb6!, seems even more provocative as it offers Black no fewer than seven different moves with which to check White's king. Each one, however, can be defended by moving the knight at c6 for a discovered checkmate. If Black moves 1 . . . Rg7 then 2 Ne7+ Ka7 3 Nc8 mate. If 1 . . . Rg5 then 2 Kb6 (threatening 3 Ne7 mate) Rxd5 3 Nc7 mate. If 1 . . . Kb7 then 2 Ne7+ Ka7 3 Nc8 mate.

THE WORLD'S MOST NEARLY IMPOSSIBLE BRAIN BAFFLER, TWENTY

Forever and ever

THE WORLD'S MOST NEARLY IMPOSSIBLE BRAIN BAFFLER, TWENTY-ONE

The envelope with the formula is Envelope 3.

THE WORLD'S MOST NEARLY IMPOSSIBLE BRAIN BAFFLER, TWENTY-TWO

Use matches to spell out the words "ten" and "five."

THE WORLD'S MOST NEARLY IMPOSSIBLE BRAIN BAFFLER, TWENTY-THREE

The series is generated by counting the number of characters in the corresponding Roman numeral, as shown for the first ten numbers below:

I	II	III	IV	V	VI	VII	VIII	IX	X
1	2	3	2	1	2	3	4	2	1

The first term to equal 10 is the 288th in the series: CCLXXXVIII. Thus the answer to the question is Brutus.

THE WORLD'S MOST NEARLY IMPOSSIBLE BRAIN BAFFLER, TWENTY-FOUR

To show the perimeter is divided into two equal lengths, whatever the angle of the arrow, let the diameter of each of the smaller semicircles (and thus the radius of the large semicircle) be d and let the arrow lie at an angle of a radians to the horizontal.

The perimeter length lying above the horizontal line is pd€2 + pd€2 = pd, which is the perimeter length lying below the horizontal line. Therefore, to prove the heart's perimeter is divided into two equal lengths, we need to show that the part of the perimeter above the horizontal line and below the arrow is equal in length to the part of the perimeter that is below the horizontal line and above the arrow.

Begin by letting C be the center of the smaller semicircle on the right as shown below:

Since triangle ABC is isosceles, angle BCD is 2a radians. Thus the length of arc BD is 2a€2p multiplied by the perimeter of the small circle = 2a€2p ? pd = ad. This is also the length of the arc of the big semicircle that is below the horizontal line and above the arrow and so the result is proven.

THE WORLD'S MOST NEARLY IMPOSSIBLE BRAIN BAFFLER, TWENTY-FIVE

Bend over backwards.

THE WORLD'S MOST NEARLY IMPOSSIBLE BRAIN BAFFLER, TWENTY-SIX

The new chart is as follows: 1. Atomic, 2. Dizzy, 3. Footloose, 4. Blockbuster, 5. Jesamine, 6. Classic, 7. Night, 8. Perfect, 9. Lamplight, 10. Emma, 11. What, 12., Obsession, 13. Autumn Almanac, 14. Gaye, 15. Reward, 16. Hello, 17. American Pie, 18. Intuition, 19. As Usual, 20. Zabadak!, 21. Another Day, 22. Kayleigh, 23. Angie Baby 24. Xanadu, 25. True, 26. Mickey, 27. YMCA, 28. Valentine, 29. Angel Eyes, 30. Ain't Nobody, 31. Amateur Hour, 32. New entry, 33. Angel Fingers, 34. Question, 35. Always Yours, 36. Adoration Waltz, 37. Alternate Title, 38. Sandy, 39. Alphabet Street, 40. Angela Jones

THE WORLD'S MOST NEARLY IMPOSSIBLE BRAIN BAFFLER, TWENTY-SEVEN

Mixed bag

THE WORLD'S MOST NEARLY IMPOSSIBLE BRAIN BAFFLER, TWENTY-EIGHT

ANGST, ABYSS, BAWDY, COMFY, DENIM, EXPEL, FAKIR, MAJOR, PIQUE, SERVE, TITLE, TOPAZ, WINCH

102. The verse asks whether 101€10 > 21€3 or, if we raise each side to the power

of 30, whether 103 > 210? The answer is "no."

THE WORLD'S MOST NEARLY IMPOSSIBLE BRAIN BAFFLER, TWENTY-NINE

The letter m

THE WORLD'S MOST NEARLY IMPOSSIBLE BRAIN BAFFLER, THIRTY

Either 1, 2, 6, 7, 9, 14, 15, 18, 20, or 1, 3, 6, 7, 12, 14, 15, 19, 20

THE WORLD'S MOST NEARLY IMPOSSIBLE BRAIN BAFFLER, THIRTY-ONE

The minimum number of moves made by White's men to reach the position shown in the question is: queen's pawn 5 (d4, c5, b6, a7, a8), new queen 2 (a7, e3), queen's knight 2 (c3, a4), king's knight 2 (f3, h2), king's rook 2 (h3, g3), king's rook's pawn 2 (h3, g4), king's bishop's pawn 1 (f3), and king 1 (f2). These total seventeen and therefore account for all of White's moves. Noting that Black's missing pieces were captured on c5, b6, a7, and g4, the position after White's ninth move would have been as follows:

The game from White's ninth move was:

9	. . .	Ra7
10	bxa7	h4
11	a8(Q)	h3
12	Qa7	h2
13	Qe3	h1(B)
14	Nh2	a5
15	f3	a4
16	Kf2	a3
17	Na4	

THE WORLD'S MOST NEARLY IMPOSSIBLE BRAIN BAFFLER, THIRTY-TWO

The traveler on the fast train sees all the trains going the other way around that left up to three hours ago or that will leave in the next two hours. The traveler on the slow train sees all the trains going the other way around that left up to two hours ago or that will leave in the next three hours. In five hours, including the beginning and end, twenty-one trains depart in each direction. Including the train they are traveling on, each traveler therefore sees twenty-two trains on his journey.

THE WORLD'S MOST NEARLY IMPOSSIBLE BRAIN BAFFLER, THIRTY-THREE

From top-to-down and left-to-right the numbers are 8, 1, 1, 2, 3, 4, 2, 4, 2, 6, 8, 0, 8, 4, 4, 2, 2, 4, 1, 6, 2, 5, 6, 8, 0, 2, 4, 4, 2, 1, 4, 1, 5, 0, 6, 2, 4, 5, 2 ,7, 4, 8, 4, 2 ,2, 2, 6, 2, and 4.

THE WORLD'S MOST NEARLY IMPOSSIBLE BRAIN BAFFLER, THIRTY-FOUR

White marbles can only be removed from the box in pairs. There is an odd number of white marbles to start with, so the last marble in the box will be white.

THE WORLD'S MOST NEARLY IMPOSSIBLE BRAIN BAFFLER, THIRTY-FIVE

At the point of no return

THE WORLD'S MOST NEARLY IMPOSSIBLE BRAIN BAFFLER, THIRTY-SIX

There are 120 socks in the drawer: 85 red ones and 35 blue ones.

THE WORLD'S MOST NEARLY IMPOSSIBLE BRAIN BAFFLER, THIRTY-SEVEN

Seventy-two hens, twenty-one sheep, seven cows

THE WORLD'S MOST NEARLY IMPOSSIBLE BRAIN BAFFLER, THIRTY-EIGHT

Pin-up

THE WORLD'S MOST NEARLY IMPOSSIBLE BRAIN BAFFLER, THIRTY-NINE

The value of 1,997 nickels is $99.85, 25 cents more than 1,992 nickels (worth $99.60).

THE WORLD'S MOST NEARLY IMPOSSIBLE BRAIN BAFFLER, FORTY

F for February. The letters are the initials of the first eight months of the year.

THE WORLD'S MOST NEARLY IMPOSSIBLE BRAIN BAFFLER, FORTY-ONE

A won against B, C, and D with scores of 3-0, 1-0, and 2-1 respectively. B won against C with a score of 1-0 and tied D with a score of 1-1. C won against D with a score of 2-0.

THE WORLD'S MOST NEARLY IMPOSSIBLE BRAIN BAFFLER, FORTY-TWO

Supplements to use are: 8, 12, 14, 17, 18, 19, 20, 21, 22, 23, 25, 26, 27, 29, 30, 31, 33, 35, 37, 39, 41, 43, 45, 47, and 49. They total 711.

THE WORLD'S MOST NEARLY IMPOSSIBLE BRAIN BAFFLER, FORTY-THREE

The solutions are 1,872,549,630 and 7,812,549,630, and are derived as follows: The 5 and 0 can be placed immediately. The sixth digit must be 4. The seventh digit is odd (since every second digit must be even), so it must be 9. The eighth digit must be 6. The ninth digit must be 3. The third digit is 1 or 7, so the fourth digit must be 2. The first three digits are therefore 187 or 781.

THE WORLD'S MOST NEARLY IMPOSSIBLE BRAIN BAFFLER, FORTY-FOUR

One step forward, two steps back

THE WORLD'S MOST NEARLY IMPOSSIBLE BRAIN BAFFLER, FORTY-FIVE

Each line describes the line above. For example, since line five is 1 1 1 2 2 1, which can be expressed as three ones (3 1), two twos (2 2), and one one (1 1), line six is 3 1 2 2 1 1.

The tenth line in the pyramid is therefore:
1 3 2 1 1 3 1 1 1 2 3 1 1 3 1 1 2 2 1 1

THE WORLD'S MOST NEARLY IMPOSSIBLE BRAIN BAFFLER, FORTY-SIX

Reading between the lines

THE WORLD'S MOST NEARLY IMPOSSIBLE BRAIN BAFFLER, FORTY-SEVEN

The solution to LAGER x 4 = REGAL is 21978 x 4 = 87912

THE WORLD'S MOST NEARLY IMPOSSIBLE BRAIN BAFFLER, FORTY-EIGHT

Bermuda Triangle

THE WORLD'S MOST NEARLY IMPOSSIBLE BRAIN BAFFLER, FORTY-NINE

						1	4	5
2	0	6	)	2	9	8	7	0
				2	0	6		
				9	2	7		
				8	2	4		
				1	0	3	0	
				1	0	3	0	

THE WORLD'S MOST NEARLY IMPOSSIBLE BRAIN BAFFLER, FIFTY

8128

THE WORLD'S MOST NEARLY IMPOSSIBLE BRAIN BAFFLER, FIFTY-ONE

Not eleven, but ten times. The times are between 1 and 2, between 2 and 3, and so on, ending with once between 10 and 11. It does not happen between 11 and 12, since it happens at exactly 12 (noon and midnight). The question excludes noon and midnight, so those occurrences don't count.

THE WORLD'S MOST NEARLY IMPOSSIBLE BRAIN BAFFLER, FIFTY-TWO

Just between you and me

THE WORLD'S MOST NEARLY IMPOSSIBLE BRAIN BAFFLER, FIFTY-THREE

The maximum number of blocks in the set is fifty-five.

If only three of the five available colors are used, then opposite faces of a block must have the same color. Thus by symmetry there is only one way in which a block can be painted with any three given colors, and there are ten different ways in which three colors can be chosen.

If four colors are used, then two pairs of opposite faces must each have the same color. By symmetry it doesn't matter which way around the other two faces are painted. The colors for the two pairs of matching faces can be chosen in ten different ways, and the other two colors can then be chosen in three ways, giving an overall total of thirty combinations.

Finally, if five colors are used then just one pair of opposite faces will have the same color. The remaining four colors can be arranged in three different ways, so using five colors gives a total of 5 x 3 = 15 combinations.

The maximum number of blocks in the set is therefore 10 + 30 + 15 = 55.

THE WORLD'S MOST NEARLY IMPOSSIBLE BRAIN BAFFLER, FIFTY-FOUR

There are twenty-six former committee members (nine of whom are women), twenty-seven committee members, and thirty-nine members who have never been on the committee. This gives a total of ninety-two members.

THE WORLD'S MOST NEARLY IMPOSSIBLE BRAIN BAFFLER, FIFTY-FIVE

The series consists of the numbers of letters in the words one, two, three, etc.

THE WORLD'S MOST NEARLY IMPOSSIBLE BRAIN BAFFLER, FIFTY-SIX

The integers are −3, −1, and 1.

THE WORLD'S MOST NEARLY IMPOSSIBLE BRAIN BAFFLER, FIFTY-SEVEN

Regrouping the series as 1, 2, 4, 8, 16, 32, 64, 128, and 256, the next two terms in this series are 512 and 1024. The answer to the question is 5121.

THE WORLD'S MOST NEARLY IMPOSSIBLE BRAIN BAFFLER, FIFTY-EIGHT

Cornerstone

THE WORLD'S MOST NEARLY IMPOSSIBLE BRAIN BAFFLER, FIFTY-NINE

Old is thirty and Young is eighteen

THE WORLD'S MOST NEARLY IMPOSSIBLE BRAIN BAFFLER, SIXTY

a4, a5, b1, b2, c1, d5, e2, e3

THE WORLD'S MOST NEARLY IMPOSSIBLE BRAIN BAFFLER, SIXTY-ONE

Five across is three factorial, which is SIX. Two-thirds of SIX or, more precisely, the last two-thirds of the word SIX, is IX, which is the Roman numeral nine.

THE WORLD'S MOST NEARLY IMPOSSIBLE BRAIN BAFFLER, SIXTY-TWO

Anyone for tennis?

THE WORLD'S MOST NEARLY IMPOSSIBLE BRAIN BAFFLER, SIXTY-THREE

Noting that the 3-5 domino can be placed uniquely, the full array is soon easily figured out, as shown.

THE WORLD'S MOST NEARLY IMPOSSIBLE BRAIN BAFFLER, SIXTY-FOUR

The players scored 5, 7, 11, 13, 17, 19, 29, 31, 37, 41, and 43 goals. Their average was 23 goals.

THE WORLD'S MOST NEARLY IMPOSSIBLE BRAIN BAFFLER, SIXTY-FIVE

Split-second timing

THE WORLD'S MOST NEARLY IMPOSSIBLE BRAIN BAFFLER, SIXTY-SIX

Despite being the worst shot of the three, Arthur has the best chance of surviving, with a probability of .5222. Allwyn has the next best chance of surviving at .3 and Aitkins the least chance at .1778.

Arthur's tactic will be to aim to miss if the other two are alive. This is because the other two, if they get the choice, will fire at each other rather than Arthur. This will leave Arthur with the first shot at the survivor. The reason that Allwyn would choose to fire at Aitkins rather than Arthur is that he would rather have Arthur shooting at him with a 50 percent hit rate than Aitkins with an 80 percent success rate. The decision for Aitkins to fire at Allwyn rather than Arthur, if he gets the choice, is because for Aitkins to fire successfully at Arthur would be to sign his own death warrant.

THE WORLD'S MOST NEARLY IMPOSSIBLE BRAIN BAFFLER, SIXTY-SEVEN

One foot in the grave

THE WORLD'S MOST NEARLY IMPOSSIBLE BRAIN BAFFLER, SIXTY-EIGHT

Yes, there are two possible ways.

THE WORLD'S MOST NEARLY IMPOSSIBLE BRAIN BAFFLER, SIXTY-NINE

93 and 87. When the digits in each number of the sequence are reversed, the sequence is the multiples of 13; that is, 13, 26, 39, 52, 65, 78, and 91.

THE WORLD'S MOST NEARLY IMPOSSIBLE BRAIN BAFFLER, SEVENTY

$4! + 5! + 7! = 24 + 120 + 5040 = (5^2 - 1) + (11^2 - 1) + (71^2 - 1) = 722$

THE WORLD'S MOST NEARLY IMPOSSIBLE BRAIN BAFFLER, SEVENTY-ONE

By factorizing 2,450 and then compiling a list of the age groups with the desired product, it is found that only two have the same sum, namely 64. Thus Jim is 32, and the three passengers are either 50, 7, and 7 or 49, 10, and 5.

When he was told there was someone older than Bob on the bus, Jim was able to determine the passengers' ages. Obviously Bob cannot be older than 49, and if he were younger than this then both groups would still have been acceptable. Thus, knowing Bob was 49, Jim was able to determine the three passengers were aged 50, 7, and 7.

THE WORLD'S MOST NEARLY IMPOSSIBLE BRAIN BAFFLER, SEVENTY-TWO

Mate in three can be forced only by 1 d4.

If 1 . . . Kh5 then 2 Qd3 Kg4 (or Kh4) 3 Qh3 mate

If 1 . . . Kg4 then 2 e4+ Kh4 3 g3 mate

THE WORLD'S MOST NEARLY IMPOSSIBLE BRAIN BAFFLER, SEVENTY-THREE

This is H. E. Dudeney's solution:

1	Nc3	d5
2	Nxd5	Nc6
3	Nxe7	g5
4	Nxc8	Nf6
5	Nxa7	Ne4
6	Nxc6	Nc3
7	Nxd8	Rg8
8	Nxf7	Rg6
9	Nxg5	Re6
10	Nxh7	Nb1
11	Nxf8	Ra3
12	Nxe6	b5
13	Nxc7+	Kf7
14	Nxb5	Kg6
15	Nxa3	Kh5
16	Nxb1	Kh4

THE WORLD'S MOST NEARLY IMPOSSIBLE BRAIN BAFFLER, SEVENTY-FOUR

2 of spades, 9 of hearts, 5 of hearts, four of diamonds, and eight of clubs

THE WORLD'S MOST NEARLY IMPOSSIBLE BRAIN BAFFLER, SEVENTY-FIVE

West Indies

THE WORLD'S MOST NEARLY IMPOSSIBLE BRAIN BAFFLER, SEVENTY-SIX

Sweet tooth

THE WORLD'S MOST NEARLY IMPOSSIBLE BRAIN BAFFLER, SEVENTY-SEVEN

On the double

THE WORLD'S MOST NEARLY IMPOSSIBLE BRAIN BAFFLER, SEVENTY-EIGHT

Create four parts using an upside-down "L" with a box attached to the tail.

THE WORLD'S MOST NEARLY IMPOSSIBLE BRAIN BAFFLER, SEVENTY-NINE

6 € (1 – 5€7) = 21

THE WORLD'S MOST NEARLY IMPOSSIBLE BRAIN BAFFLER, EIGHTY

96,420 x 87,531 = 8,439,739,020

THE WORLD'S MOST NEARLY IMPOSSIBLE BRAIN BAFFLER, EIGHTY-ONE

Income tax

THE WORLD'S MOST NEARLY IMPOSSIBLE BRAIN BAFFLER, EIGHTY-TWO

The diagram contains 47 triangles in total, as below:

1 triangle of full size	06 triangles of $^1/_2$ size
3 triangles of $^1/_3$ size	10 triangles of $^1/_4$ size
6 triangles of $^1/_6$ size	12 triangles of $^1/_8$ size
3 triangles of $^1/_{12}$ size	06 triangles of $^1/_{24}$ size

THE WORLD'S MOST NEARLY IMPOSSIBLE BRAIN BAFFLER, EIGHTY-THREE

Receding hairline

THE WORLD'S MOST NEARLY IMPOSSIBLE BRAIN BAFFLER, EIGHTY-FOUR

```
            6     6     .     3     7     5
  1     6     )     1     0     6     2
                           9     6
                         ─────────
                     1     0     2
                           9     6
                         ─────────
                                 6     0
                                 4     8
                               ─────────
                           1     2     0
                           1     1     2
                               ─────────
                                 8     0
                                 8     0
```

THE WORLD'S MOST NEARLY IMPOSSIBLE BRAIN BAFFLER, EIGHTY-FIVE

Position	Team	Captain	Color
1	United	Cooke	Red
2	Rovers	Allen	Blue
3	County	Dixon	White
4	Albion	Evans	Yellow
5	Thistle	Boyle	Green

THE WORLD'S MOST NEARLY IMPOSSIBLE BRAIN BAFFLER, EIGHTY-SIX

Unfinished symphony

THE WORLD'S MOST NEARLY IMPOSSIBLE BRAIN BAFFLER, EIGHTY-SEVEN

Other than rotations and reflections there is only one solution. The best way to start is with the central number, which must be a factor of 45, the sum of all nine numbers.

THE WORLD'S MOST INTENSE FALSE LOGIC PUZZLES

THE WORLD'S MOST INTENSE MULE PUZZLE

CONSIDERATIONS: Consider that each farmer made one true and one false statement. Assume that A is the owner. If so, both of A's statements are false. Therefore, A is not the owner. Assume that C is the owner. If so, both of C's statements are true. Therefore C is not the owner. Therefore, B is the owner.

SUMMARY SOLUTION: It is B's mule.

THE WORLD'S MOST INTENSE WRITINGS OF HOMER PUZZLE

CONSIDERATIONS: Assume B is guilty. If so, A's second and third statements are true. Therefore, B did not do it. Assume C is guilty. If so, B's first and second statements are true. Therefore, C did not do it. Therefore, A is guilty.

SUMMARY SOLUTION: A is the thief.

THE WORLD'S MOST INTENSE OPEN CELLAR DOOR PUZZLE

CONSIDERATIONS: Consider that three statements are true, and five are false. Assume that A is guilty. If so, A's first and second statements are both false; B's statements are both true; C's first statement is false, and second is true; and D's first statement is true, and second is false. Therefore, since, if A did it, there are four true statements. A is not guilty.

Assume that B is guilty. If so, A's first statement, C's first and second statement, and D's first statement are true. Therefore B did not do it.

Assume that C is guilty. If so, A's first and second statement, B's first statement, C's second statement, and D's first statement are true. Therefore, D did not do it. By elimination, D is guilty.

SUMMARY SOLUTION: D is guilty.

THE WORLD'S MOST INTENSE SECRET OBSERVER PUZZLE

CONSIDERATIONS: Assume A is the observer. If so, A's statements are true. C's second statement, which refers to A, confirms A's second statement. Therefore, A is not the observer. Also, in confirming A's second statement, C's second statement verifies that D is not the observer.

Assume C is guilty. If so, A's first statement, which refers to C, must be false. However, D's second statement confirms A's first statement. Therefore, C is not the observer. Therefore, D's first statement, which claims C's first statement is false, is true. B is the observer.

SUMMARY SOLUTION: B is the observer.

THE WORLD'S MOST INTENSE STATUE OF ATHENA PUZZLE

CONSIDERATIONS: Consider that one suspect made three true statements.

A's second statement is false, as it was given that all four suspects were in Athens when the crime occurred. C's second statement is false, as there was evidence that the thief acted alone. From D's first statement, we know that at least one of D's statements is false. Therefore, B is the one with three true statements.

From B's third statement, C was seen at the Acropolis late that night. This agrees with D's second statement. Therefore, since we know that at least one of D's statements is false, D's third statement must be false. D did it.

SUMMARY SOLUTION: D is the thief.

THE WORLD'S MOST INTENSE VICTORY PARADE LEADER PUZZLE

CONSIDERATIONS: Consider that one made one false statement, one made two false statements, and one made three false statements.

Assume that A should lead the parade. If so, A's first two statements are true. Therefore, A's third statement must be false. If so, C's third statement must be true, and C must be the one with one true statement. Therefore, C's second statement must be false. Therefore, B's third statement must be true. Therefore, since each soldier would have at least one true statement, A is not the correct choice.

Assume that B should lead the parade. If so, B's first two statements are true and third statement must be false. Therefore, C's second statement must be true. Therefore, C's third statement must be false. This means that A's third statement must be true. Again, each soldier would have at least one true statement.

Therefore, C is the correct choice. A has made three false statements; B has made two false statements; and C has made one false statement.

SUMMARY SOLUTION: C should lead the parade.

THE WORLD'S MOST INTENSE TRIP OF SOCRATES PUZZLE

CONSIDERATIONS: Consider that the disciple Socrates selects made three true or three false statements. One of the other two made two true and one false statement. The remaining one made one true and two false statements.

C's first and third statements are contradictory. One is true and one is false. Therefore, C is not the one who is selected.

Assume that B is selected. If so, C is the one with two true statements, and A has made one true statement either his first or second one. However, A's first and second statements contradict B's third and first statements. One of A's two statements and one of B's statements must be true. Therefore, since B's second statement is false, B is not the one with three true or three false statements. B was not selected.

A is the disciple selected. C has made one true statement, and B is the one with two true statements. Since B's second statement is false, his first and third statements are true; and A's three statements are false.

SUMMARY SOLUTION: Socrates selects A.

THE WORLD'S MOST INTENSE STATUE REPAIR PUZZLE

CONSIDERATIONS: Consider that each of the four craftsmen made the same number of true statements and the same number of false statements.

Assume that A is the most qualified. If so, B has at least two true statements; and each of the other three has at least two false statements. Therefore, A is not the most qualified. Assume that B is the most qualified. If so, A's and C's first and third statements are consistent. However, their second statements are not. Therefore, each of these two has a different number of true statements. Therefore, B is not the most qualified.

Assume that D is the most qualified. If so, D's first and third statements are false. D's second and A's first statements agree, and A's second statement is true. Therefore, A and D each has a different number of true statements. Therefore, D is not the most qualified.

C is the most qualified. A's first and second statements are false, and third statement is true; B's first and second statements are false, and third statement is true; C's first statement is true, and second and third statements are false; D's first statement is true, and second and third statements are false.

SUMMARY SOLUTION: C is the most qualified.

THE WORLD'S MOST INTENSE DISCUS THROW PUZZLE

CONSIDERATIONS: Since no two made the same number of true statements, it is apparent that one made three true statements, one made two true statements, one made one true statement, and one made no true statements.

Assume that A was the winner. If so, only A's first statement and B's first statement confirm this. B must be the one with all true statements, since, if A was the winner, his second statement is false. If so, B was second and B and C trained together; A's third statement is false; D's first and third statements are false, and second statement is true. Therefore, A and D would each have made only one true statement. Therefore, A was not the winner.

Assume that C was the winner. If so, D must be the one with all true statements. If so, B was second, and C and D trained together. If so, A's three statements and C's three statements are false. Therefore, C was not the winner.

Assume that D was the winner. If so, either A or D could be the one with three statements. Assume it is A. If so, A was second, and A and C trained together. If so, both C and D would each have made only one true statement. Therefore, if D was the winner, A was not the one with three true statements.

Assume D was the winner, and D was the one with three true statements. If so, B was second, and C and D trained together. If so, A and B have each made only one true statement. Therefore, D was not the winner.

Therefore, B was the winner; C was the one with all true statements; A was second; and C did not train with anyone.

SUMMARY SOLUTION: B was the winner.

THE WORLD'S MOST INTENSE FOOD PRODUCE THEFT PUZZLE

CONSIDERATIONS: Consider that the one who delivered the milk made three true statements; the one who delivered the cheese made two true statements and one false statement; the one who delivered the honey made one true and two false statements; the one who delivered the nuts, and the one who delivered the bread, each made three false statements.

A is the one who delivered the bread and D is the one who delivered the nuts. We know this, since the two who delivered these two food products made only false statements, and neither B, C, nor E could have delivered the bread or nuts as the first statement or statements would be true. A and D, who each accuse each other, are both innocent.

E's first statement must be true, since it would be false only if made by the citizen who delivered the milk, and that citizen made three true statements. Therefore, E must be the one who delivered the goats' cheese, or the one who delivered the honey. If E is the one who delivered the honey, his second and third statements must be false. However, since we know E's third statement to be true, E is the one who delivered the cheese. E's second statement must be false. Therefore, C is not the thief. Since we know that D is not the thief, C's third statement is true. C is either the one who delivered the milk or the one who delivered the honey.

If C is the one who delivered the milk from C's second statement B is guilty. If C is the one who delivered the honey, C's first and second statement are false, and B is innocent. From A's third statement, which we know to be false, B did not deliver the honey. Therefore, B, whose statements are all true, delivered the milk; C, whose first and second statements are false, delivered the honey; and E is the thief.

SUMMARY SOLUTION:
   A. bread
   B. milk
   C. honey
   D. nuts
   E. cheese; E is the thief

THE WORLD'S MOST INTENSE OPEN MARKET THEFT PUZZLE

CONSIDERATIONS: Since none of the suspects is completely truthful, and no two suspects made the same number of true statements, we can conclude that one made three true statements, one made two true statements, one made one true statement, and one made no true statements.

A's fourth statement is false as, if it were true, it would be a contradiction. Therefore, A made at least one true statement. A's second statement is clearly false, as it was a given that one of the four is guilty. Therefore, either or both of A's first and third statements must be true.

D's second and fourth statements are contradictory: either one is true and one is false, or both are false. If D's third statement is true, A's first statement is false and his third statement must be true. However, this makes D's fourth statement false. If A's first statement is true, D's third statement is false. Therefore, either D's third or fourth statements are false, or both are false.

C's first statement is false, as either or both of A's first and third statements must be true. Also, C's fourth statement is false, as none of the four suspects is completely truthful.

The suspect with no true statements must be B, C, or D. Assume that B is the suspect with no true statements. If so, B's first statement is false and A is guilty. If so, D's second statement claiming B is guilty must be false. Since we know that either or both of D's third and fourth statements are false, D has made at least two false statements. Since either B or D must be the suspect with three true statements (A and C each have made at least two false statements), we can eliminate B as the suspect with no true statements.

Therefore, the suspect with no true statements must be either C or D. Since C's second statement and D's first statement both agree, they must both be false. Since C's third statement, and D's third statement agree, they must also be false. Since C's third statement and D's third statement agree, they must also be false. Therefore, C is the suspect with no true statements.

We know that D's first and third statements are false. Since we know that either D's second or fourth statements are false, D must be the suspect with one true statement, and B is the suspect with three true statements.

Therefore, A is the suspect with two true statements, the first and the third ones. Therefore, since D's fourth statement disagrees with A's third statement, which is true, D's only true statement is the second one, B is guilty.

SUMMARY SOLUTION: B is guilty.

THE WORLD'S MOST INTENSE NEPTUNE COMMUNICATION PUZZLE

CONSIDERATIONS: A must be the Midravian. Only a Midravian could answer "no" to the question, "Are you the Soravian?" A Soravian, who always speaks truthfully, would answer "yes;" a Noravian, who always speaks falsely, would also answer "yes."

Since A's first response was truthful, his second response is false; B is the Soravian and C is the Noravian.

SUMMARY SOLUTION:
   A. Midravian
   B. Soravian
   C. Noravian

THE WORLD'S MOST INTENSE TWO AVIANS PUZZLE

CONSIDERATIONS: B's statement must be false, since, if truthful, it would confirm that B is a Noravian. A truthful statement would not be possible for a Noravian. B is a Midravian. Since the two represent different groups, A, whose statement is false, is a Noravian.

SUMMARY SOLUTION:
   A. Noron
   B. Midron

THE WORLD'S MOST INTENSE UMBRELLA SELLING PUZZLE

CONSIDERATIONS: If C were the Noravian or the Soravian, A's statement would be denied, as Noravians always speak falsely and Soravians always speak truthfully. Therefore, C is the Midravian. A, who has made a false statement, is the Noravian and B is the Soravian.

SUMMARY SOLUTION:
   A. Noravian

B. Soravian
C. Midravian

THE WORLD'S MOST INTENSE HIPPOGRIFF PUZZLE

CONSIDERATIONS: C's statement infers that A is the Soravian. If true, C is the Midravian and B is the Noravian. However, it was given that this was the first visit from a hippogriff. Therefore, B is the Soravian, and, from A's second statement, which is false, A is the Noravian and C is the Midravian.

SUMMARY SOLUTION:
A. Noravian
B. Soravian
C. Midravian

THE WORLD'S MOST INTENSE ASPIDOCHELON CATCHING PUZZLE

CONSIDERATIONS: C's second statement is false, since it claims that C is a Noravian. If true, it would be impossible, as Noravians always speak falsely. Therefore, C must be a Midravian, and his statement is true.

Therefore, A's first statement is false, since it is contradicted by C's first statement. Therefore, A's second statement is also false. A must be a Noravian.

Since we know A's first statement to be false, B's third statement, which confirms this, is true. Therefore, B's first statement must also be true. Therefore, since B is not a Midravian, he must be a Soravian.

SUMMARY SOLUTION:
A. Noravian
B. Soravian
C. Midravian

THE WORLD'S MOST INTENSE DISGUISED NEPTUNE VISITOR PUZZLE

CONSIDERATIONS: C's second statement is false, since it claims A is a Soravian, which A's second statement denies. Therefore, neither A nor C is a Soravian.

If A's second statement is truthful, he is a Midravian and his third statement is false. If so, at least one of B's statements is truthful. If B's third statement is truthful, B must be a Soravian. If so, this refutes A's second statement. If B's second statement is truthful, B must be a Soravian, since we know that neither A nor C is a Soravian. Therefore, A's second statement is false. One of the three speakers is a Soravian, and, again, it must be B.

Since A's third statement is refuted, A is a Noravian. Since B's first statement refutes C's first statement, C is a Noravian.

SUMMARY SOLUTION:
A. Noravian
B. Soravian
C. Noravian

THE WORLD'S MOST INTENSE TRUTHFUL STATEMENT PUZZLE

CONSIDERATIONS: A's statement is truthful, since each of the three possibilities is covered. A is either a Soravian or a Midravian, since a Noravian can not speak truthfully. C's statement must be truthful, as it could be false only if C were a Soravian, and a Soravian can not make a false statement. C must be a Midravian, as a Noravian can not make a truthful statement.

Therefore, B and D are the two who have made false statements. B must be a Noravian, as the statement would be truthful for either a Soravian or a Midravian.

D must be a Midravian, as the statement would be true if made by a Soravian or a Noravian. Therefore, A must be the Soravian.

SUMMARY SOLUTION:
  A. Soravian
  B. Noravian
  C. Midravian
  D. Midravian

THE WORLD'S MOST INTENSE SEA MONSTER PROBLEM PUZZLE

CONSIDERATIONS: If A's third statement is truthful, C is the Midravian, A must be the Soravian, and B must be the Noravian. If so, C's first statement must be false, since it contradicts A's second statement. If so, C's second statement is truthful and third statement is false. However, C's third statement contradicts B's third statement. One is truthful and the other is false. Therefore, A's third statement must be false. Therefore, A's first statement is also false. The Soravian is either B or C. B's first statement contradicts A's first statement. Therefore, B's first statement is truthful.

Since B's first statement is truthful, his third statement, which contradicts C's third statement, is also truthful. C is not the Soravian. Therefore, B is the Soravian; C, who has made three false statements, is the Noravian; A, whose first and third statements are false and second statement is truthful, is the Midravian.

SUMMARY SOLUTION:
  A. Midravian
  B. Soravian
  C. Noravian

THE WORLD'S MOST INTENSE VILLAGE FAIR PUZZLE

CONSIDERATIONS: Statement 1 suggests that the sheep must have won in the daybreak to midmorning showing. From statement 6, Edvo's animal was entered in the daybreak to midmorning showing. From these two statements we would conclude that Edvo's animal was the sheep. However, statement 2 indicates that Edvo's animal was the goat. Therefore, the false statement is either 1, 2, or 6. From statement 4, the goat's showing must have been from midmorning to midday. Therefore, the false statement must be either 2 or 6.

From statements 1 and 3, Dor, who did not own the sheep, must have won the midmorning to midday showing. From statement 4, Dor's animal is the goat. Therefore, the false statement is 2. From statement 6, Edvo's animal is the sheep.

From statements 4 and 5, Frer's animal, the cow, was entered in the mid-afternoon to sundown showing; Har's animal, the pig, was entered in the midday to mid-afternoon showing, and from statement 4, was the blue ribbon winner.

Dor	goat	midmorning to midday
Edvo	sheep	daybreak to midmorning
Frer	cow	midafternoon to sundown
Har	pig	midday to midafternoon (blue ribbon winner)

THE WORLD'S MOST INTENSE DRAGON MEDUSO PUZZLE

CONSIDERATIONS: From statement 1, Sir Hector's attempt to use his peripheral vision was not his fourth one. From statement 3, the attempt by Sir Hector to slip into the dragon's cave was not his fourth one. From statements 4 and 5, we can conclude that neither the attempt to use his polished shield nor the attempt to use a blindfold was the fourth one. Since one of these four attempts had to be the fourth one, it is apparent that one of statements 1, 3, 4, and 5 must be the false one.

Assume that statement 3 is the false statement. If so, shield was the third attempt and the blindfold was either the first or second attempt, as was the attempt to use peripheral vision. However, from statement 6, the blindfold and peripheral vision attempts were not in consecutive order. Therefore, statement 3 is not the false one.

Assume that statement 4 is the false one. If so, from statement 5, the blindfold attempt was before the polished shield attempt; and from statements 1 and 6, the peripheral vision attempt must have followed the polished shield attempt, leaving the attempt to slip into the cave as the fourth one. However, from statement 2, this was not the case. Therefore, statement 4 was not the false one.

Assume that statement 5 is the false statement. If so, from statement 4, the polished shield attempt was immediately before the attempt to slip into the cave. If so, from statements 1 and 6, the peripheral vision attempt must have been the first, and the blindfold attempt the fourth one. However, from statement 2, the blindfold attempt did not immediately follow the attempt to slip into the cave. Therefore, statement 5 is not the false one. Therefore, statement 1 is the false statement.

Therefore, from statements 5 and 4, the blindfold attempt was first, followed by the polished shield attempt, then the attempt to slip into the cave. The fourth attempt was the peripheral vision one.

SUMMARY SOLUTION:

First:	blindfold
Second:	polished shield
Third:	slip into cave
Fourth:	peripheral vision

THE WORLD'S MOST INTENSE DRAGON WATCH PUZZLE

CONSIDERATIONS: From statement 1, Har was not the youngest. From statement 3, neither Edvo nor Frer was the youngest. From statement 4, Tolo was not the youngest. Therefore, if these statements are true, Winn must be the youngest. Also from statements 1, 3, and 4, Winn held the fifth watch. However, from statement 2, Win could not have held the fifth watch and be the youngest. One of these statements must be false.

Assume that statement 1 is false. If so, Har could be either the youngest or have held the fifth watch. However, from statements 4 and 6, Har was not the youngest, and from statements 3 and 6, Har did not hold the fifth watch. Therefore, the false statement is not statement 1.

Assume that statement 3 is false. If so, Edvo could be either the youngest or have held the fifth watch, as could Frer. However, from statement 2, Edvo was not the youngest, and from statements 7 and 5, since he was younger than Frer, he did not hold the fifth watch. From statement 6, Frer was neither assigned a later watch nor was he younger than Edvo. Therefore, statement 3 is not false.

Assume that statement 4 is false. If so, Tolo could have stood the fifth watch or be the youngest. However, from statement 2, Tolo was not the youngest, and from statement 7, he was not the tallest. Therefore, the false statement is statement 2.

Therefore, Winn stood the fifth watch. Har did not stand the first watch, and Tolo stood an earlier watch than Frer or Edvo. Tolo stood the first watch. Since Har was not the oldest, from statement 8, he was not assigned the second watch. Therefore, Frer, who stood an earlier watch that Edvo (statement 3), stood the second watch and, from statement 8, was the oldest.

From statements 4 and 7, Tolo was not the second oldest, the fourth oldest, or the youngest. Therefore, Tolo was the third oldest. Also, from statement 7, Edvo was not the fourth oldest or the youngest. Therefore, Edvo was the second oldest. Since the fourth oldest stood an earlier watch than Edvo, Har must have been the fourth oldest and Winn was the youngest. Since the fourth oldest stood an earlier watch than Edvo, Har had the third watch and Edvo had the fourth watch.

SUMMARY SOLUTION:

Edvo	fourth watch	second oldest
Frer	second watch	oldest
Har	third watch	fourth oldest
Tolo	first watch	third oldest
Winn	fifth watch	youngest

THE WORLD'S MOST INTENSE NEW PONY PUZZLE

CONSIDERATIONS: From statement 1, Tolo was not the Son of Fergy or Son of Evel. From statements 1 and 5, since Tolo's new pony was not black, he was not Son of Alfo. Therefore, if both statements 1 and 5 are true, Tolo was Son of Dirk.

However, statements 2 and 3 indicate that Boro was second to acquire a new pony, as was Son of Dirk. Either Tolo was not Son of Dirk, or Boro was not second to acquire a pony, or Son of Dirk was not second to acquire a pony.

From statements 2 and 4, if both are true, Boro's pony must have been eleven hands. From statement 3, if true, Son of Dirk's new pony was not eleven hands. Therefore, the false statement must be 2, 4, or 3.

Therefore, statements 1 and 5 are true; Tolo was Son of Dirk. From statements 1 and 6, Tolo's pony was not ten or twelve hands. Therefore, it was nine or eleven hands. Therefore statement 3, which states that Son of Dirk's pony was neither nine hands nor eleven hands, is false.

Therefore, Boro was the second to acquire a pony. From statement 1, since Tolo's pony was acquired immediately after Kover's, Tolo was the fourth to acquire a pony, Kover was third, and Jes was first.

From statements 2 and 5, Boro, who acquired the white pony, was the Son of Fergy, and Jes was the Son of Alfo. His pony was black.

From statement 4, Tolo did not acquire the pony that was eleven hands. Therefore, Tolo's pony was nine hands. From statement 2, Kover, Son of Evel, whose pony was not twelve hands or eleven hands, acquired the pony that was ten hands. Boro, whose pony was not twelve hands, acquired the pony that was eleven hands; Jes' pony was twelve hands.

From statement 1, Tolo's pony was not palomino; it was gray, and Kover's was palomino.

SUMMARY SOLUTION:

Boro	Son of Fergy	eleven hands	white
Jes	Son of Alfo	twelve hands	black
Kover	Son of Evel	ten hands	palomino
Tolo	Son of Dirk	nine hands	gray

THE WORLD'S MOST INTENSE WORK AND RECREATION PUZZLE

CONSIDERATIONS: From statement 1, the carpenter's favorite activity was singing. From statement 2, the cobbler's favorite activity was dancing. From statement 6, the weaver enjoyed instrumental music most. Therefore, either the blacksmith or the miller mist have enjoyed storytelling most. However, from statement 4, neither enjoyed storytelling. Therefore, the false statement must be 1, 2, 4, or 6.

From statement 5, Winn was not the cobbler or the miller. From statement 8, he was not the carpenter or weaver. (From statement 5, his second-favorite activity was dancing.) Therefore, Winn was the blacksmith, and, from statement 5, he enjoyed storytelling most. Therefore, statement 4 is the false one.

The miller's favorite activity must have been puzzles.

From statements 3 and 8, Zett, whose second favorite was storytelling, was the carpenter. From statement 7, Hober was the weaver. From statement 6, his second favorite was singing.

From statement 3, since Fram's second favorite, which was not dancing (it was Winn's), was the same as Dok's favorite, Dok was not the cobbler. Therefore, Fram was the cobbler and Dok was the miller.   Fram's second favorite was puzzles, and Dok's favorite activitiy was also puzzles. Fram's favorite activitiy was dancing and Dok's second favorite was instrumental music.

SUMMARY SOLUTION:

Name	Trade	Favorite Recreation	Second-favorite Recreation
Dok	miller	puzzles	instrumentals
Fram	cobbler	dancing	puzzles
Hober	weaver	instrumentals	singing
Winn	blacksmith	storytelling	dancing
Zett	carpenter	singing	storytelling

THE WORLD'S MOST INTENSE GIANT IN THE SHIRE PUZZLE

CONSIDERATIONS: From statements 2, and 5, Alf was not the Son of Rup, Son of

Tas, Son of Quin, or Son of Edno. Therefore, if the two statements are valid, Alf's second name was Son of Lor.

From Statement 6, Son of Lor did not raise goats or pigs. Therefore, if true, he must have raised cattle or sheep. However, from statement 7, Alf did not raise sheep and from statement 1, he must have raised goats. (Since neither of the two who wielded pitchforks raised sheep or goats, one raised cattle and the other raised pigs.) Therefore, either Alf was not Son or Lor, in which case, either statement 2 or statement 5 is false; or Alf did not raise goats, in which case either statement 1 or statement 7 is false; or Son of Lor raised goats, in which case, statement 6 is false.

Assume that statement 2 is false. If so, this statement does not validate that Alf was not Son of Rup or Son of Tas. However, from statement 1, both wielded pitchforks, and from statement 7, Alf wielded an ax. Therefore, statement 2 is not false.

Assume statement 5 is false. If so, Alf could be either Son of Edno or Son of Quin. However, from statement 7, Alf did not raise sheep, and from statement 3, both Son of Edno and Son of Quin raised sheep. Therefore, statement 5 is not false. Therefore Alf was son of Lor.

From statement 6, if true, Son of Lor must have raised sheep or cattle. However, from statement 7, Alf did not raise sheep (which is validated by statement 3) or cattle (which is validated by both statements 1 and 2). Therefore, statement 6 is the false statement. Therefore, Alf raised goats.

From statement 1, Son of Rup and Son of Tas raised cattle and pigs. From statement 2, Hon, who was not Son of Tas raised cattle. Therefore, Hon was Son of Rup, and Son of Tas raised pigs. Both wielded pitchforks. From statement 3, Son of Edno and Son of Quin raised sheep.

From statements 2 and 5, since Dek was one of the leaders in organizing the group, he was not Son of Quin, and, from statement 4, he was not Son of Tas. Therefore, Dek was Son of Edno. Also, from statement 4, since Forber wielded a spade, Dek wielded a club. Since Bord must have wielded a pitchfork, he was Son of Tas, and Forber was Son of Quin.

SUMMARY SOLUTION:

Alf Son of Lor	goats	ax
Bord Son of Tas	pigs	pitchfork
Dek Son of Edno	sheep	club
Fober Son of Quin	sheep	spade
Hon Son of Rup	cattle	pitchfork

THE WORLD'S MOST INTENSE PONY RACING PUZZLE

CONSIDERATIONS: FIRST RACE: From statements 2 and 1, Lak finished before Pro, who finished before Pen and Ismo, and, from statement 4, Adus finished in third place. From statement 3, Pir must have finished in sixth place. Therefore, if statements 1, 2, 3, and 4 are valid, Lak was first, Pro was second, Adus was third, Pen was fourth, Isom was fifth, and Pir was sixth.

SECOND RACE: From statements 6 and 7, if valid, Pro finished in second place and Pir finished in fifth place. In the four remaining places, from statements 5 and 8, if valid, Pen was first, Lak was third, Ismo was fourth, and Adus was sixth.

THIRD RACE: From statements 9 and 11, if valid, Lak was second (He was not first, since he won the 3rd race and no rider won more than one race.), Pen was third, and Pro was fourth. From statement 10, if valid, Pir was fifth and Ismo was sixth. Adus, who was not named in these statements was first.

However, statement 12 presents a contradiction, since from the existing statements Pir finished in fifth place in both the 2nd and 3rd races. Therefore, either statement 12 is false, or one of the statements placing Pir in fifth place in either the second or third race is false.

FOURTH RACE: From statements 14, 15, and 16, since Pir finished ahead of Lak, Pen, Pro, and Adus, he must have finished in first or second place. However, from statement 13, his position in either the second or third race must have been second or third. Therefore, statement 12 is not the false statement.

Assume that statement 9 (3rd race) is the false statement. If so, from statements 10 and 11, Pir could not have finished in second or third place. Therefore, statement 9 is not the false one.

Assume that statement 10 is the false statement. If so, from statementse 9 and 11, again, Pir could not have finished in second or third place.

Assume that statement 11 is the false statement. If so, from statements 9 and 10, Pir could not have finished in second or third place.

Therefore, the false statement is one describing the finish in the second race, and is clearly statement 7. Therefore, the second race was won by Pen; Pro finished in second place; Pir finished in third place; and Lak, Ismo, and Adus finished in fourth, fifth, and sixth places.

Therefore, in the fourth race, Pir was second, Lak was third, Pro was fourth, Pen was fifth, Adus was sixth, and Ismo was first.

SUMMARY SOLUTION:

	Race 1	Race 2	Race 3	Race 4
1.	Lak	Pen	Adus	Ismo
2.	Pro	Pro	Lak	Pir
3.	Adus	Pir	Pen	Lak
4.	Pen	Lak	Pro	Pro
5.	Ismo	Ismo	Pir	Pen
6.	Pir	Adus	Ismo	Adus

THE WORLD'S MOST INTENSE VALLEY OF LIARS VISITOR PUZZLE

CONSIDERATIONS: From B's second statement we know immediately that it is true. Therefore, B's first statement is also true; A is not a Pemtru. A is an Amtru who has spoken falsely. Therefore, it must be afternoon. Therefore, since B's statement is true, B is a Pemtru.

SUMMARY SOLUTION: It is afternoon; A is an Amtru; B is a Pemtru.

THE WORLD'S MOST INTENSE ROUTE TO THE VALLEY OF LIARS PUZZLE

CONSIDERATIONS: From A's second statement, we can conclude that A is an Amtru. Only an Amtru, true or false, can say it is morning. If it is morning, a Pemtru would lie, saying it is afternoon. If it is afternoon, a Pemtru would truthfully say so. From B's second statement we can conclude that it is morning, whether the statement is true or false. If it were afternoon, a Pemtru would speak the truth, and an Amtru would claim to be a Pemtru. Therefore, A's second statement is true, it is morning, and it follows that his first statement is true, it is morning, and it follows that his first statement must also be true; the road leading East is the correct one.

Since B disagrees, B must be a Pemtru, in the morning, falsely claiming to be an Amtru.

SUMMARY SOLUTION: The road leading East is the correct one. It is morning; A is an Amtru; B is a Pemtru.

THE WORLD'S MOST INTENSE TWO VALLEY LIARS PUZZLE

CONSIDERATIONS: Assume it is morning. If so, A's statement could be true. If so, A and B would both be Pemtrus. B's statement, however, that A is not a Pemtru, would be false—not possible for a Valley Pemtru referring to an inhabitant in the same group in the morning. If it is morning, assume that A is a Pemtru and B is an Amtru. Again, however, B's statement would not be possible, since B would be an Amtru in the morning referring to an inhabitant not in the same group and, therefore, would have to be truthful. The other possibility, that A is an Amtru and B is a Pemtru, could not be made by A, who would have to speak the truth.

Therefore, it is afternoon. A must be an Amtru, since the statement could not be made by a Valley Pemtru in the afternoon. If B is also an Amtru, A would have to truthfully state so. Therefore, B is a Pemtru. B's statement, that A is not a Pemtru, is true.

SUMMARY SOLUTION: It is afternoon; A is an Amtru, and B is a Pemtru.

THE WORLD'S MOST INTENSE TWO MORE VALLEY LIARS PUZZLE

CONSIDERATIONS: Assume it is afternoon. If so, if A is a Pemtru, his first statement could not be made. A would deny that B is a Pemtru. If it is afternoon, A must be an Amtru. If so, if B were a Pemtru, A would falsely claim that B is an Amtru. If B were an Amtru, A would truthfully confirm this.

Therefore, it is morning. Assume A is an Amtru. If so, if B is an Amtru, A's first statement is false, which is consistent for a Valley Amtru in the morning. However, A's second statement, implying that A and B are both Amtrus would be true, which is an impossible assertion for a Valley Pemtru, which would be consistent with his first statement. However, A's second statement would be false, which is not consistent.

Therefore, it is afternoon. Assume A is an Amtru. Again, A's statement could not be made. (If B were an Amtru, it would confirm it; if B were a Pemtru, A would falsely indicate that B and he belong to the same group.)

Therefore, A is a Pemtru. If B were a Pemtru, he would confirm A's statements. Since he rejects them, B is an Amtru, who has told the truth.

SUMMARY SOLUTION: It is morning; A is a Pemtru; B is an Amtru.

THE WORLD'S MOST INTENSE THREE VALLEY LIARS PUZZLE

CONSIDERATIONS: Assume it is morning, and assume A is a Pemtru. If so, A's statement could not be made (If B were a Pemtru, A would confirm it; if B were an Amtru, A would falsely infer that B and he belong to the same group). If it is morning, A must be an Amtru. If so, if B were an Amtru, his statement would be true, making C an Amtru. (If C were a Pemtru, B would truthfully indicate that C would claim it is afternoon.) This is not a possible statement for an Amtru to make in the morning, referring to another Amtru.

Therefore, if it is morning, and if A is an Amtru, B must be a Pemtru. If so, if C were an Amtru, B's statement would be true, not a possible statement for a Pemtru in the morning. If C were a Pemtru, B would speak truthfully, indicating that C would claim it is afternoon.

Therefore, it is afternoon. Assume A is an Amtru. Again, A's statement could not be made. (If B were an Amtru, A would confirm it; if B were a Petru, A would falsely indicate that B and he belong to the same group.)

Therefore, A is a Pemtru, who has spoken truthfully. B is an Amtru, who has also spoken truthfully. C is an Amtru, whose statement about a Pemtru (A) is false.

SUMMARY SOLUTION: It is afternoon; A is a Pemtru; B and C are Amtrus.

THE WORLD'S MOST INTENSE THREE VALLEY LIARS PUZZLE, AGAIN

CONSIDERATIONS: From A's statement, we can conclude that, if it is morning, A must be an Amtru who has spoken truthfully, since a Pemtru in the morning would speak truthfully referring to another Pemtru, falsely if referring to an Amtru. If it is afternoon, A must be a Pemtru, who has spoken truthfully about an Amtru, or falsely about another Pemtru.

From B's statement, we can conclude that B is either an Amtru in the afternoon or a Pemtru in the morning. If B's statement is true, C belongs to the same group. If B's statement is false C is either an Amtru in the morning or a Pemtru in the afternoon.

From C's statement, we can conclude that C is either an Amtru in the morning or a Pemtru in the afternoon.

Therefore, if it is morning, A has spoken truthfully about another Amtru. However, an Amtru in the morning mentioning another Amtru would not tell the truth. Therefore, it is not morning; it is afternoon.

B, whose statement is false, is an Amtru, and C is a Pemtru. From A's statement, we can conclude that A is a Pemtru, who has made a false statement about two Pemtrus.

SUMMARY SOLUTION: It is afternoon; A and C are Pemtrus; B is an Amtru.

THE WORLD'S MOST INTENSE FOUR VALLEY LIARS PUZZLE

CONSIDERATIONS: Assume it is afternoon. If so, if B's statement is true; B is the only Pemtru. If so, D's statement must be false, and D must be an Amtru. If so, A must be an Amtru, and his statement, referring to another Amtru, would have to be true. However, A's statement would be false, an inconsistency.

Therefore, if it is afternoon, B's statement is false; B must be an Amtru. If so, from D's statement, D is an Amtru, since, in the afternoon, a Pemtru referring to an Amtru would speak truthfully. If so, A's statement could not be made. If A were an Amtru, in the afternoon, referring to another Amtru, his statement would have to be true. If A were a Pemtru, in the afternoon, again, his statement would have to be true. In either case, D would not refer to A as a Pemtru.

Therefore, it is morning. Assume that B's statement is false. If so, B is a Pemtru. If so, D, whose statement is false, must also be a Pemtru. However, in the morning, a Pemtru mentioning another Pemtru must speak truthfully.

Therefore, B's statement is true; B is the only Amtru. D's statement is false, and D is a Pemtru. A is also a Pemtru, whose statement regarding D is true. C is also a Pemtru, whose statement referring to an Amtru is false.

SUMMARY SOLUTION: It is morning. A, C, and D are Pemtrus; B is an Amtru.

THE WORLD'S MOST INTENSE IMPOSTOR PUZZLE

CONSIDERATIONS: Consider B's statement. The implication is that if it is afternoon, he is an Amtru; if it is morning he is a Pemtru. If it is afternoon, B must be an Amtru who has spoken truthfully. However, in the afternoon, an Amtru would speak falsely, and for the statement to be false, B would be a Pemtru. In the afternoon, a Pemtru would speak truthfully. In either case that would be an impossibility. If it is morning, B must be either a Pemtru, who has spoken truthfully, or an Amtru, who has spoken falsely, again, an impossibility. Therefore, whether it is morning or afternoon, B's statement is not possible. Therefore, B must be the impostor.

Consider that Amtrus and Pemtrus are equally represented. Assume that it is morning. If so, C's statement could not be made. If C were an Amtru, the inference that A is an Amtru would have to be false, making A a Pemtru; however, if A were a Pemtru, C would speak truthfully and confirm it. If C were a Pemtru, the statement, referring to an Amtru in the morning would not be possible. If A were an Amtru, C would falsely refer to A as a Pemtru. If A were a Pemtru, C would truthfully indicate so.

Therefore, it is afternoon. A's statement could only be made by a Pemtru (If A were an Amtru he would claim the same group as C, whether true or false.) C's statement is false; it could be made by am Amtru or a Pemtru.

Since we know that A is a Pemtru, if D were an Amtru, his statement would be true, not possible for an Amtru in the afternoon. Therefore, D is a Pemtru, who has spoken falsely about another Pemtru in the afternoon.

If E's statement is true, E is a Pemtru; if it is false he is an Amtru. Therefore, since there are two Amtrus, we can conclude that C and E are both Amtrus who have spoken falsely.

SUMMARY SOLUTION: B is the impostor. It is afternoon; A and D are Pemtrus; C and E are Amtrus.

THE WORLD'S MOST TAXING FALSE LOGIC PUZZLES

THE WORLD'S MOST TAXING STRADIVARIUS THEFT PUZZLE

CONSIDERATIONS: The guilty suspect's statement is false; the others are true.

Assume that A is guilty. If so, A's statement is false. If so, this means that the other three must have made true statements. However, B says C is guilty; if A is guilty, A and B have both made false statements. Therefore, A is not guilty.

Assume that C is guilty. If so, B's statement, indicating that C is guilty, is true. However, if C is guilty, C's and D's statements are both false. Therefore, C is not guilty.

Assume that D is guilty. If so, B's statement indicating that C is guilty is false. Therefore, D is not guilty.

B is guilty. The other three make true statements:

A. T
B. F
C. T
D. T

SUMMARY SOLUTION: B is the thief.

THE WORLD'S MOST TAXING FOREST ROBBER PUZZLE

CONSIDERATIONS: One suspect makes two true statements; one makes one true and one false statement; one makes two false statements.

Assume that A is guilty. If so, A's first and second statements are both false; B's first and second statements are both true; and C's first and second statements are both true. Therefore, A is not guilty.

Assume that B is guilty. If so, each of the three suspects makes one true and one false statement. Therefore B is not guilty. Therefore, C is guilty.

SUMMARY SOLUTION: C is the robber.

THE WORLD'S MOST TAXING TWO PICKPOCKET PUZZLE

CONSIDERATIONS: The two guilty ones each make only one true statement.

Assume that B is guilty. If so, B's first statement is true, as is either the second or third statement. Therefore, B is not one of the guilty ones. Assume that C is guilty. Since C's second statement indicates that B is not guilty, it is true. Also, if C is guilty, C's third statement must also be true. Therefore C is not guilty and the two guilty ones are A and D.

SUMMARY SOLUTION: A and D are the guilty ones.

THE WORLD'S MOST TAXING POACHER PUZZLE

CONSIDERATIONS: Consider that the guilty suspect makes only one true statement.

Assume that A is guilty. If so, A's first statement indicating that D is innocent is true, as is his third statement, confirming that hunting is a source of food. Therefore, A is not guilty.

Assume that B is guilty. If so, B's second statement confirming that A is not the poacher is true, as is B's third statement indicating that his statements are not all true. Therefore B is not guilty.

Assume that D is guilty. D's first statement indicates that A's statements are not all true. If the statement is false, then A's first statement that D is innocent must be true. D's second statement, that at least one of C's statements is true, must itself be true if D is the poacher as claimed by C's second statement. Either D is innocent as confirmed by A's first statement, or else D has made two true statements. Therefore, D is not guilty.

Therefore, C is guilty.

SUMMARY SOLUTION: C is the poacher.

640

THE WORLD'S MOST TAXING PROPERTY DESTRUCTION PUZZLE

CONSIDERATIONS: The butcher's first statement is false, as all five were present. The baker's first statement agrees with the butcher's false first statement. Therefore, it also is false.

The blacksmith's second statement is clearly false, from the description of the incident. The cobbler's first and third statements are contradictory. One is true and the other is false.

Therefore, the candlestick maker must be the one who makes no false statements. As indicated by his third statement, the baker did it.

SUMMARY SOLUTION: The baker is guilty.

THE WORLD'S MOST TAXING GUILTY TWO PUZZLE

CONSIDERATIONS: Consider that one of the two culprits makes two true statements; the other makes two false statements.

Assume that A is guilty. If so, both statements are false. If so, B is also guilty. If so, B's statements must both be true. However, B's first statement claims innocence. Therefore, A is not guilty.

Assume that B is guilty. If so, since B claims innocence, both statements must be false. Therefore, if B is guilty, E's first statement must be true. However, since we know that at least A is innocent, E's first statement is false, as truthfully indicated by B. Therefore, B is not guilty.

Assume that E is guilty. If so, since we know E's first statement is false, both of his statements must be false. However, since we know that D's second statement is true, E's second statement is true. Therefore E is not guilty.

Therefore, the guilty ones are C, both of whose statements are false, and D, both of whose statements are true.

SUMMARY SOLUTION: C and D are the guilty ones.

THE WORLD'S MOST TAXING PICKPOCKET THEFT PUZZLE

CONSIDERATIONS: If either A or C is guilty, each of the four suspects makes two true statements.

Assume that A is guilty. If so, his first statement is false, since it was given that all four suspects were in town at the time of the last known theft. A's second statement would also be false. Therefore, A is not guilty.

Assume that C is guilty. If so, A's first and third statements are false, as are C's first and second statements. Therefore, C did not do it.

The guilty suspect must be B or D. Therefore, no two of the suspects make the same number of true statements. Therefore, one makes three true statements, one makes two true statements, one makes one true statement, and one makes no true statements.

Assume that B is guilty. If so, B's second and third statements are false and first statement is true; C's first and second statements are false and third statement is true. Therefore, B did not do it.

Therefore, D is guilty. C's statements are all false; A makes one true statement; D makes two true statements; and all three of B's statements are true.

SUMMARY SOLUTION: D is the pickpocket.

THE WORLD'S MOST TAXING MISSING D PUZZLE

CONSIDERATIONS: Each suspect makes two true and one false statement.

A's second statement and C's second statement are contradictory. One is true and one is false. Assume that C's second statement is false. If so, C's first and third statements must be true. If so, B's second statement is false, and first and third statements are true. This means that A's third statement and second statement are true, and first statement is false. However, if A's first statement is false, this contradicts B's first statement. Therefore, C's second statement is true.

A's second statement is false, and first and third statements are true. B's second statement is false, and first and third statements are true. C's second and third statements are true, and first statement is false. C is guilty.

SUMMARY SOLUTION: C is the burglar.

THE WORLD'S MOST TAXING UNLUCKY CAR THIEF PUZZLE

CONSIDERATIONS: Consider that six statements are false. A's first statement and C's first statement contradict each other. One of them is false. C's third statement and D's second statement contradict each other. One of them is false. Therefore, there are four additional false statements.

Assume A is guilty. If so, A's second statement, B's second statement, and D's first statement are the additional false statements. This makes a total of five false statements. Therefore, A is not guilty.

Assume C is guilty. If so, A's second statement and D's first and third statements are false. This makes a total of five false statements. Therefore, C is not guilty.

Assume that D is guilty. If so, A's second statement, B's first statement, and D's third statement are false. Again, this makes a total of five false statements. Therefore, D did not do it.

Therefore, B is the culprit. B's third statement, C's second statement, and D's first and third statements are the additional false statements.

SUMMARY SOLUTION: B did it.

THE WORLD'S MOST TAXING OLDEST/YOUNGEST PUZZLE

CONSIDERATIONS: Each suspect makes only one true statement.

B's first statement and C's first statement are contradictory. One is true and one is false. B's second statement and C's third statement are contradictory. One is true and one is false. Since each makes only one true statement, B's third statement and C's second statement are both false. D is not the youngest, and C is not the oldest.

If A's first statement is true, the conclusion from A's second statement, which would be false, would be that B, the oldest, is guilty. From A's third statement, also false, we would conclude that C was also guilty. Therefore, A's first statement is false; B is not the oldest.

If D's second statement is true, B is guilty. However, from D's first statement, which would be false, we would conclude that the oldest was guilty. Since we know that B is not the oldest (A's false first statement), D's second statement is false. D's third statement is false, since it agrees with B's third statement, which we know to be false. Therefore D's first statement is true; the guilty one is the youngest.

Conclusions at this point are:

A's second statement agrees with D's first statement. Therefore, it is true, and A's third statement, that C is innocent, is false; C did it.

SUMMARY SOLUTION: C, the youngest, is guilty.

THE WORLD'S MOST TAXING HYPERBOREAY OUTLIER PUZZLE

CONSIDERATIONS: Assume that A's first statement is true. If so, B's first statement is false and second statement must be true. If so, this means that C's second statement is true and first statement is false, which means that C is a Nororean. This contradicts A's second statement, which would be false. Therefore, A's first statement is false.

A is either a Midrorean or a Nororean. Assume A is a Midrorean, whose second statement is truthful. If so, B is a Sororean, since the only other possibility would be Nororean, which would be inconsistent with B's true first statement. If so, B's second statement is also true. However, this is inconsistent with A's second statement. Therefore, A's second statement is false; A is a Nororean.

Our conclusions, so far, are:

C's first statement disagrees with A's second statement, which we know to be false. Therefore, C's first statement is true and, since C is not a Nororean (which A is), his second statement is false; C is a Midrorean.

Assume B's second statement is true. If so, B is a Midrorean, and his first statement is false. However, since A is a Nororean, for B's first statement to be false, B would have to be a Nororean. Therefore, B's second statement is false; B must be a Nororean, whose first statement is also false.

SUMMARY SOLUTION:
  A. Nororean
  B. Nororean
  C. Midrorean

THE WORLD'S MOST TAXING OUTLIER PUZZLE

CONSIDERATIONS: Assume A's first statement, that he is the Outlier, is true. If so, A's second statement could be true or false. If A is the Outlier, B is the Sororean or the Midrorean. C, who claims not to be the Outlier, must be the Sororean or the Midrorean. If so, D must be the Nororean. However, D's statement confirms C's statement. Therefore, A's first statement must be false, as is B's statement.

Since there is a Sororean, it must be C or D, and since C's first statement and D's statement agree, both are true. Therefore, A must be the Nororean. Since C's first statement is true, C is not the Outlier. If C were the Midrorean, his second statement would be false, making B the Midrorean. Therefore, C must be the Sororean. Thus, from C's second statement, B is not the Midrorean. Therefore, B is the Outlier, and D is the Midrorean.

THE WORLD'S MOST TAXING ONE OF EACH PUZZLE

CONSIDERATIONS: A's first statement claims that he is the Outlier. If true, A's third statement must be false. If so, B is not the Sororean. From B's third statement, if A is the Outlier, B must be the Midrorean, who has spoken falsely. (For a Nororean, the statement would be true, which is not possible.) If so, B's first statement must also be false. However, B's first statement asserts that A is the Outlier. Therefore, A is not the Outlier. B must be either the Outlier, whose first statement is false and third statement is truthful, or the Midrorean, whose first and third statements are false.

C's first and second statements and D's first statement are truthful. Therefore, A is the only one of the four who can be the Nororean and, if B is the Outlier, C must be the Sororean, and D is the Midrorean. If so, D's third statement must be truthful. However, it asserts that C's third statement is false. Therefore, B is not the Outlier; B is the Midrorean.

Our conclusions, so far, are:

From B's second statement, which truthfully claims C is not the Sororean, we can conclude that C, whose third statement is false, is the Outlier, and D is the Sororean.

SUMMARY SOLUTION:
A. Nororean
B. Midrorean
C. Outlier
D. Sororean

THE WORLD'S MOST TAXING OLYMPIC GAME PUZZLE

CONSIDERATIONS: Assume that A was the winner of the one-half league run as indicated by his first statement. If so, his third statement must also be true. If so, A is a Sororean. However, A's second statement implies that C is a Sororean, while C's second statement indicates that A did not win the one-half league run, which is a contradiction. Therefore, A's first statement is false. Since A's third statement would be true for a Nororean, A must be either the Outlier or a Midrorean.

B's first statement and C's third statement are both truthful. However, B's third statement and C's first statement disagree; one is truthful and the other is false. Either B or C must be the Outlier. Therefore, A is a Midrorean, whose second statement must be truthful; C is a Sororean. Therefore, B is the Outlier.

SUMMARY SOLUTION:
A. Midrorean
B. Outlier
C. Sororean

THE WORLD'S MOST TAXING OUTLIER PUZZLE, AGAIN

CONSIDERATIONS: Assume that B is the Outlier. If so, B's first statement is false.

B's second statement must be false, since A's first statement must be true. B's third statement must be true (otherwise, B would be a Nororean). However, if not a Midrorean, C must be a Sororean, as the only other option would be for C to be a Nororean, and C's first statement would be true, not possible for a Nororean. C's second statement must be true. Therefore, B is not the Outlier. B's first and third statements must be true.

C could be a Sororean. However, C's third statement, claiming that D is a Sororean, must be false, as D's second statement is clearly false. C has made two consecutive true statements followed by a false statement. C is the Outlier.

At this point our conclusions are:

A, who has made three false statements, is a Nororean; B is a Sororean, and D is a Nororean, having made all false statements.

SUMMARY SOLUTION:
  A. Nororean
  B. Sororean
  C. Outlier
  D. Nororean

THE WORLD'S MOST TAXING OLIVE PICKING PUZZLE

CONSIDERATIONS: From A's second statement and B's first statement we can conclude that neither is the Sororean. If B's first statement is truthful, B is the Midrorean and, from B's third statement, C is the Outlier. However, if so, A must be the Nororean, and A's third statement, asserting that C is the Outlier, must be false. Therefore, B's first statement is false. If B's third statement were true, he'd be the Outlier, so the third statement must be false. Thus, B must be the Nororean.

The Sororean must be either C or D. Since C's second statement and D's first statement agree, both statements are true. Therefore, A's first statement is false. Therefore, A's second statement must be true; A is the Midrorean.

Since we know that B is the Nororean, with all false statements, D's third statement, agreeing with B's false second statement, is false. Therefore, since D's first statement is true and third statement is false, D is the Outlier. Therefore, C is the Sororean.

SUMMARY SOLUTION:
  A. Midrorean
  B. Nororean
  C. Sororean
  D. Outlier

THE WORLD'S MOST TAXING FOUR FOR THE RACES PUZZLE

CONSIDERATIONS: Assume that A's third statement is truthful and C is the Outlier. If so, A's first statement is also truthful. If so, A is either the Sororean or the Midrorean. If A is the Sororean, his second statement is truthful and D's first statement is false. If so, D's third statement should also be false. However, it affirms that A is the Sororean. Therefore, A is not the Sororean. If C is the Outlier and A is the Midrorean, A's second statement is false. If so, D's first statement is truthful and third statement is false. Therefore, C is not the Outlier.

A's third statement is false. Assume A is the Outlier; if so, his first statement must

645

be truthful. If so, B's first statement is also truthful. However, B's second statement indicates that he is the Midrorean. If so, B's first statement is false, and if B's second statement is false, B is the Nororean. In either case, his first statement is false. Therefore, A is not the Outlier.

Therefore, A's first statement is false. If A is the Midrorean, his second statement is truthful. If so, D's first statement is false and D must be the Nororean. If so, B must be the Outlier, and C must be the Sororean. However, C's second statement confirms that B is the Midrorean. Therefore, B is not the Outlier, and A is not the Midrorean; A is the Nororean.

Our conclusions at this point are as follows:

Therefore, the Outlier must be D. His third statement is false and first statement is truthful. B is the Midrorean as claimed by his truthful second statement, and C is the Sororean, with three truthful statements.

SUMMARY SOLUTION:
A. Nororean
B. Midrorean
C. Sororean
D. Outlier

THE WORLD'S MOST TAXING SIX HYPERBOREANS PUZZLE

CONSIDERATIONS: Philemon's first and third statements are contradictory, since Hesperus claims that Cadmus is the tax collector, the job also claimed by Philemon. Either Philemon's first statement or his third statement is false, or both of Philemon's statements are false, or Philemon is the Outlier.

Agenor's second and third statements are inconsistent, since he agrees that Hesperus' statements are all true, yet he claims that Cadmus is the chariot maker, although Hesperus' third statement indicates that Cadmus is the tax collector. At least one of Agenor's statements is false. It follows that Callisto's second statement, indicating that Agenor's statements are all true, is false.

Cadmus' first and fourth statements are inconsistent. Either or both are false, as he claims to be the olive grower, which agrees with Philemon's fourth statement, and also indicates that all of Philemon's statements are false.

Since Philemon, Agenor, Callisto and Cadmus have each made at least one false statement, the remaining candidates for the Sororean must be Alphenor and Hesperus.

Assume that Hesperus is the Sororean. This would mean that Alphenor is an Outlier, whose first statement is true, and second and third statements are false. It would also mean that Agenor is an Outlier, whose first and second statements are false and third statement is true. It would also mean that Philemon is an Outlier, whose first and fourth statements are false and third statement is true. Therefore, since there is only one Outlier, Hesperus is not the Sororean. Therefore, Alphenor is the Sororean. He is the tax collector, as claimed, and Hesperus is the chariot maker.

Cadmus, who makes at least two consecutive true statements, his second and third, is the Outlier. Hesperus, whose first, third, and fourth statements are contradicted by Alphenor's second and third statements, is a Nororean. Agenor, whose second statement contradicts Alphenor's true third statement, and whose third statement agrees with Philemon's false third statement, is a Nororean.

Callisto and Philemon are the two Midroreans. Callisto's first and third statements are true, and second statement is false. Philemon's second and fourth statements are true, and first and third statements are false. Cadmus' one false statement is his fourth one.

Our conclusions so far are:

Cadmus is the olive grower, as claimed. Callisto is the musician, as implied by her true first statement, as well as Philemon's true second statement. Since Hesperus falsely infers that Agenor is the wine maker, he must be the fishnet weaver, and Philemon is the wine maker.

SUMMARY SOLUTION:

Agenor	Nororean	fishnet weaver
Alphenor	Sororean	tax collector
Cadmus	Outlier	olive grower
Callisto	Midrorean	musician
Hesperus	Nororean	chariot maker
Philemon	Midrorean	wine maker

THE WORLD'S MOST TAXING CHARIOT RACE WINNER PUZZLE

CONSIDERATIONS: Assume that Agathon's third statement is truthful. If so, Agathon's first statement is also true, unless he is the Outlier. Lysis' third statement contradicts Agathon's first statement. Therefore, if Agathon's third statement is truthful, then Lysis' third statement is truthful, and Agathon's first statement is false. Agathon could be the Outlier.

Lysis, however, claims that Phaedrus is a Sororean. Phaedrus' fourth statement, claiming that Protagoras is the Outlier, contradicts Lysis' first statement that Sosias is the Outlier. Therefore Lysis cannot be a Sororean. Therefore, Agathon's third statement is false and, unless he is the Outlier, his first statement is also false, and Lysis' third statement is true. Therefore, Lysis' first statement, claiming that Sosias is the Outlier, is also true, unless Lysis is the Outlier. Therefore, we can conclude that the Outlier is either Agathon, Lysis, or Sosias.

Phaedrus' fourth statement, claiming that Protagoras is the Outlier, is false. Therefore, Phaedrus' second statement, that Agathon is the Grand Champion, must also be false. Therefore, Lysis' fourth statement, that Agathon is not the Grand Champion, is true. Since we know that Lysis' second statement is false, Lysis is the Outlier. Therefore, Agathon's first and third statements are false. Therefore, Lysis is not the Grand Champion. Since we know that Phaedrus is not the Outlier, Agathon's fourth statement, agreeing with this, is true, as is his second statement, that Protagoras has had 15 wins. Agathon is a Midrorean. Also, we can conclude that Protagoras could not be the Grand Champion, since the Grand Champion would have to have had at least 18 wins.

Protagoras' third statement, that Lysis is the Outlier, is true. His second statement that Sosias has had 15 wins is false, as we know that Protagoras has had fifteen wins, and no two racers have had the same number of wins. Therefore, Protagoras is a Midrorean, whose first and third statements are truthful and second and fourth statements are false. Agathon has had fewer wins than either Lysis or Protagoras.

Sosias' second statement, asserting that Agathon has had more wins than Protagoras, is false, as is his third statement, claiming that Phaedrus is the Outlier. Therefore, Sosias is a Nororean, with all false statements. From Sosias' first statement, we can conclude that he has had six wins. Therefore, the Grand Champion is Phaedrus. From Sosias' fourth statement, we can conclude that Phaedrus' third statement, that Lysis has had the third-highest number of wins, is true. Therefore, Phaedrus' first statement is also true. Phaedrus, who has had 18 wins, is a Midrorean.

Since we know that Lysis has had the third-highest number of wins, that number must be 12, and Agathon, who has had fewer wins than Lysis, has had nine wins.

SUMMARY SOLUTION:

Agathon	Midrorean	9 wins	
Lysis	Outlier	12 wins	
PhaFedrus	Midrorean	18 wins	Grand Champion
Protagoras	Midrorean	15 wins	
Sosias	Nororean	6 wins	

THE WORLD'S MOST TAXING MIDVILLE MUDDLERS PUZZLE

CONSIDERATIONS: From statement 6, Henry must be the center fielder. However, the indication that his batting average is lower than that of the catcher cannot be correct, considering statement 1. Statements 3 and 5 are also contradictory to statement 6. Therefore, statement 6 is false.

From statements 1 and 3, since Leo is not the catcher, he is the center fielder who bats .295. From statements 2 and 4, Leo must be one of the three players who are neighbors. Therefore Leo's surname is Clements. From statements 1 and 4, Ken, whose batting average is 30 points below Stan's, is the catcher, whose batting average is .280; Stan's batting average is .310. From statements 2 and 5, Stan's surname is Brooks, and he is the right fielder.

From statement 5, Henry's surname is not Ashley. Therefore, Henry is Dodson, the left fielder, whose batting average is .325. Ken's surname is Ashley.

SUMMARY SOLUTION:

Henry Dodson	left fielder	.325
Ken Ashley	catcher	.280
Leo Clements	center fielder	.295
Stan Brooks	right fielder	.310

THE WORLD'S MOST TAXING FISHING VACATION PLANS PUZZLE

CONSIDERATIONS: From statements 1, 3, 6, and 7, Barrott's first name is neither Andy, Bill, Carl, nor Dennis. Therefore, one of these four statements is the false one. From statement 5, Barrott was one of the two who are not married. This is contradictory to statement 3. Therefore, statement 3 is false.

Therefore, Barrott's first name is Carl. From statements 4 and 6, Dennis is not Whelan or Crowley. Therefore, Dennis is Cole.

From statements 4, 6, and 7, Whelan's favorite destination was the third, Crowley's was the last, and Barrott's was the first. Therefore, Cole's favorite destination was the second one.

From statement 4, the third destination was neither Patagonia nor New Zealand. Therefore, it was either Alaska or Iceland. From statement 6, the trip to New Zealand was not planned to be the first or the fourth destination. From statement 2, the trip to Iceland was planned for the year before the trip to Alaska. Therefore, the first trip must have been planned for Patagonia; the second trip, New Zealand; the third trip, Iceland; and the fourth trip, Alaska.

From statement 2, Andy's favorite destination was not Alaska (which, from statement 6, was Crowley's favorite). Therefore, Andy is Whelan and Bill is Crowley.

SUMMARY SOLUTION:

Andy Whelan	Iceland	third
Bill Crowley	Alaska	fourth
Carl Barrott	Patagonia	first
Dennis Cole	New Zealand	second

THE WORLD'S MOST TAXING WHITE-WATER RAFTING PUZZLE

CONSIDERATIONS: From statement 5, Henry and Hughes were on the same raft. However, this is inconsistent with statement 7, which states that Alan and Hughes were on the same raft. One of these two statements is false. Statement 7, which states that they were the first to finish, is inconsistent with statement 10, which indicates that they were last. Therefore, statement 7 is the false one.

From statement 6, Hawley was with Frank on the second-place yellow raft. From statements 2, 4, 6, and 10, Paul and Alan Wilson were on the third-place blue raft. From statement 1, Phil and Cook must be on the yellow raft, so they must be Phil Hawley and Frank Cook. From statements 2 and 5, Walt (who was not on the red raft) was on the green raft. From statements 2, 5, and 9, the partners on the red raft were Henry Gladstone and Don Hughes. From statements 3 and 8, the two on the green raft must have been LeRoy Sands and Walt Smith. O'Brien is Paul's surname.

SUMMARY SOLUTION:

Alan Wilson / Paul O'Brien	blue raft	3rd place
Phil Hawley / Frank Cook	yellow raft	2nd place
Walt Smith / LeRoy Sands	green raft	1st place
Henry Gladstone / Don Hughes	red raft	did not finish

THE WORLD'S MOST TAXING SPELLING CONTEST PUZZLE

CONSIDERATIONS: From statements 7 and 8, Jennings, who is one of the three young ladies, is not Lois or Helen. Therefore, Eleanor must be Jennings. However, this is inconsistent with statement 3. One of statements 3, 7, and 8 is false. Statement 5 is also inconsistent with statement 3. Therefore, statement 3 is false. Eleanor is Jennings.

From statements 6 and 7, Helen is not Knudson or Olsen, and from statement 1, she is not North. Therefore, Helen is Salisbury. From statement 4, Eric placed second. Therefore, from statement 6, he is not Knudson. From statement 4, Eric is not Olsen. Therefore, Eric is North. From statement 5, Gordie did not win, but placed higher than Jennings. Therefore, since Knudson placed fifth (statement 6), Gordie is Olsen and Lois is Knudson. Eleanor Jennings placed fourth, Gordie Olsen placed third, and Eric North placed second (statement 5). Helen Salisbury was the winner.

From statements 1 and 2, Lois misspelled "physiognomy," Eleanor misspelled "bivouac," Gordie misspelled "vicissitude," and Eric misspelled "isthmus."

SUMMARY SOLUTION:

Eleanor Jennings	bivouac	4th place
Eric North	isthmus	2nd place
Gordie Olsen	vicissitude	3rd place
Helen Salisbury		1st place (winner)
Lois Knudson	physiognomy	5th place

THE WORLD'S MOST TAXING AUDOBON FIELD TRIP PUZZLE

CONSIDERATIONS: From statement 5, Curtis' spouse is an active Audubon member. From statement 3, Curtis' spouse is not Rosemary or Nancy. However, from statement 7, Nancy's husband is Curtis. Either statement 3, 5, or 7 is false. Statement 7 is also inconsistent with statement 10. Therefore, statement 7 is false. From statements 5 and 6, Angela is not married to Curtis. Therefore, Curtis' spouse is Susan (statements 3 and 5).

From statement 8, a pine siskin and a yellow warbler were sighted by the Dwyers. From statement 6, a lazuli bunting was sighted by Angela, and from statement 3, neither Rosemary nor Nancy is Dwyer. Therefore, Susan and Curtis are the Dwyers. From statement 10, Curtis was the last to sight his bird. Therefore, since the pine siskin was sighted early in the day (statement 8), it was sighted by Susan, and Curtis sighted the yellow warbler.

From statements 1 and 2, neither James nor William, who sighted a golden-crowned kinglet, is Brinkley. Therefore, Harold, who sighted a white-crowned sparrow (from statement 9), is Brinkley. From statement 3, neither Rosemary nor Nancy is Valentine. Therefore, Angela is Valentine. Since, from statement 1, James is not Valentine, William is Valentine and Angela's spouse. Therefore, James must be Eng. From statement 9, Nancy, who is not Harold Brinkley's spouse, must be the spouse of James Eng. Rosemary's spouse is Harold.

From statements 4 and 9, Nancy was not the first to sight a western tanager or a black-headed grosbeak. Therefore, she was first to sight an acorn woodpecker. Since, from statement 1, James was not the first to sight a western tanager, he was the first to sight a black-headed grosbeak. Rosemary was the first to spot a western tanager.

SUMMARY SOLUTION:

Angela Valentine	lazuli bunting
William Valentine	golden-crowned kinglet
Curtis Dwyer	yellow warbler
Susan Dwyer	pine siskin
Harold Brinkley	white-crowned sparrow
Rosemary Brinkley	western tanager
James Eng	black-headed grosbeak
Nancy Eng	corn woodpecker

THE WORLD'S MOST TAXING CAR POOL PUZZLE

CONSIDERATIONS: From statement 1, Amarol must be one of the three women. This, however, is inconsistent with statement 7. Also, from statement 1, Amarol is the first to be dropped off in the evening. This is inconsistent with both statements 3 and 6. Therefore, statement 1 is false.

From statement 2, neither Neal nor Florence is the secretary. From statements 3 and 4, since the secretary is the second to be picked up in the morning, Paul, who is the sixth to be picked up in the morning, is not the secretary. From statement 6, since Gloria is dropped off immediately after Avenal, who is dropped off first (statement 3), she is dropped off second, and Evelyn, who is dropped off two people later, is the fourth to be dropped off in the evening. Since the secretary is the fifth to be dropped off in the evening (statement 4), neither Gloria nor Evelyn is the secretary. Therefore, Milton, the secretary, is the second to be picked up in the morning and the fifth to be dropped off in the evening.

From statement 7, Avenal and Amarol are two of the three men. Since Paul is not Avenal (statement 3), and, from statement 6, Amarol is the third to be dropped off (immediately before Evelyn, who is the fourth to be dropped off), Milton is not Amarol. Therefore, Paul is Amarol, and Neal is Avenal, the first to be dropped off. Therefore, Florence is Adams the attorney, who is the first to be picked up in the morning and the sixth to be dropped off in the evening (statement 5). From statement 6, Gloria, who is picked up immediately after Neal and before Paul, is the fifth to be picked up, and Neal is the fourth to be picked up in the morning. Therefore, Evelyn is the 3rd to be picked up in the morning.

From statement 2, the secretary (who is Milton) is neither Agassi nor Atwater. Therefore, Milton is Altchech. From statement 4, Paul Amarol, who is the third to be dropped off in the evening, is the word processing supervisor. From statement 8, the personnel manager, who is not the fourth or fifth to be picked up in the morning, is Evelyn; since she is not Atwater, she is Agassi, and Gloria is Atwater. From statement 7, since Neal Avenal is not the systems analyst, he is the computer programmer, and Gloria Atwater is the systems analyst.

SUMMARY SOLUTION:

carpoolers	positions	A.M. pickup	P.M. drop-off
Evelyn Agassi	personnel manager	3rd	4th
Florence Adams	attorney	1st	6th
Gloria Atwater	systems analyst	5th	2nd
Milton Altchech	secretary	2nd	5th
Neal Avenal	computer programmer	4th	1st
Paul Amarol	word processing supervisor	6th	3rd

THE WORLD'S MOST TAXING SUMMER STUDENT PUZZLE

CONSIDERATIONS: From statement 5, Professors Harrison and White teach in buildings at the two ends of the row. This is contradictory to statement 8, which is also contradictory to statement 7. Therefore, statement 8 is false.

From statements 4, 5, 6, and 7, Professors Harrison and White teach in buildings A and F, not necessarily in that order. Professor Landers teaches in building B. Professor Carson does not teach in building D. Therefore, he teaches in building C or E, and Professor Denton, whose building is not adjacent to that of Professor Carson, must also teach in C or E. Therefore, Professor Bradford's building is D.

From statements 4, 5, 6, and 7, Professor Denton does not teach music; neither Professor Harrison nor Professor White teach music or psychology; Professor Landers does not teach music, and Professor Carson teaches law. Therefore Professor Bradford teaches music in building D with Sawyer as his student (statement 11). From statement 2, Carl, who is not attending class in buildings A or F (he is between Sawyer and Burt), is studying history. Therefore, Professors Harrison and White teach economics and English, not necessarily in that order.

From statement 10, John's class is in the building next to Professor Harrison's building. Therefore, John's building is either B or E. Since Rogers, who is not John, attends class in building B (Professor Landers' building), John's building is E. Therefore, Professor Harrison's building is F, and Professor White's building is A.

From statement 2, Carl, whose class is in the building between those of Sawyer and Burt, is studying history (statement 2) from Professor Denton in building C. Therefore, John is studying law under Professor Carson in building E. Burt Rogers is studying psychology (the remaining subject) under Professor Landers in building B.

From statement 9, Fran's building is not A or F (nor is Williams'). Therefore, her surname is Sawyer. She is studying music under Professor Bradford in building D. From statement 1, Louise, whose class is in building A, must be studying economics from Professor White. Victoria is studying English under Professor Harrison in building F. From statement 3, since Peterson's building is adjacent to Victoria's, John is Peterson, Carl is Williams (statement 9), Louise is West (statement 1), and Victoria is Karr.

SUMMARY SOLUTION:

first name	surname	subject	professor	building
Burt	Rogers	psychology	Landers	B
Carl	Williams	history	Denton	C
Fran	Sawyer	music	Bradford	D
John	Peterson	law	Carson	E
Louise	West	economics	White	A
Victoria	Karr	English	Harrison	F

THE WORLD'S MOST TAXING CHESS PLAYER PUZZLE

CONSIDERATIONS: Of the six members of the City Chess Club, Edith is the only female. From statement 9, she usually opens with the Stonewall System. However, from statement 6, Edith always opens with a king's pawn; the Stonewall System is a queen's pawn opening. One of statements 6 and 9 is false. However, from statement 2, Draper, who is a male, prefers the Stonewall System, and since no two players prefer the same opening, statement 9 is the false one.

From statements 3, 4, and 7, the two strongest players are Harry Duvall and Fred Evans. From statements 1 and 5, George's surname is not Gruber or Campbell. Therefore, George is either Davis or Draper. Besides George, the other possibilities for Draper are Dan and Jeff. From statement 5, Campbell is not Edith or Jeff. Therefore, Dan's surname is Campbell. Since, from statement 5, Jeff prefers to open with the Ruy Lopez, and, from statement 2, Draper prefers the Stonewall System, George's surname is Draper.

From statement 5, Dan Campbell favors the King's Gambit opening. Since Jeff prefers the Ruy Lopez, from statement 6, Edith prefers the third king's pawn opening, the Bishop's opening. From statement 4, Edith prefers the Pirc Defense against king's pawn openings and the Meran Defense against queen's pawn openings.

Therefore, Edith is Gruber and Jeff is Davis (statements 1, 3, and 4).

From statement 2, Draper prefers to open with the Stonewall System. From statement 7, Evans does not favor the Queen's Gambit opening. Therefore, he prefers the Colle System and Harry prefers the Queen's Gambit opening.

Our conclusions so far are:

From statement 1, Jeff Davis must be the player who prefers the Sicilian Defense against king's pawn openings and the Tarrasch Defense against queen's pawn openings. From statement 10, Dan Campbell prefers the King's Indian Defense against queen's pawn openings. From statements 3 and 8, Fred Evans does not favor the French Defense, the Caro-Kann Defense, or Petroff's Defense against king's pawn openings. Therefore, he prefers the Two Knights Defense. From statements 7 and 10, Fred prefers the Benoni Defense against queen's pawn openings. From statement 2, Draper uses the Nimzo-Indian Defense against queen's pawn openings, and Harry Duvall uses the remaining defense against queen's pawn openings, the Cambridge Springs Defense.

From statements 2 and 3, Dan Campbell uses the French Defense against king's pawn openings, and Harry Duvall favors Petroff's Defense. The remaining defense against king's pawn openings, the Caro-Kann Defense, is preferred by George Draper.

SUMMARY SOLUTION:

full name	preferred opening move	preferred king's pawn defense	preferred queen's pawn defense
Dan Campbell	King's Gambit	French Defense	King's Indian Defense
Edith Gruber	Bishop's Opening	Pirc Defense	Meran Defense
Fred Evans	Colle System	Two Knights	Benoni Defense Defense
George Draper	Stonewall System	Caro-Kann Defense	Nimzo-Indian Defense
Harry Duvall	Queen's Gambit	Petroff's Defense	Cambridge Springs Defense
Jeff Davis	Ruy Lopez	Sicilian Defense	Tarrasch Defense

THE WORLD'S MOST MYSTIFYING LOGIC PUZZLES

THE WORLD'S MOST MYSTIFYING EDUCATIONAL ACCOMPLISHMENT PUZZLE

CONSIDERATIONS: From statement 1, if Prince Tal excelled in chivalry, his second subject was horsemanship. However, from statement 3, if he did especially well in horsemanship, he excelled in fencing. From these two statements we can conclude that the hypothesis in statement 1 is invalid. Prince Tal did not excel in chivalry.

From statements 4 and 5, if Prince Tal excelled in fencing, his second subject was chivalry. However, if his second subject was chivalry, he excelled in horsemanship. Therefore, he did not excel in fencing. Therefore, statement 2 is valid.

THE WORLD'S MOST MYSTIFYING DRAGON BATTLE PUZZLE

CONSIDERATIONS: From statement 2, Sir Aard encountered neither Flame Thrower nor Old Smoky. From statement 4, Sir Bolbo encountered neither Flame Thrower nor Black Heart. Therefore, Sir Delfo encountered Flame Thrower.

From statement 6, Sir Delfo did not encounter Biter or Old Smoky. Therefore, Sir Bolbo must have encountered Old Smoky.

From statements 3 and 1, since we know that Sir Delfo encountered Flame Thrower, Sir Aard did not encounter Dante and Sir Delfo did not encounter Black Heart. From statement 5, since Sir Delfo encountered Flame Thrower, he did not encounter Dante. Therefore, Sir Bolbo encountered Dante and Sir Aard encountered Biter and Black Heart.

SUMMARY SOLUTION:
Sir Aard encountered Biter and Black Heart.
Sir Bolbo encountered Dante and Old Smoky.
Sir Delfo encountered Flame Thrower.

THE WORLD'S MOST MYSTIFYING TILTING PUZZLE

CONSIDERATIONS: According to statement 1, if either Prince Tal or Sir Aard tilted with Sir Keln, Sir Bolbo tilted with Sir Gath. However, from statements 4 and 3, if Sir Gath and Sir Bolbo tilted, so did Sir Delfo and Prince Tal, and then Sir Keln tilted with Sir Gath. Therefore, Sir Keln did not tilt with Prince Tal or Sir Aard.

From statement 6, if Sir Keln tilted with Sir Gath, Prince Tal tilted with Sir Aard. However, from statement 5, if Prince Tal and Sir Aard tilted, so did Sir Bolbo and Sir Gath. Therefore, Sir Keln did not tilt with Sir Gath.

From statement 3, since Sir Keln did not tilt with Sir Gath, Prince Tal did not tilt with Sir Delfo, and from statement 7, since Sir Keln did not tilt with Sir Aard, Prince Tal did not tilt with Sir Bolbo. Therefore, Prince Tal must have tilted with either Sir Aard or Sir Gath. From statements 5 and 4, if Prince Tal tilted with Sir Aard, then Sir Bolbo and Sir Gath tilted; this, however, means that Sir Delfo and Prince Tal tilted— an impossibility. Therefore, Prince Tal tilted with Sir Gath. From statement 2, Sir Keln tilted with Sir Delfo.

The remaining knights, Sir Bolbo and Sir Aard, tilted with each other.

SUMMARY SOLUTION:
Sir Bolbo tilted with Sir Aard.
Sir Keln tilted with Sir Delfo.
Prince Tal tilted with Sir Gath.

THE WORLD'S MOST MYSTIFYING FEARSOME BEAST ENCOUNTER PUZZLE

CONSIDERATIONS: According to statement 3, if Sir Aard was prostrate on the ground, Prince Tal and Sir Bolbo were not thrown. If this was the case, Sir Delfo was the one who climbed a tree. However, from statement 2, if Sir Delfo climbed a tree, Sir Aard was not thrown. Therefore, Sir Aard was not the one who was prostrate on the ground.

According to statement 1, if Sir Bolbo climbed a tree, Prince Tal and Sir Delfo were not thrown. If so, Sir Aard was the one who was prostrate on the ground. However, since we know that Sir Aard was not the one who was prostrate on the ground, Sir Bolbo was not the one who climbed a tree.

According to statement 2, if Sir Delfo climbed a tree, Sir Aard and Prince Tal were not thrown. If so, Sir Bolbo was the one who was prostrate on the ground. However, from statement 6, if Sir Bolbo was prostrate on the ground, Sir Delfo was not thrown. Therefore, Sir Delfo did not climb a tree.

According to statement 5, if Prince Tal did not climb a tree, either Sir Bolbo or Sir Delfo climbed a tree. Since we know that neither Sir Bolbo nor Sir Delfo climbed a tree, Prince Tal was the one who climbed a tree. Therefore, Sir Aard must have been one of the two adventurers who were not thrown.

Our conclusions so far are:

According to statement 4, if Sir Aard was not thrown, which we know to be the case, Sir Bolbo was not thrown and Sir Delfo was prostrate on the ground.

SUMMARY SOLUTION:

Sir Aard was not thrown.
Sir Bolbo was not thrown.
Sir Delfo was prostrate on the ground.
Prince Tal climbed a tree.

THE WORLD'S MOST MYSTIFYING STRANGE CREATURE PUZZLE

CONSIDERATIONS: From statement 7, since Sir Delfo saw either a basilisk or a monoceros, Sir Delfo did not see a bonnacon, a satyr, or a leucrota. Therefore, from statement 1, Sir Bolbo did not see a monoceros, and from statement 6, Prince Tal did not see a monoceros. From statement 8, Sir Bolbo did not see a leucrota. From statement 4, since Sir Delfo saw either a basilisk or a monoceros, neither Sir Bolbo nor Sir Aard saw a basilisk. From statement 2, since we know that Prince Tal did not see a monoceros, Sir Bolbo did not see a bonnacon. Therefore, Sir Bolbo saw a satyr.

Conclusions so far are:

From statement 3, since Sir Aard did not see a satyr, Sir Keln was the one to see a leucrota. From statement 5, since Sir Aard did not see a basilisk, Prince Tal did not see a bonnacon. Therefore, Sir Aard is the one who saw a bonnacon, and Prince Tal saw a basilisk. Therefore, Sir Delfo saw a monoceros.

SUMMARY SOLUTION:

Sir Aard saw a bonnacon.
Sir Bolbo saw a satyr.
Sir Delfo saw a monoceros.
Sir Keln saw a leucrota.
Prince Tal saw a basilisk.

THE WORLD'S MOST MYSTIFYING ENCHANTRESS PUZZLE

CONSIDERATIONS: From statement 5, if the noblemen stormed the castle, Prince Tal was imprisoned for three days. But this contradicts statement 6, so the noblemen did not storm the castle. If he broke the door, from statement 4, Prince Tal was imprisoned for one week or two weeks. But from statement 6, if his imprisonment was for one week, he did not break the door, so if he broke the door, his imprisonment was for two weeks. This contradicts statement 7, though, so he did not break the door.

If the ransom was paid, then Prince Tal was imprisoned for one week or two weeks, according to statement 4. However, statement 3 says that it's impossible for an imprisonment of two weeks and a ransom payment, so if the ransom was paid, Prince Tal was imprisoned for one week. This contradicts statement 2, though, so the ransom was not paid. Therefore, the dungeon keeper left the door open. From statement 1, Prince Tal was imprisoned for one day or three days. But, from statement 2, it couldn't have been for one day, so it must have been for three days.

SUMMARY SOLUTION: Prince Tal was imprisoned for three days and the dungeon keeper left the door open.

THE WORLD'S MOST MYSTIFYING RESCUE PUZZLE

CONSIDERATIONS: From statement 1, if Sir Keln rescued Maid Marion or Maid Mary, Sir Aard rescued Maid Muriel or Maid Marie. Following through statements 3, 5, and 7, if Sir Aard rescued Maid Muriel or Maid Marie, then Prince Tal rescued Maid Mary or Maid Morgana, Sir Bolbo rescued Maid Matilda or Maid Marion, and Sir Delfo rescued both Maid Muriel and Maid Marie, which is a contradiction. Therefore, Sir Keln did not rescue Maid Marion or Maid Mary.

From statement 6, since we know that Sir Keln did not rescue Maid Marion or Maid Mary, Sir Aard rescued either Maid Marion or Maid Muriel. From statements 3, 5, and 7, Sir Aard did not rescue Maid Muriel or Maid Marie. Therefore, he rescued Maid Marion. From statement 8, since Sir Aard did not rescue Maid Marie, but did rescue Maid Marion, Prince Tal rescued both Maid Matilda and Maid Muriel.

Our conclusions so far are as follows:

From statement 2, since Prince Tal rescued Maid Matilda, Sir Bolbo rescued Maid Mary. From statement 4, since Sir Bolbo rescued Maid Mary, Sir Keln rescued Maid Morgana. The remaining maiden, Maid Marie, was rescued by Sir Delfo.

SUMMARY SOLUTION:

Sir Aard	Maid Marion
Sir Bolbo	Maid Mary
Sir Delfo	Maid Marie
Sir Keln	Maid Morgana
Prince Tal	Maid Matilda and Maid Muriel

THE WORLD'S MOST MYSTIFYING FOUR DRAGON ENCOUNTER PUZZLE

CONSIDERATIONS: From statement 8, Prince Tal must not have forgotten his shield during the first and third encounters, since from statements 5, 6, and 7, it is apparent that he did not feign death during his second encounter. Therefore, the encounter in which Prince Tal forgot his shield and left without fighting must have been the second or fourth one. From statements 5 and 7, if the second encounter was with Dante, Quicksilver, or Vesuvius, Prince Tal did not forget his shield at that time.

Further, if the second encounter was with Meduso, it was not the time that Prince Tal left without fighting, since we know that Prince Tal fought Meduso using his peripheral vision. Therefore, Prince Tal forgot his shield at the fourth encounter, and that encounter was not with Meduso.

From statements 1 and 4, Vesuvius was not the first or fourth dragon confronted, since Prince Tal's fellow noblemen did not arrive to save him during the fourth encounter, and if they arrived to save him during the first encounter, it was with Quicksilver. From statement 3, since Prince Tal did not feign death during the fourth encounter, it was not with Dante. Therefore, the fourth encounter was with Quicksilver.

From statement 2, since the fourth encounter was not with Meduso, the first encounter was not with Dante. Therefore, the first encounter was with Meduso.

From statement 6, since the encounter with Meduso was the first one, Prince Tal did not feign death in his confrontation with this dragon. From statement 4, Prince Tal's fellow noblemen did not arrive to save him during the encounter with Meduso. Therefore, the outcome of the encounter with Meduso was that the dragon suffered a coughing fit.

Conclusions so far are:

Either the encounter with Vesuvius or the one with Dante resulted in Prince Tal's fellow noblemen arriving in time to rescue him. From statement 7, the encounter with Vesuvius was not the second one. Therefore, the second encounter was with Dante, and from statement 5, the outcome was that Prince Tal's fellow noblemen rescued him. Therefore, the third encounter was with Vesuvius and the outcome was that Prince Tal feigned death.

SUMMARY SOLUTION:

1st encounter	Meduso	coughing fit
2nd encounter	Dante	help arrived
3rd encounter	Vesuvius	feigned death
4th encounter	Quicksilver	forgot shield

THE WORLD'S MOST MYSTIFYING ONE-DRAGON PUZZLE

CONSIDERATIONS: If either part of A's statement is true, the statement is true. A is not blue, as all blue dragons lie. If the statement is true, A is a gray rational; if it is false, A must be a red rational.

SUMMARY SOLUTION:
    The dragon is a rational.

THE WORLD'S MOST MYSTIFYING TWO-DRAGON PUZZLE

CONSIDERATIONS: A is not from Wonk, as blue dragons always lie. A's first statement is false, so A is either a red rational or a gray predator. A's second statement is false; at least one of A and B is a rational.

B, who also claims to be from Wonk, has lied. From B's second statement, B is a gray predator. Therefore, A must be a red rational.

SUMMARY SOLUTION:
    A is a red rational.

B is a gray predator.

THE WORLD'S MOST MYSTIFYING THREE-DRAGON PUZZLE

CONSIDERATIONS: A's second statement is true. If it were false, A would be a red predator, and red predators always tell the truth. A is a gray rational. Therefore, from A's first statement, C is blue. We know that B's statements are false, since B's first statement claims that A is from Wonk. From B's second statement, since A is a rational, C must be a predator. From C's two statements, which are false, we can conclude that B is a red rational.

SUMMARY SOLUTION:
A is a gray rational.
B is a red rational.
C is a blue predator.

THE WORLD'S MOST MYSTIFYING DRAGONS FROM WONK PUZZLE

CONSIDERATIONS: Consider that two of the three dragons are blue.
Since blue dragons from Wonk always lie, one of A's and B's first statements, asserting that B and C are from Wonk, must be true and the other false. Thus, one of B and C is not blue. Therefore, A has lied; he must be one of the two from Wonk. Therefore, B has told the truth. B is a gray rational, and A and C are blue predators.

SUMMARY SOLUTION:
A is a blue predator.
B is a gray rational.
C is a blue predator.

THE WORLD'S MOST MYSTIFYING COLORFUL DRAGON FROM WONK PUZZLE

CONSIDERATIONS: Consider that one dragon is blue.
Assume A is a gray rational as indicated by his second statement. If so, C must be a gray rational, as A's first statement claims. However, from C's first statement, A is not a gray rational. Therefore, A's statements are false, and C's statements are true. C must be a red predator. From C's second statement, B is blue; and, from B's third statement, B is a predator. From B's first and second statements, A is a red rational.

SUMMARY SOLUTION:
A is a red rational.
B is a blue predator.
C is a red predator.

THE WORLD'S MOST MYSTIFYING AT-LEAST-ONE FROM WONK PUZZLE

CONSIDERATIONS: Consider that at least one dragon is blue.
A must be blue. Only a blue dragon can claim that he is a gray predator or a red rational. B's second statement must be false, since if it were true, C's second statement would be impossible. From B's third statement, B is not gray, and from A's second statement, which is false, B is not red. Therefore, B is blue.
D's third statement correctly asserts that both A and B are blue. Therefore, D is a

red predator, as claimed.

C, whose statements are false, is a gray predator. From C's third statement, B is a rational, and from B's first statement, A is a predator.

SUMMARY SOLUTION:
A is a blue predator.
B is a blue rational.
C is a gray predator.
D is a red predator.

THE WORLD'S MOST MYSTIFYING THREE DRAGONS PUZZLE, AGAIN

CONSIDERATIONS: If A's first statement is true, A is either a gray rational or a red predator. If his first statement is false, he is either a blue rational or a blue predator. If B's second statement is true, C is blue and from C's first statement, which would be false, A's statements are true. If B's first statement is false, A is red and, again, C's first statement is false. Therefore, in either case, A's statements are true. A is either a gray rational or a red predator.

From A's second statement, C is either gray or red. Therefore, since at least one dragon is blue, it must be B. From B's first statement, which is false, A is a red predator. From A's second statement, C is red, and must be a rational. From C's second statement, B is a rational.

SUMMARY SOLUTION:
A is a red predator.
B is a blue rational.
C is a red rational.

THE WORLD'S MOST MYSTIFYING PROTECTION PUZZLE

CONSIDERATIONS: Assume A's second statement is true. If so, B's statements are false; B is either a red rational or a blue rational. If so, from B's second statement, C could be a red rational or a blue rational. However, C's third statement would be true and first statement would be false, which is not possible. Therefore, A's statements are false.

From A's second statement, at least one of the three must be a predator. From A's first statement, he is either red or blue, and from A's third statement, C is either gray or blue.

Assume that C's statements are true. If so, C is a gray rational; and from C's second statement, A must be a red rational. However, C's first statement indicates that he and A are different types, an inconsistency. Therefore, C's statements are false; A is not red. Therefore, A is blue.

From C's third statement, B is a predator, which is consistent with B's first statement. Therefore, B is a red predator. From B's second statement, C must be a gray predator. From C's first statement, A is a predator.

SUMMARY SOLUTION:
A is a blue predator.
B is a red predator.
C is a gray predator.

THE WORLD'S MOST MYSTIFYING DRAGON COLORING PUZZLE

CONSIDERATIONS: Assume that A's statements are true. If so, from A's second statement, A must be a gray rational. From C's second statement, which agrees with A's second statement, C's statements are also true, and C is either a gray rational or a red predator. If so, from C's first statement and A's third statement, B is a red rational, with all false statements.

However, B's first statement is in agreement with the type that C would claim for A. This statement would not be possible for a red rational. Therefore, A's statements are false.

Therefore, from A's statements, B would claim that C is a rational, A is either red or blue, and B is a predator. C, who asserts that A is gray, is also a liar. From C's first statement, A would claim that B is not red. Therefore, B is red.

B's first statement, that C would claim that A is a rational, is correct. Therefore, B is a red predator, and from B's second statement, C is a red rational. A is a predator, and since we have established that A is a liar and is not gray, A is blue.

SUMMARY SOLUTION:
A is a blue predator.
B is a red predator.
C is a red rational.

THE WORLD'S MOST MYSTIFYING PUZZLE FROM THE ADDLED ARITHMETICIAN, I

CONSIDERATIONS: Each letter above the line represents a digit that has a difference of one from the digit represented by the same letter below the line.

The digits are 0, 1, 2, 3, 4, and 5.

	(4)	(3)	(2)	(1)
	A	F	C	E
+	A	D	D	B
	B	F	B	F

Since the largest available digit is 5, A must be 1 or 2, and B below the line is 2 or 4. From column 3, since F above the line and F below the line must be one number different, D must be 1. Therefore, A is not 1; A is 2. B below the line is 4, and B above the line is 3 or 5. From column 2, C must be 3, since C plus 1 equals 4. Therefore, B above the line is 5.

Considering the digits left, F above the line must be 4. Therefore, F below the line is 5; and E is 0, the remaining digit.

SUMMARY SOLUTION:

A	B	C	D	E	F
2	5	3	1	0	4

	4				5

	2	4	3	0
+	2	1	1	5

4	5	4	5

THE WORLD'S MOST MYSTIFYING PUZZLE FROM THE ADDLED ARITHMETICIAN, II

CONSIDERATIONS: The digits are 0, 1, 2, 3, 4, and 5.

	(5)	(4)	(3)	(2)	(1)
	F	B	A	C	B
−	D	A	F	E	B
	C	F	D	E	

From column 1, E below the line equals 0, and E above the line must be 1. From column 5, D above the line is one less than F above the line, since the answer disappears in that column. D above the line must be 4, 3, or 2.

From column 4, since there was a carry from column 5, B must represent a smaller digit than A. Since the largest available digit is 5, the only possibility is A is 5, and B is 0 and C below the line is 5. Therefore, C above the line is 4.

From column 2, D below the line must be 3. From column 5, D above the line cannot be 4, since that digit is taken. Therefore, D above is 2, and F above is 3. From column 3, A minus F equals F. Therefore, since A above is 5, and F above is 3, F below is 2.

SUMMARY SOLUTION:

A	B	C	D	E	F
5	0	4	2	1	3

		5	3	0	2
	3	0	5	4	0
−	2	5	3	1	0
		5	2	3	0

THE WORLD'S MOST MYSTIFYING PUZZLE FROM THE ADDLED ARITHMETICIAN, III

CONSIDERATIONS: The digits are 0, 1, 2, 3, 4, 5 and 6.

	(5)	(4)	(3)	(2)	(1)
	D	G	A	E	C
+	E	F	B	A	C
C	F	G	D	G	F

C below the line reprints a carry from column 5. C below the line must be 1. Therefore, C above the line is 0 or 2. Therefore, from column 1, F below the line is 0 or 4. If F below is 4, from column 5, then D plus E must equal 14. This is not possible with the available digits. Therefore, F below is 0 and C above is also 0. F above must be 1.

From column 5, since F below is 0, D and E are 6 and 4, or 4 and 6. From column 2, E plus A equals G. Since we know that F below is 0 and C below is 1, there is no combination of digits available in which E could be 6. Therefore, E is 4 and D above is 6. Therefore, D below is 5. The only possible digit available to A is 2, and G below is 6. Therefore, G above is 5. B is 3, the remaining digit.

SUMMARY SOLUTION:

A	B	C	D	E	F	G
2	3	0	6	4	1	5
		1	5		0	6
	6	5	2	4	0	
+	4	1	3	2	0	
1	0	6	5	6	0	

THE WORLD'S MOST MYSTIFYING PUZZLE FROM THE ADDLED ARITHMETICIAN, IV

CONSIDERATIONS: The digits are 0, 1, 2, 3, 4, 8, and 9.

	(5)	(4)	(3)	(2)	(1)
	E	D	B	D	D
	E	D	B	D	D
+	E	D	B	D	D
C	F	A	B	D	E

D above the line, column 2, must be 4 or 9. No other available digits above the line will equal D below the line given a carry from column 1. However, if D above the line were 9, the carry from column 1 would be 2, and D below the line, column 2, would be 9, the same as D above the line. Therefore, D above the line is 4 and D below the line is 3. E below the line, column 1, must be 2.

Since A represents 4 plus 4 plus 4 plus a different carry than 1, that carry must be 2, and A equals 4.

B above the line must be 9, and B below the line is 8 (9 plus 9 plus 9 plus a carry of 1 from column 2). Given what's left, E above the line is 3, F is 0 (3 plus 3 plus 3 plus a carry of 1 from column 4), and C is 1.

SUMMARY SOLUTION:

A	B	C	D	E	F
	9		4	3	
4	8	1	3	2	0
	3	4	9	4	4

	3	4	9	4	4
+	3	4	9	4	4
1	0	4	8	3	2

THE WORLD'S MOST MYSTIFYING PUZZLE FROM THE ADDLED ARITHMETICIAN, V

CONSIDERATIONS: Each letter in the problem (above the line) represents a digit that has a difference of one from the digit represented by the same letter in the answer (below the line).

The digits are 0, 1, 2, 3, 4, and 5.

		C	A	E	(1)
x		E	C	E	(2)
		E	C	A	(3)
	D	F	B		(4)
E	C	A			(5)
E	B	B	B	A	(6)

E above the line can't be 0, since it starts a three-digit number. It can't be 3 or 4, since that would make A below be 9 or 6. It can't be 5, since E below would then be 4, and row 1 times 5 can't start with a 4 since C can't be 0. If E above the line were 1, A below the line would also be 1, making A above the line 0 or 2. If A above the line were 0, C below the line, row 3, would also be 0, making C above the line, row 2, 1, which is already taken. If A above the line were 2, C below the line, row 3, would also be 2, making C above the line 3. This would not fit, since F would be 6. Therefore, E above is 2. Therefore, A below the line, is 4.

E, row 2, times C, row 1, equals E, row 3. Therefore, there must be a carry from E times A (since E below must be an odd number). Therefore, E below the line must be 3, and A above the line must be 5.

The remaining letter above the line, C, is 1.

SUMMARY SOLUTION:

A	B	C	D	E	F
5		1		2	
4	2	0	1	3	5
		1	5	2	
	x	2	1	2	
		3	0	4	
	1	5	2		
3	0	4			
3	2	2	2	4	

THE WORLD'S MOST MYSTIFYING PUZZLE FROM THE ADDLED ARITHMETICIAN,

VI

CONSIDERATIONS: The digits are 0, 1, 2, 3, 4, 5, and 6.

	(7)	(6)	(5)	(4)	(3)	(2)	(1)
	B	D	C	A	B	F	B
−	E	E	B	G	E	A	E
	G	E	E	F	C	F

From column 7, B is one more than E, since the column disappears in the answer to the problem. Therefore, from column 1, F below the line equals 1.

Therefore, F above the line is 0 or 2. From column 3, it is apparent that no carry to column 2 is required, since the digit in the answer is the same as for column 1. Therefore, F above the line must be 2, and A is 0 or 1. C below the line must be 2, since 1 is taken. Therefore, A is 0. C above the line must be 1 or 3.

From column 6, considering that a carry from column 7 was required, E above the line must be 5, 4, or 3, and D must be 0, 1, or 2. Therefore, since 0 and 2 are taken, D is 1. Therefore, C above the line is 3, and E above the line is 5 or 4.

From column 6, if E above the line is 4, G below the line must be 6, and B must be 5. If so, however, G above the line must also be 5. Therefore, E above the line is 5, B is 6, and G above the line is 4, the remaining digit above the line. Subtracting yields the rest.

SUMMARY SOLUTION:

	A	B	C	D	E	F	G
	0	6	3	1	5	2	4
		2		6	1	5	
	6	1	3	0	6	2	6
−	5	5	6	4	5	0	5
	5	6	6	1	2	1

THE WORLD'S MOST MYSTIFYING PUZZLE FROM THE ADDLED ARITHMETICIAN, VII

CONSIDERATIONS: The digits are 0, 1, 2, 3, 4, 5, and 6.

	(6)	(5)	(4)	(3)	(2)	(1)
				F	C	C
			F	A	C	C
		B	A	E	C	A
+	A	D	C	F	A	A
	A	C	B	A	C	A

From column 6, A below the line represents A above the line plus a carry from column 5. Therefore, the sum of B above the line, D, and the carry into column 5 has to be 10 or more. The carry into column 5 can be no more than 1, so the sum of B above and D has to be 9 or more, and C below is either 0, 1, or 2. That means that C above is 0, 1, 2, or 3, but looking at columns 1 and 2, the only one that makes a value of A above that works in both columns is C above, equal to 0. In this case, A above must be 1, and A below is 2. This makes C below equal to 1.   Column 4, with a 1 and a 0, doesn't have enough to carry into column 5, so the sum of B above and D is 11; thus one is 5 and one is 6. Looking at column 3, F + 1 + E + F sums to either 2 or 12. The only numbers left for E and F are 2, 3, and 4, and the only combination that works is F = 4 and E = 3. This makes B below in column 4 equal to 6, which means E above is 5 and D is 6.

SUMMARY SOLUTION:

	A	B	C	D	E	F
	1	5	0	6	3	4
	2	6	1			
				4	0	0
			4	1	0	0
			5	1	3	0	1
+	1	6	0	4	1	1
	2	1	6	2	1	2

THE WORLD'S MOST MYSTIFYING PUZZLE FROM THE ADDLED ARITHMETICIAN, VIII

CONSIDERATIONS: The digits are 0, 2, 3, 5, 6, 8, and 9.

		D	E	B	(1)
x			D	G	(2)
		E	E	E	(3)
B	F	G			(4)
A	E	C	E		(5)

There is no digit 1 in the problem. Therefore, 0 must be represented by a letter that is not both above and below the line. The possibilities for 0 are A, C, D, and F. D can be eliminated, since it is located at the left end of lines 1 and 2. A can be eliminated, since it represents a digit one number greater than B below the line, resulting from a carry from E below plus F. Additionally, since there is a carry from E below plus F, F must be greater than 0. Therefore, C is 0.

The multipliers, D and G above, line 2, must be 2 and 3 or 3 and 2, since neither digit creates a carry that results in a fourth digit in rows 3 or 4. D must be 2, since if it were 3, D times D plus a carry from E above times D would create a fourth digit in line 4. Therefore, G above the line is 3, and G below the line must be 2 since there is no 4 available. B below the line must be 5 or 8 and A must be 6 or 9. B above the line must be 6 or 9. However, 3 times 9 (B above times G above) would yield 7, a digit not available. Therefore, B above the line is 6, B below the line is 5, and A is 6.

E below the line must be 8 since B above times G above equals 18 (lines 1, 2 and 3). Therefore, E above the line is 9, and F equals 9, since E below plus F plus a carry equals E below (lines 3, 4, and 5).

SUMMARY SOLUTION:

A	B	C	D	E	F	G
	6		2	9		3
6	5	0		8	9	2
		2	9	6		
		x	2	3		
		8	8	8		
	5	9	2			
		6	8	0	8	

THE WORLD'S MOST MYSTIFYING FOUR HORSE PUZZLE

CONSIDERATIONS: From statement 2, Mary did not own or ride the horse named Charger. From statements 1 and 4, Danielle rode Charger, so neither Danielle nor Harriet owned Charger. Therefore, Charger was owned by Alice.

From statements 3 and 5, since Alice did not ride El Cid or Silver, she rode Champ. Since Champ's owner rode El Cid, and El Cid's owner rode Silver, Danielle owned Silver. Then, from statement 1, Harriet owned El Cid and rode Silver, and Mary owned Champ and rode El Cid.

SUMMARY SOLUTION:

	owned	**rode**
Alice	Charger	Champ
Danielle	Silver	Charger
Harriet	El Cid	Silver
Mary	Champ	El Cid

THE WORLD'S MOST MYSTIFYING FIVE THESPIAN PUZZLE

CONSIDERATIONS: From statements 4 and 5, Roland did not play the victim, the murderer, the sheriff, or the witness. Therefore, Roland played the magistrate. From statements 6 and 2, we can conclude that Ronald played Roland the murderer. From statements 1 and 8, we can conclude that Raymond's character was Ronald the victim.

From statement 7, Rodney played the part of Raymond. Since the two remaining parts are the sheriff and the witness, and since from statement 3, Rupert did not play the sheriff, it is evident that Rodney played the sheriff and Rupert played the role of Rodney, the witness. The remaining character, Rupert, was the magistrate.

SUMMARY SOLUTION:

actor	**character**	**role**
Raymond	Ronald	victim
Rodney	Raymond	sheriff
Roland	Rupert	magistrate
Ronald	Roland	murderer
Rupert	Rodney	witness

THE WORLD'S MOST MYSTIFYING FIVE AUTHOR PUZZLE

CONSIDERATIONS: From statement 4, Milton writes general fiction. From statements 2 and 3, neither John, Sarah, nor Florence write mystery novels. Therefore, James writes mystery novels, and uses Montague as his pseudonym (statement 2). From statement 6, John must be the author of travel books.

At this point our conclusions are:

From statement 1, Sarah does not write historical novels. Therefore, Florence writes historical novels, and Sarah writes biographies. Also from statement 1, Florence's pseudonym is Blackledge, and from statement 5, John's pseudonym is Williams. Sarah's pseudonym is Quincy, and Milton's pseudonym is Hastings.

SUMMARY SOLUTION:

James Blackledge	Montague	mystery novels
Sarah Hastings	Quincy	biographies
John Montague	Williams	travel books
Milton Quincy	Hastings	general fiction
Florence Williams	Blackledge	historical novels

THE WORLD'S MOST MYSTIFYING ST. BERNARD AND DALMATION PUZZLE

CONSIDERATIONS: From statement 1, we can conclude that Simon's St. Bernard is not named Sidney. Therefore, the name is Sam or Smitty, and Sam or Smitty owns the Dalmatian named Sidney. From statement 2, we can conclude that Smitty's Dalmatian is not named Sam. Therefore, the name is either Sidney or Simon, as is Sam's St. Bernard. From statement 4, we can conclude that Sam's Dalmatian is not named Simon. Therefore, the name is either Sidney or Smitty, and Sidney or Smitty owns the St. Bernard named Simon.

From statement 5, we can conclude that Sidney's Dalmatian is not named Smitty. Therefore, the name is either Sam or Simon, and Sam or Simon owns the St. Bernard named Smitty. From statement 3, we can conclude that the Dalmatian named Sam is not owned by Smitty. Therefore, the owner is Sidney or Simon. Also, Smitty's St. Bernard must be named Sidney or Simon.

From statement 5, we know that Sam or Simon owns the St. Bernard named Smitty. From statement 2, we know that Sam's St. Bernard is named Sidney or Simon. Therefore, Simon must own the St. Bernard named Smitty.

From statement 4, we know that Sam's Dalmatian is named either Sidney or Smitty. Therefore, Sam must own the Dalmatian named Smitty, since the name is not available to any of the other three owners.

From statement 4, we know that Sidney or Smitty owns the St. Bernard named Simon. From statement 2, we know that Sam's St. Bernard is named Sidney or Simon. Therefore, Sam's St. Bernard must be named Sidney. Therefore, Smitty's Dalmatian is named Sidney (from statement 2), and his St. Bernard is named Simon (from statement 3). Our conclusions at this point are:

Therefore, Sidney's St. Bernard is named Sam, Simon's Dalmatian is named Sam, and Sidney's Dalmatian is named Simon.

SUMMARY SOLUTION:

owner   St. Bernard   Dalmation

Sam	Sidney	Smitty
Sidney	Sam	Simon
Simon	Smitty	Sam
Smitty	Simon	Sidney

THE WORLD'S MOST MYSTIFYING ISLANDERS' BOAT PUZZLE

CONSIDERATIONS: From statement 2, O'Byrne's daughter is Ophelia. Therefore, his fishing boat is not named Ophelia. From statement 4, O'Brien's fishing boat is not named Ophelia, and from statement 5, O'Bradovich's fishing boat is not named Ophelia. Therefore, that name belongs to O'Boyle's fishing boat. Therefore, O'Boyle's sailboat is not named Ophelia.

From statement 4, O'Brien's sailboat is not named Ophelia, and, since O'Byrne's sailboat is not named Ophelia (his daughter's name), that name belongs to O'Bradovich's sailboat.

From statement 3, O'Byrne's sailboat is not named Olivia. From statement 2, O'Boyle's daughter is named Olivia. Therefore, O'Brien's sailboat is named Olivia. From statement 4, O'Brien's fishing boat is not named Olga. Therefore, his fishing boat must be named Odette.

Our conclusions, so far, are:

O'Brien's daughter, who is not named Odette, must be named Olga, and O'Bradovich's daughter is Odette.

From statement 1, O'Byrne's fishing boat and O'Boyle's sailboat have the same name. Therefore, the name is not Olivia or Ophelia (their daughters' names). Since O'Brien's fishing boat is named Odette, O'Byrne's fishing boat and O'Boyle's sailboat are both named Olga. Therefore, O'Byrne's sailboat is named Odette, and O'Bradovich's fishing boat is named Olivia.

SUMMARY SOLUTION:

owner	**daughter**	**sailboat**	**fishing boat**
O'Boyle	Olivia	Olga	Ophelia
O'Bradovich	Odette	Ophelia	Olivia
O'Brien	Olga	Olivia	Odette
O'Byrne	Ophelia	Odette	Olga

THE WORLD'S MOST MYSTIFYING CLASSIC BOOK WRITER PUZZLE

CONSIDERATIONS: From statement 1, the Conrads gave or received a book by Dickens and gave or received a book by Kafka. From statement 2, since the Tolstoys were the ones who received a book by Dickens, it must have been given by the Conrads, who received a book by Kafka. According to statement 4, the Brontës received a book by Conrad from the namesakes of the author of the book given by the Conrads. Therefore, since we know that the Conrads gave a book by Dickens, the Brontës received a book by Conrad from the Dickenses. Since we know that the Conrads were the couple who received a book by Kafka, from statement 3, a book by Forster was received by the Kafkas. Also, from statement 3, since we know that the Conrads gave a book by Dickens, and that it was given to the Tolstoys, the Forsters received a book by Tolstoy.

Conclusions at this point:

A book by Brontë must have been received by the Dickenses, since this is the remaining possibility. From statement 5, since we know that the Dickenses received a book by Brontë, the Brontës gave a book by Forster to the Kafkas. Since (also from statement 5) the namesakes of the book given by the Kafkas (the remaining choices are a book by Brontë or a book by Tolstoy) gave a book by Kafka, the gift given by the Kafkas must have been a book by Tolstoy, and the Tolstoys gave a book by Kafka. Therefore, the Forsters gave a book by Brontë.

SUMMARY SOLUTION:

gave	received	
Brontës	Forster	Conrad
Conrads	Dickens	Kafka
Dickenses	Conrad	Brontë
Forsters	Brontë	Tolstoy
Kafkas	Tolstoy	Forster
Tolstoys	Kafka	Dickens

THE WORLD'S MOST MYSTIFYING TWO INHABITANT PUZZLE

CONSIDERATIONS: From A's statement, we know that A is a Pemtru. Only a Pemtru can, truthfully or falsely, state that it is afternoon.

From B's statement, we know that it is afternoon, whether B's statement is truthful or not. In this case, B has made a false statement.

SUMMARY SOLUTION: It is afternoon, A is a Pemtru, and B is an Amtru.

THE WORLD'S MOST MYSTIFYING TRUE STATEMENT PUZZLE

CONSIDERATIONS: Consider that two are Pemtrus.

Assume it is morning. If so, and if A is an Amtru, his statement is true, and B is a Pemtru. However, B's statement would be impossible for a Pemtru in the morning. Therefore, if it is morning, A must be a Pemtru. If so, A's statement is false, and B is an Amtru. However, since A's statement would be false, B's statement would be impossible for an Amtru in the morning.

Therefore, it is afternoon. If A is an Amtru, B is also an Amtru. However, since we know that two are Pemtrus, A is not an Amtru. A is a Pemtru, as is B. C, whose statement is false, is an Amtru.

SUMMARY SOLUTION: It is afternoon, A and B are Pemtrus, and C is an Amtru.

THE WORLD'S MOST MYSTIFYING THREE INHABITANT PUZZLE

CONSIDERATIONS: Consider that there are two Pemtrus and one Amtru.

Assume it is afternoon. If so, two of the three are Pemtrus, who have told the truth, and one is an Amtru, who has lied. If so, since A claims that B is a Pemtru and B claims that C is a Pemtru, one of A and B must be the Amtru. It must be A, as stated by C. This means that B and C are the two Pemtrus. However, this means that A, who claims that B is a Pemtru, has spoken truthfully, an impossibility for an Amtru in the afternoon.

Therefore, it must be morning. A and C, who have both lied, are the two

Pemtrus, and B, who has told the truth, is the Amtru.

SUMMARY SOLUTION: It is morning, A and C are the Pemtrus, and B is the Amtru.

THE WORLD'S MOST MYSTIFYING FOUR INHABITANT PUZZLE

CONSIDERATIONS: Consider that two are Amtrus and two are Pemtrus.

Assume it is afternoon. If so, if A is an Amtru, A's statement is false and B is a Pemtru. If so, B's statement is true and C is a Pemtru. If so, C's statement is true and D is a Pemtru. However, D's statement would be false. Therefore, if it is afternoon, A is a Pemtru. If so, B is an Amtru, C is an Amtru, and D is a Pemtru. Again, D's statement would be false, not possible for a Pemtru in the afternoon.

Therefore, it is morning. Assume A is an Amtru. If so, B is an Amtru, C is a Pemtru, and D is an Amtru. However, this would mean only one Pemtru. Therefore, A is a Pemtru, B is a Pemtru, C is an Amtru, and D is an Amtru.

SUMMARY SOLUTION: It is morning, A and B are Pemtrus, and C and D are Amtrus.

THE WORLD'S MOST MYSTIFYING FIVE INHABITANT PUZZLE

CONSIDERATIONS: Assume it is afternoon, and assume A's statement is true. If so, A is a Pemtru. If so, D, who claims A is an Amtru, must be an Amtru. If it is afternoon, B's statement must be true, and B is a Pemtru. If so, E, who asserts that B is a Pemtru, is also a Pemtru. C, who falsely asserts that D and E belong to the same group, is an Amtru. However, this would mean two Amtrus and three Pemtrus. Since we know there are three Amtrus and two Pemtrus, if it is afternoon and A's statement is not true.

Assume it is afternoon and A's statement is false. If so, A is an Amtru. If so, D, who claims A is an Amtru, is a Pemtru. B must be a Pemtru, as is E. If so, C, who truthfully claims D and E are in the same group, is a Pemtru. However, this would mean four Pemtrus and one Amtru. Therefore, it is not afternoon.

It is morning. Assume B's statement is false. If so, B is a Pemtru. E, who truthfully states B is a Pemtru, is an Amtru. A must be an Amtru. D, who claims A is an Amtru, is an Amtru. C, who truthfully asserts that D and E belong to the same group, is an Amtru. However, this would mean four Amtrus and one Pemtru.

Therefore, since we know it is morning, B's statement is true and B is an Amtru. E, who falsely claims that B is a Pemtru, is a Pemtru. A's statement is true, and A is an Amtru. D, who truthfully asserts that A is an Amtru, is an Amtru. C, who falsely claims that D and E belong to the same group, is a Pemtru.

SUMMARY SOLUTION: It is morning, A, B, and D are Amtrus, and C and E are Pemtrus.

THE WORLD'S MOST MYSTIFYING FOUR VALLEY INHABITANT PUZZLE

CONSIDERATIONS: Consider that both groups are represented equally by the four valley inhabitants.

Assume it is afternoon. If so, if C were an Amtru, he would truthfully or falsely assert that B is an Amtru. If C were a Pemtru, again he would truthfully or falsely assert that B is an Amtru. It would be impossible for C to refer to B as a Pemtru. Therefore, since C claims that B is a Pemtru, it can not be afternoon.

It is morning. Whether C is an Amtru or a Pemtru, he has truthfully or falsely stated that B is a Pemtru. From B's statement in the morning, that he and A belong to the same group, we know that B is a Pemtru. (If B were an Amtru, truthfully or falsely he would deny that he and A belong to the same group.)

For the same reason, from A's statement, A is a Pemtru and D could be an Amtru or a Pemtru. However, since both groups are represented equally, D and C must both be Amtrus.

SUMMARY SOLUTION: It is morning, A and B are Pemtrus, and C and D are Amtrus.

THE WORLD'S MOST MYSTIFYING THREE VALLEY INHABITANT PUZZLE

CONSIDERATIONS: Assume it is afternoon. If so, from A's statement we can conclude that A is an Amtru, as a Pemtru in the afternoon could not refer to another valley inhabitant as a Pemtru. If it is afternoon, C must be a Pemtru, as an Amtru would be truthfully referred to as such by A. However, B's statement that he and C are not both Amtrus would be true, which is not a possible statement in the afternoon.

Therefore, it is morning. A is either a Pemtru who has spoken truthfully or falsely about C, or an Amtru who has spoken falsely in a statement referring to another Amtru (if C were a Pemtru, A would truthfully say so).

Assume A is a Pemtru. If so, if C is a Pemtru, C's statement, which refers to A, must be true: A would say that B is an Amtru. However, as a Pemtru in the morning, A's reference to B as an Amtru must be false. Therefore, B must be a Pemtru. However, this is a contradiction, as A's reference to another Pemtru in the morning must be true.

Therefore, if A is a Pemtru, C must be an Amtru. If so, again, C's statement would be true: A would falsely say that B is an Amtru, which leads to the same contradiction as in the previous paragraph.

Therefore, A and C are both Amtrus. C's statement referring to A must be false: A would not say that B is an Amtru. B must be an Amtru who has spoken falsely about another Amtru.

SUMMARY SOLUTION: It is morning, and A, B, and C are Amtrus.

THE WORLD'S MOST MYSTIFYING LIAR ON THE HILL PUZZLE

CONSIDERATIONS: Consider that the hill inhabitant will speak the truth only if none of the other speakers are truthful. Otherwise, he will lie. Also consider that it is afternoon.

If C is the hill inhabitant as claimed, B has spoken falsely and, therefore, must be an Amtru. A, who truthfully confirms this, must be a Pemtru. As the hill inhabitant, C could not have spoken truthfully. Therefore, C is not the hill inhabitant.

C, who has spoken falsely, must be an Amtru. B, who falsely claims C is a Pemtru, could be an Amtru or the hill inhabitant. If B is the hill inhabitant, A's statement is false and A is an Amtru. D, who falsely states that A is a Pemtru, must be an Amtru. Therefore, since A, C, and D all make false statements, B, if the hill inhabitant, would speak truthfully. Since B falsely claims C to be a Pemtru, B is not the hill inhabitant.

Therefore, the hill inhabitant must be A or D. Assume D is the hill inhabitant. If so, since A truthfully states that B is an Amtru, he is a Pemtru. If D is the hill inhabitant, his statement would be false. However, it is not. Therefore, A, who has spoken truthfully, is the hill inhabitant. B, C, and D have spoken falsely; all three are Amtrus.

SUMMARY SOLUTION: A is the hill inhabitant, and B, C, and D are Amtrus.

THE WORLD'S MOST MYSTIFYING ONE FROM THE HILL PUZZLE

CONSIDERATIONS: Consider that the hill inhabitant will speak the truth only if none of the other speakers are truthful. Otherwise, he will lie.

Assume that A is the hill inhabitant. If so, if it is morning, D's statement is true, and A's statement about D is also true. But a hill inhabitant lies if others speak the truth, so if A is the hill inhabitant, it must be afternoon. If so, B's statement is true, so A's statement must be false. This means D is a Pemtru and his statement is true. But since C's statement is not true, C is an Amtru, which contradicts D's statement. Therefore, A does not live on the hill.

Assume that B is the hill inhabitant. If so, B's statement about C must be true. But C's statement is also true. Therefore, B is not the hill inhabitant.

Assume that C is the hill inhabitant. If so, C's statement is true, and D's statement is true too. Therefore, C is not the hill inhabitant.

Therefore, D lives on the hill. B's statement is true, so D's statement must be false. Since C's statement is false, from D's false statement C must be an Amtru, and it must be afternoon. So B is a Pemtru, and A, whose statement is true, is also a Pemtru.

SUMMARY SOLUTION: It is afternoon, D is the hill inhabitant, A and B are Pemtrus, and C is an Amtru.

THE WORLD'S MOST DAUNTING MATH PUZZLES

THE WORLD'S MOST DAUNTING FISHING PUZZLE

Fred, using worms, caught one fish. Sammy, using dry flies, caught three fish. Torkel, using eggs, caught two fish. Joe, using flatfish, caught no fish at all.

THE WORLD'S MOST DAUNTING JUMP ROPE PUZZLE

Danielle made 12 jumps; Gary made 9 jumps; Jan jumped 20 times; Arnie jumped 17 times; and Ruth made 25 jumps before missing a jump.

THE WORLD'S MOST DAUNTING POCKET CHANGE PUZZLE

Alex started with $4 and ended with 40¢. Scott started with $3 and ended with 95¢. Dan started with $2 and ended with 10¢. Jim started with $1 and ended with 70¢. Duane started with $2 and ended with $1.65.

THE WORLD'S MOST DAUNTING TEMPERATURE PUZZLE

The lowest temperature is at the 10:30 A.M. reading. The drop in temperature then is due to all the open doors as the students take their morning break.

THE WORLD'S MOST DAUNTING COAST TO COAST PUZZLE

The route that Jacques and Chi Chi travelled took them in order to: Phoenix, Los Angeles, San Francisco, Portland, Salt Lake City, Denver, Dallas, St. Louis, Chicago, Pittsburgh, and finally to Washington, D.C.

THE WORLD'S MOST DAUNTING COFFEE PUZZLE

Max drinks 4 cups, with 2 sugars, no milk.
Doris drinks 5 cups, with 1 sugar, milk.
Blizzo drinks 1 cup, with no sugar, no milk.
Jan drinks 6 cups, with 6 sugars, milk.
Boris drinks 8 cups, with 4 sugars, no milk.

THE WORLD'S MOST DAUNTING DECIMAL RULER PUZZLE

The length of the lines are: a 3.3; b 1.3; c 3.9; d 2.8; e 0.6; f 3.8; g 1.8.

THE WORLD'S MOST DAUNTING DESTRY'S MISSING NUMBERS PUZZLE

The squares are: A 22.34; B 11.93; C 25.17; D 13.47; E 25.71.

THE WORLD'S MOST DAUNTING E.F. BINGO PUZZLE

Wanda won when $^{16}/_{18}$ was called.

THE WORLD'S MOST DAUNTING FAMOUS PERSON PUZZLE

J O H N F K E N N E D Y

THE WORLD'S MOST DAUNTING FLIGHTY DECIMALS PUZZLE

In the square:	4.39	4.01	2.60	1.42	total: 12.42
In the circle:	5.20	1.16	.07	.03	total: 6.46
In the rectangle:	3.71	1.01	.72	.30	total: 5.74

THE WORLD'S MOST DAUNTING HEATHER'S GARDEN PUZZLE

Heather has: 3 rows of carrots, 4 rows of cabbages, 1 row of turnips, 2 rows of pole beans, 5 rows of spinach, and 6 rows of cucumbers.

THE WORLD'S MOST DAUNTING MATHATHON PUZZLE

The girls defeated the boys 80 to −10.

THE WORLD'S MOST DAUNTING MOUNTAIN CLIMB PUZZLE

Dacon climbed Mirre (7500-foot elevation). Drakon climbed Old Baldy (4500).

Macom climbed Goat (8000). Bacon climbed Sleepy (9000). Jake climbed Raleigh (11,000).

THE WORLD'S MOST DAUNTING MOUNTAIN RACE PUZZLE

Andy Stiller climbs Mt. Stewart carrying 20 lbs.
Gerald Brown climbs Mt. Morgan carrying 40 lbs.
Dale Dorsey climbs Mt. Waring carrying 50 lbs.
Paul Anderson climbs Mt. McIntire carrying 30 lbs.
Jim McGee climbs Mt. Picard carrying 10 lbs.

THE WORLD'S MOST DAUNTING NED'S NEWSPAPER ROUTE PUZZLE

The Joneses live in the green house and get a *daily only* (clue #4).
The Johnsons live in the blue house and get a Sunday only.
The Smiths live in the grey house and get a Sunday only.
The Browns live in the white house and get both daily and Sunday.
The Simpsons live in the yellow house and also get both papers.

THE WORLD'S MOST DAUNTING WILD NUMBERS PUZZLE

$1/4$	$1/2$	$3/4$	1
$4/16$	.5	$6/8$	$5/5$
one-fourth	50%	.75	100%
$3/12$	$4/8$	three-fourths	$1.00
.250	half a dollar	$9/12$	whole
$6/24$	$7/14$	75%	$10/10$
$5/20$	$3/6$	75¢	$4/4$

THE WORLD'S MOST DAUNTING ZOX PUZZLE

Of 750 Zoxians, the island of Zog has 75 residents, Zod has 250, Zob has 150, Zop has 175, and Zoz has 100.

THE WORLD'S MOST DAUNTING AUCTION PUZZLE

Irene Black bought cheese ($5). Denise Green bought pie ($4). Duane Grey bought coffee ($7). Dan White bought cake ($6). Elroy Brown bought fruit ($3.50).

THE WORLD'S MOST DAUNTING BIOLOGY CLASS PUZZLE

Kate adopted Willy, the mole (18 cm). Kristen adopted Weldon, the ladybug (1.3 cm). Kurt adopted Walter, the fly (1 cm). Kristi adopted Wendy, the rat (14 cm). Kyle adopted Warren, the bat (11 cm). Kevin adopted Wanda, the hamster (23 cm).

THE WORLD'S MOST DAUNTING CALEB'S CHECKBOOK PUZZLE

Caleb Jones started with $1987 but now has $681.
Barbara Jackson started with $1749 but now has $423.
Sam Brown stated with $1699 but now has $1004.

Joyce Wilson started with $1940 but now has $970.

Millard Smith started with $2050 but is now overdrawn $45!

THE WORLD'S MOST DAUNTING CHICKEN MOUNTAIN PUZZLE

Chicken-grading formula results: Saffola 242.5; McSanders 257.6 (winner); McPlume 172.2; McCombe 224.9; Poularde 196.6.

THE WORLD'S MOST DAUNTING CHOCOLATE CHIP COOKIES PUZZLE

Ms. Effie Bundt puts in 5 chips and bakes for 16 min 17 sec.

Ms. Ruby Strudel puts in 7 chips and bakes for 17 min 7 sec.

Ms. Themla Spicer puts in 8 chips and bakes for 16 min 9 sec.

Ms. Miriam Applestreet puts in 9 chips and bakes for 17 min.

Ms. Georgia Honeydew puts in 10 chips, baking for 17 min 8 sec.

THE WORLD'S MOST DAUNTING DESSERT PUZZLE

Jane Brown ate $2/3$ of the custard.

Pete Smith ate $1/6$ of the apple pie.

Tom Grey ate $3/4$ of the fig cookie.

Sarah Jones ate $1/8$ of the chocolate cake.

THE WORLD'S MOST DAUNTING DOG APARTMENTS PUZZLE

Name	Apt. No.	Food/Week	Baths/Months
MacTavish	408	2 lbs.	9
Chico	103	10 lbs.	3
Ivan	609	8 lbs.	12
Wilfred	512	4 lbs.	2
Taz	221	12 lbs.	6
Spunky	341	6 lbs.	4

THE WORLD'S MOST DAUNTING FIELD TRIP PUZZLE

Jorn weighs 45.1 qinae, or 4.1 Earth ounces (Eo), Duloc weighs 42.9 qinae (3.9 Eo), Phren weighs 63.8 qinae (5.8 Eo), Sio weighs 50.6 qinae (4.6 Eo), and Ontrus weighs 15.4 qinae (1.4 Eo).

THE WORLD'S MOST DAUNTING FLEA MARKET LEFTOVERS PUZZLE

Dan took the nut. Sandy took the bolt. Bob took the pencil. Irene took the pencil sharpener. Doris took the compass.

THE WORLD'S MOST DAUNTING FOUR CUPS PUZZLE

Cup A has 8 oz. of apple juice, B has 3 oz. of water, C has 11 oz. of oil, and D has 5 oz. of vinegar.

THE WORLD'S MOST DAUNTING FRACTIONS PROM PUZZLE

Table 1:	$^1/_3$	$^2/_3$	$^1/_6$	$^5/_6$
Table 2:	$^1/_4$	$^1/_8$	$^3/_8$	$^7/_8$
Table 3:	$^1/_5$	$^1/_{10}$	$^2/_5$	$^3/_5$

THE WORLD'S MOST DAUNTING FUND-RAISER PUZZLE

Tinzen won the CD player; and room 125 won the field trip to the amusement park.

THE WORLD'S MOST DAUNTING GOLF PUZZLE

Player	1	2	3	4	5	6	7	8	9	Total
Jim	5	5	4	4	6	6	5	3	4	42
Jan	4	7	3	4	5	5	5	4	3	40
Jon	6	5	4	5	5	6	4	5	3	43
Jed	5	6	3	4	5	6	5	6	4	44

Jed was the lazy scorekeeper.

THE WORLD'S MOST DAUNTING GRADE BOOK PUZZLE

	Score			
Student	Missed	Total	Average	Grade
Alban	18	495	55	C
Astrid	62	495	55	C
Amos	48	549	61	B
Angus	68	558	62	A
Avril	33	531	59	B

THE WORLD'S MOST DAUNTING HOT DOGS PUZZLE

Gerald Jones, in room 205, ate 20 hot dogs.
Isabella Smith, in room 202, ate 12 hot dogs.
Germaine Brown, in room 201, ate 24 hot dogs.
Tony Green, in room 204, ate 16 hot dogs.
Ginger White, in room 203, ate 22 hot dogs.

THE WORLD'S MOST DAUNTING LONGEST DRIVE PUZZLE

Desmond Rivers drove 257m/236yds with a 3-wood.
Simon Bates drove 263m/242yds with a 2-iron.
Lyle Reed drove 244m/224yds with a 5-wood.
Lester Baring drove 283m/260yds with a driver.
Henry Jenkins drove 282m/259yds with a 3-wood.
Jake Pym drove 261m/240yds with a driver.

THE WORLD'S MOST DAUNTING MULTIPLICATION JEOPARDY PUZZLE

Sue Jensen   8 x 15 = 120
June James   9 x 16 = 144
Dale Johnson   5 x 14 = 70
Neil Johns   7 x 18 = 126
Tina Jones   11 x 13 = 143

THE WORLD'S MOST DAUNTING OLD HOUSE PUZZLE

The Barneses lived 11 years in the red-painted house.
The Carpenters lived 44 years in the green-painted house.
The Lewises lived 5 years in the blue-painted house.
The Parkers lived 2 years in the yellow-painted house.
The Smiths lived 22 years in the brown-painted house.
The Warners lived 4 years in the white-painted house.

THE WORLD'S MOST DAUNTING PLAY BALL PUZZLE

Teddie has a white soccer ball that weighs 16 oz.
Teresa has an orange golf ball that weighs 1.5 oz.
Toddy has a yellow Ping-Pong ball that weighs .8 oz.
Tanya has a green tennis ball that weighs 2 oz.
Tom has a brown basketball that weighs 22 oz.
Tillie has a red football that weighs 15 oz.

THE WORLD'S MOST DAUNTING POTATO CHIPS PUZZLE

Elmo Glitzwhizzle ate 18 bags. Gazelda Kettledrummel ate 6 bags. Amos Grugenminer ate 12 bags. Gerald Crackenberry ate 9 bags. Sally Witteyspooner ate 3 bags. Hubert Jones at 24 bags!

THE WORLD'S MOST DAUNTING QUEEN RACHEL'S BRIDGE TOLL PUZZLE

Chiquita wears black shoes and pays 18¢ bridge toll.
Cindy wears blue shoes and pays 36¢ bridge toll.
Kurt wears red shoes and pays 14¢ bridge toll.
Taber wears white shoes and pays 38¢ bridge toll.
Caleb wears green shoes and pays 24¢ bridge toll.

THE WORLD'S MOST DAUNTING RHODA TILLER PUZZLE

	Figure Name	Inside Angle	Outside Angle
A	Rhoda Tiller	17	163
B	Ed Able	58	122
C	Val Veda	75	105
D	Asper Gus	85	95
E	Ruta Baggy	61	119

THE WORLD'S MOST DAUNTING SAND PUZZLE

Mr. Logan took 21.875%, or 26.25 lbs.
Mr. Driver took 3.125%, 3.75 lbs.
Mr. Thomas took 6.25%, 7.5 lbs.
Mr. Lang took 37.5%, 45 lbs.
Mr. Antonelli took 12.5%, 15 lbs.
Mr. Waters took 18.75%, 22.5 lbs.

THE WORLD'S MOST DAUNTING SHAPES PUZZLE

A trapezoid with the following measurements: 1.0, 3.25, 3.75, and 1.75

THE WORLD'S MOST DAUNTING SKATEBOARD CONTEST PUZZLE

Jimmy Cooper rode 8 blocks, from Elm St. Sally Mander rode 3, from Main St.
Lenny Linden rode 11, from Chestnut Ave. Roger Chapman rode 7, from Acorn Dr.
Kenny Lyle rode 1, from 11th St.

THE WORLD'S MOST DAUNTING SLUG CRAWL PUZZLE

Gerald's Slig, who wears a red leash, crawled 1.5 cm.
Walter's Oozey, who wears a yellow leash, crawled 1.8 cm.
Jack's Slippo, who wears a blue leash, crawled 2.3 cm.
Bob's Woozey, who wears a white leash, crawled 1.2 cm.
Harry's Gooey, who wears a purple leash, crawled 2.1 cm.
Bill's Slimeball, who wears a green leash, crawled .6 cm.

THE WORLD'S MOST DAUNTING SQUARE COUNT PUZZLE

The number of squares in the sections are: 1. 23; 2. 14; 3. 20; 4. 20; 5. 26; 6. 32; 7. 30.

THE WORLD'S MOST DAUNTING TABER'S BIRDHOUSE PUZZLE

The measurements in centimeters are: the top is 3.25, the side is 6.4, the front is 4.0, the bottom is 5.5, and the back is 2.8.

THE WORLD'S MOST DAUNTING TIME ZONE PUZZLE

Nick, as you know, is in Boston. Lori is in Mazatlan. Deb is in Nairobi. Jan is in Wellington. Duke is in London. Cary is in Perth. Alex is in Honolulu. Gene is in Cape Town.

THE WORLD'S MOST DAUNTING TURKEYS IN THE ROAD PUZZLE

Crate 1: 45; 2: 36; 3: 42; 4: 35; 5: 43; and 6: 32

THE WORLD'S MOST DAUNTING VEGETABLE SOUP CONTEST PUZZLE

	Corn	Peas	Carrots	Asparagus	Beans	Spent
Benny	2	1	4	5	3	$6.43
Lily	1	5	3	4	2	$6.09
T-Bone	5	3	2	1	4	$7.75

Slim	3	4	1	2	5	$7.42 (winner)
Joshua	4	2	5	3	1	$6.66

THE WORLD'S MOST DAUNTING BOXES PUZZLE

Bryce had 2, 6, 10, and 13 for 31 total.
Jeremy had 1, 5, 9, and 14 for 29 total.
Boyd had 3, 7, 11, and 15 for 36 total.
Kevin had 4, 8, 12, and 16 for 40 total.

THE WORLD'S MOST DAUNTING ELEVATOR PUZZLE

	Morning	Noon	Evening	Total	Average
Ives	78	44	121	243	81
Newell	84	52	98	234	78

THE WORLD'S MOST DAUNTING FIGS PUZZLE

The number of figs in the five boxes are: A 60; B 280; C 20; D 70; E 120.

THE WORLD'S MOST DAUNTING FOUL SHOTS PUZZLE

Player #12 made 36 foul shots out of 45 attempts, for 80%.
Player #18 made 58 foul shots out of 98 attempts, for 59%.
Player #22 made 94 foul shots out of 113 attempts, for 83%.
Player #27 made 89 foul shots out of 134 attempts, for 66%.
Player #34 made 102 foul shots out of 176 attempts, for 57%.
Player #49 made 132 foul shots out of 184 attempts, for 71%.

THE WORLD'S MOST DAUNTING GARAGE SALE PUZZLE

Ms. McGaskin bought the sweater for $0.50; original price $3.
Mr. Pazzini bought the tires for $8.00; originally $9.
Mr. Schmidt bought the dresser for $6; originally $12.
Ms. Cullen bought the telephone for $12; originally $15.
Ms. Higgins bought the dress for $0.75; originally $2.
Mr. Havill bought the bicycle for $10; originally $20.

THE WORLD'S MOST DAUNTING GREAT PENCIL SALE PUZZLE

Mr. Pendip sold 413 at 10¢ each for a $26.30 profit (front row seats).
Ms. Glenwhip sold 500 at 10 for 75¢, for a profit of $22.50.
Ms. Rimdrip sold 219 at 15¢ each, for a profit of $17.85.
Mr. Slimhip sold 371 at 5 for 40¢ for a profit of $15.00.

THE WORLD'S MOST DAUNTING HIDDEN GRADES PUZZLE

Dan scored 90 (B+); Bernard got 80 (C+); Jason got the highest grade, 93 (A-);
Dexter got 87 (B).

THE WORLD'S MOST DAUNTING HIGH RENT PUZZLE

Adrienne Drake lives on 24 and pays $650.
Peter Adams lives on 17 and pays $525.
Danielle Stuart lives on 12 and pays $450.
Farah Price lives on 25 and pays $700.
Sarah Jordan lives on 14 and pays $475.
Jacob Falk lives on 21 and pays $600.

THE WORLD'S MOST DAUNTING HUNDRED-MILER PUZZLE

Chet Brown rode the tan bike in 6:09 hours to average 16.42.
Dave Johns rode the grey bike in 6:39 hours to average 15.65.
Bob Day rode the blue bike in 6:21 hours to average 16.10.
Kurt White rode the red bike in 6:32 hours to average 15.82.
Rick Seig rode the green bike in 6:40 hours to average 15.62.

THE WORLD'S MOST DAUNTING MOTORCYCLE PUZZLE

Luke bought the helmet and got 90¢, Jake bought the tire and got $1.50. Swizzle bought the motorcycle and earned $3.75. Jeremiah bought the goggles and earned 45¢. Malcolm bought the outfit and 90¢. The "handsome prize" was $7.50.

Notes: The puzzle "key" is the prize money promised by old Mrs. Frizzle. Knowing from clue #4 that 90¢ represents 12%, you divide $.90 by .12 to get $7.50, the "handsome prize." Then, you can determine that 50% of $7.50 is $3.75, that 20% is $1.50, and that 6% is 45¢. From clue #2, you know that Malcolm can have only 90¢, because any other amount plus 60¢ would not total any of the other amounts. Therefore, Jake has $1.50, meaning he bought the tire.

THE WORLD'S MOST DAUNTING PARTY TIME PUZZLE

Guest	Distance in Miles	Average mph	Hours Away	Departure Time
Great Aunt Lucille	208	64	3 1/4	11:45 A.M.
Nephew Fredrick	196	49	4	11:00 A.M.
Uncle Jed	60	40	1 1/2	1:30 P.M.
Niece Gwendolyn	319	58	5 1/2	9:30 A.M.
Cousin Ansel	348	58	6	9:00 A.M.

THE WORLD'S MOST DAUNTING ROOMMATES PUZZLE

Greg and Jason live in green #4.
Dawn and Sue live in pink #1.
Terry and Kris live in yellow #6.
April and Sandra live in white #5.
Diane and Tina live in beige #3.
Gary and Duke live in blue #2.

THE WORLD'S MOST DAUNTING RUNNERS PUZZLE

Runner	Distance (km)	Average Time (min)
Sandy	10	8.5
Peter	5	7.0
Wendy	18	11.0
Kerry	8	8.0
Todd	12	9.5
Bob	4	7.5
Darlene	11	9.0
Lynn	9	10.5

THE WORLD'S MOST DAUNTING STEPHANIE'S INVESTMENTS PUZZLES

Smith and Co. sold paint. Stephanie's profit on $500 was $50.

Alaco sold siding, and Stephanie lost $10 on her $200 investment.

Dowin Products sold soft drinks. Stephanie's profit on the $100 she invested was $30.

Corbett & Sons Co. sold aluminum. Stephanie lost $160 on her $800 investment in that company.

Cortell Co. sold paper products and made Stephanie a $45 profit on her investment of $300.

Sadly, the outcome of all Stephanie's various investments was a total loss of $45.

THE WORLD'S MOST DAUNTING TALLEST PUZZLE

The heights of the six friends are: Duane tallest at 75 inches; Tom 2nd at 74 in.; Kevin 3rd at 73 in.; Monte 4th at 72 in.; Kris 5th at 71 in.; Brad shortest at 69 in.

THE WORLD'S GREATEST CRITICAL THINKING PUZZLES

THE WORLD'S GREATEST BRAIN NET PUZZLE

There are twenty routes. Although you can chart them all out, there is a less confusing way. Starting at the left, identify the number of routes that can get you to a circle. You can arrive at this number by adding the numbers found in the connecting circles to the left. Keep going until you get to the finish.

THE WORLD'S GREATEST PREDICTING PATHS PUZZLE

a. It creates a "bouncing ball" path.

b. It creates a square-like shape with extended lines radiating from the points.

THE WORLD'S GREATEST WHO'S THAT? PUZZLE

Position the mirrors so that they are arranged like an open book. The right side of your face will reflect on the right side of the mirror. This image does not reflect back to that eye. Instead, it bounces to the other mirror. From there, the image is reflected back to the other eye.

THE WORLD'S GREATEST LEFTOVERS AGAIN PUZZLE

There are thirty-one statues. The 25 ounces are used directly to make twenty-five statues. During this process, 5 ounces of excess clay are produced. This extra clay is used to make five additional statues. While making these five additional statues, there is enough unused clay to make one more statue with one-fifth of the clay left over.

THE WORLD'S GREATEST BROWNIE CUT PUZZLE

She makes one cut to create three portions. Two of the portions are in two pieces.

THE WORLD'S GREATEST BALANCING GOLD PUZZLE

The answer is nine pounds. Examine the objects on the right side of the balance. If we looked at the balance pan containing the two bars, we'd see that $^1/_{10}$ of the gold bar is absent. In its place we have $^9/_{10}$ of a pound. From this we can infer that $^1/_{10}$ of a gold bar weighs $^9/_{10}$ of a pound. Therefore, a complete gold bar would weigh ten times as much. $^9/_{10}$ pound x 10 = $^{90}/_{10}$, or 9 pounds.

THE WORLD'S GREATEST THRIFTY TECHNIQUE PUZZLE

First, divide the coins into three groups of three. Then, balance any one group against another group. If the counterfeit is contained in either of the groups, the coins will not balance. If, however, they balance, the counterfeit coin must be in the third pile. Now that we have identified the pile with the counterfeit coin, remove one coin from the pile and balance the other two. The lighter coin will not balance. If the two coins do balance, the counterfeit coin is the one not selected.

THE WORLD'S GREATEST TRICKY TIDE PUZZLE

Five rungs will still remain exposed. As the tide comes in, the boat will rise up.

THE WORLD'S GREATEST BREAKING UP IS HARD TO DO PUZZLE

The shapes are a box, a "t," an upside-down "l," an "l" on its back, and a straight line.

THE WORLD'S GREATEST DISORDER PUZZLE

From left-to-right, top-to-bottom, the numbers are 7, 3, 1, 4, 5, 8, 6, and 2.

THE WORLD'S GREATEST TRUE OR FALSE PUZZLE

The answer is tarsal. To figure this one out, we need to look at each alien's response.

If the first alien was a tarsal, it would identify itself as a tarsal. If it was a carpal, it would still identify itself as a tarsal. Either way, the mumbling alien would identify itself as a "tarsal." Therefore, the second alien had to be lying. The third alien truthfully identified the carpal, making him a truth-telling tarsal.

THE WORLD'S GREATEST PACK UP YOUR TROUBLE PUZZLE

The "trick" is using the same block in the rows of two adjacent sides.

THE WORLD'S GREATEST DON'T COME BACK THIS WAY AGAIN! PUZZLE

Start at the upper-most square's right-hand side and follow the exterior lines. Finish with the interior lines.

THE WORLD'S GREATEST MEET ME ON THE EDGE PUZZLE

The answer is one in six. The ant (or fly) can take any one of the six available routes. It doesn't matter. Now, the other insect must select the "collision route" from its own six possible choices. Therefore, the odds are one in six.

THE WORLD'S GREATEST ONLY THE SHADOW KNOWS PUZZLE

They can never cast shadows of equal size.

Any difference in their altitude would be negligible compared to their distance to the sun. It's those 93,000,000 miles from our planet to the sun that affect the shadows' size much more than their puny distances apart.

THE WORLD'S GREATEST MORE SHADOW STUFF PUZZLE

At that time of day, the shadow is two-fifths of the object's height. If the tree's shadow (two-fifths of the unknown height) is 25 feet, then the height of the tree is 62 ½ feet.

THE WORLD'S GREATEST TRIP TIME PUZZLE

Since it takes her 1 hour to reach the top (while traveling at 30 mph), the hill is a 30-mile route. Traveling at 60 mph, she'll cover that distance in only 30 minutes.

The average speed is the total distance/total time = 60 miles/1.5 hours or 40 mph.

THE WORLD'S GREATEST AVERAGE PUZZLE

There is no way that she can average 20 mph for the whole trip. Like the uphill path, the downhill path is only 10 miles. This distance is too short to achieve an average speed (for the whole trip) of 20 mph.

Consider this: If she completed her trip by traveling the downhill path at 600 mph, then her average speed would be the total distance divided by the total time, or 20 miles/61 minutes, or an average of about 19.6 mph.

By examining this equation, you'll see that there will be no way for her to decrease the denominator (time) below the 60 minutes she has already spent cycling up the hill.

THE WORLD'S GREATEST PALINDROME PUZZLE

The answer is 55 mph. The next palindrome that the odometer can display is 14,041. To reach this value, Bob will have had to travel 110 miles. If it took him 2 hours to reach this point, his average speed will be 55 mph.

All other palindromes would have required too many miles to produce a logical speed. For example, the odometer's next palindrome is 14,141. From this, you can calculate an average speed of 105 mph—highly unlikely.

THE WORLD'S GREATEST STACKING UP PUZZLE

From left-to-right, top-to-bottom, the numbers are: 1, 2, 3, 4, 6, 4, 9, 7, 8 or 1, 2, 3, 6, 4, 5, 8, 9, 7.

THE WORLD'S GREATEST STAR BIRTH PUZZLE

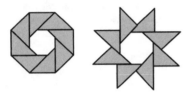

THE WORLD'S GREATEST FLIP FLOP PUZZLE

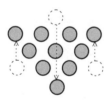

THE WORLD'S GREATEST CROSSING HAND PUZZLE

The answer is eleven times. For each hour up until 11:00, the clock's hands will cross once. Between 11 A.M. and 1 P.M., they'll only cross once (at noon). For each remaining hour between 1 P.M. and 5 P.M. the clock's hands will cross once. That gives us a total of 6 + 1 + 4 = 11 times.

THE WORLD'S GREATEST WHAT'S NEXT? PUZZLE

The sequence is based on the expanding geometric figures. After each figure reaches the outside perimeter, it starts again at the center.

THE WORLD'S GREATEST TRYING TRIANGLE PUZZLE

The answer is thirty-five triangles.

THE WORLD'S GREATEST FLIPPING PAIR PUZZLE

The first move is: heads, heads, tails. The second move is: tails, heads, heads. The third move is: tails, tails, tails.

THE WORLD'S GREATEST MISSING BLOCK PUZZLE

a. Twenty-three blocks. None are missing from the bottom layer, six are missing from the second layer, eight are missing from the third layer, and nine are missing from the top layer.

  b. Seventeen blocks. Eight are hidden in the bottom layer, six are hidden in the second layer, three are hidden in the third layer, and none are hidden in the top layer.

THE WORLD'S GREATEST MATCHSTICK MEMORY PUZZLE

The equations are:
I = III - II
I x I = I
III + I = IV

THE WORLD'S GREATEST SUM CIRCLE PUZZLE

From left-to-right and top-to-bottom, the numbers are 5, 1, 4, 3, 2, and 6.

THE WORLD'S GREATEST MANY RIVERS TO CROSS PUZZLE

First, the two children row to the far side. There, one gets out. The other child returns and gives the boat to an adult. The adult crosses the river. On the far side, the adult gets out and the child gets in the boat. The child brings the boat across the river and transports the other child back to the far side. This pattern continues until the four adults have crossed.

THE WORLD'S GREATEST TRAIN TRAVEL PUZZLE

The answer is 15 minutes and 32 seconds. This problem is not as simple as it may appear. The distance from pole one to pole ten is nine units. As stated, it takes the train 10 minutes to travel this distance. Therefore, it takes the train 1 minute and one-ninth (about 6.6 seconds) to travel each inter-pole distance.

  From the first pole to the fifteenth pole is fourteen inter-pole distances. It should take 14 x 1 minute and 6.6 seconds, or 14 minutes and 92 seconds, or about 15 minutes and 32 seconds.

THE WORLD'S GREATEST MILES APART PUZZLE

The answer is 120 miles. This problem is full of extra (and unneeded) information.

  Think it backwards. One hour before they meet, one train is 65 miles away from the meeting point, while the other is 55 miles. Add the two distances together and you'll get 120 miles.

THE WORLD'S GREATEST PASSING TRAIN PUZZLE

The answer is 792 feet. The length of the freight train can be calculated by knowing its relative passing speed and the time it took for it to move by. The passing speed is equal to the sum of both train speeds (60 mph +30 mph = 90 mph).

Here's where some conversion comes in. By dividing by 60, we find that 90 mph is equal to 1.5 miles per minute. By dividing by 60 again, we find that this is equivalent to 0.025 miles per second.

The freight train takes 6 seconds to pass. Therefore, its length is 0.15 miles. To change this into feet, multiply 0.15 by the number of feet in a miles (5,280).

THE WORLD'S GREATEST SOUPED-UP SURVEY PUZZLE

The numbers do not add up correctly. The agency stated that only 100 people were interviewed. Yet, according to a logical breakdown of the results, they received 120 responses. You can see by making a diagram of the data.

THE WORLD'S GREATEST TOASTY PUZZLE

Fry one side of two slices for 30 seconds. Flip one slice over and replace the other slice with a fresh slice of bread. At the end of 1 minute, remove the completely fried bread. Return the unfried side of the previous slice to the pan and flip the other slice over for 30 seconds.

THE WORLD'S GREATEST CIRCLE GAME PUZZLE

When added together, the numbers at the opposite ends of this sequence equal 10 (1 + 9, 2 + 8, etc.). By placing a 5 in the middle circle, we ensure that all the sums must equal 15 (10 + 5).

THE WORLD'S GREATEST FARE SPLIT PUZZLE

The answer is $12.50. One-fourth of the total round trip fare ($5.00) was taken by Michelle alone. Three-fourths of the round trip was shared (half of $15.00). Therefore, Michelle should pay $5.00 + $7.50 or $12.50.

THE WORLD'S GREATEST PENTAGON PART PUZZLE

Six patterns

THE WORLD'S GREATEST BAGEL FOR FIVE PUZZLE

Yes; the cuts intersect creating two measly pieces, and three substantial ones.

THE WORLD'S GREATEST COIN MOVE PUZZLE

Move the two left-hand coins on the top row, and move the first right-hand coin on the bottom row.

THE WORLD'S GREATEST TRAPEZOID TRAP PUZZLE

Make a mark dividing it in half, then create four trapezoids by drawing four angles extending outward from the center line.

THE WORLD'S GREATEST A+ TEST PUZZLE

The large piece is at an angle; the triangles are , side-by-side, two-by-two to each long side of the large piece.

THE WORLD'S GREATEST MISMARKED MUSIC PUZZLE

Select the box labeled "Rap & Jazz." Listen to one tape. If the marble is jazz, then you must have the box full of jazz cassettes. (Remember that since all the boxes are mislabeled, this box could not contain the mix of rap and jazz.) Likewise, if the tape is rap, you have selected the all-rap box. Since all three names are mismatched, then just switch the names of the other two boxes to correctly identify the contents of all boxes.

THE WORLD'S GREATEST MEASURING MUG PUZZLE

Fill the mug about two-thirds full of water. Then tilt it so that water pours off. When the level of water reaches the same height as the uplifted mug bottom, the vessel is then half full.

THE WORLD'S GREATEST COIN ROLL PUZZLE

   a. The same direction—to the left
   b. Two

THE WORLD'S GREATEST PAINTING ON THE SIDE PUZZLE

The answer is ten ways. 1 = all sides white, 1 = one red face, 1 = two adjacent red faces, 1 = two opposite sides red faces, 1 = three sides red (in line), 1 = three faces red (in right-hand and left-hand L-shape design), 1 = four faces red (in line), 1 = four faces red (two pairs of two in line), 1 = five red faces, 1 = all faces red.

THE WORLD'S GREATEST MAGIC TRIANGLE PUZZLE

23, 20, and 17

THE WORLD'S GREATEST PATTERN PUZZLE

The answer is fourteen. Add the upper left number, lower left number, and lower right number together. Then multiply this sum by the number in the upper right corner. The product is in the center of the square.

THE WORLD'S GREATEST FROG JUMP PUZZLE

The answer is four days. During the first day, the frog jumps up 6 feet and at night slides down 2 feet. The frog begins day two at a height of 4 feet, jumps to 10 feet, but slides back to 8 feet. On day three, the frog jumps to 14 feet, but slides back to 12 feet. On day four, the frog jumps to 18 feet and leaves the well.

THE WORLD'S GREATEST ARMY ANT PUZZLE

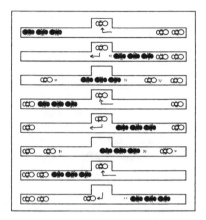

THE WORLD'S GREATEST NO SWEAT PUZZLE

Five girls and two boys. First, subtract the coach's 9 cups from the total amount. Therefore, the boys and the girls together drank 34 cups. The winning combination is five girls (who together drink 20 cups) and two boys (who together drink 14 cups). 20 + 14 = 34 cups.

THE WORLD'S GREATEST GO FIGURE! PUZZLE

It is statement 4. The confusing relationship may best be understood by putting the information in a graphic layout. From the drawing, you can see that only statement 4 is true.

THE WORLD'S GREATEST SQUARE PATTERN PUZZLE

There are only three distinguishing patterns. All other patterns are obtained by rotating the square.

THE WORLD'S GREATEST BOUNCING BALL PUZZLE

Approximately 3 meters. The first fall is 1 meter. It rebounds to $1/2$ meter, than falls $1/2$ meter. So now we're at 2 meters. Then the ball goes up and down $1/4$ meter, then $1/8$ meter, then $1/16$ meter, and so on. It continues this pattern until it comes to rest (theoretically it would keep going, but in the real world it stops). If we were to add all these distances up, we'd get: $1 + 1/2 + 1/2 + 1/4 + 1/4 + 1/8 + 1/8 + 1/16 + 1/16 + \ldots = < 3$ meters.

THE WORLD'S GREATEST COMPLETE THE PATTERN PUZZLE

The answer is X = 22; Y = 25. Each circle equals 1, each square equals 5, each triangle equals 10, and the pentagon equals 2. The numbers represent the sums of the values in each row or column.

THE WORLD'S GREATEST CHECKERBOARD PUZZLE

Thirty squares

THE WORLD'S GREATEST CUTTING EDGE PUZZLE

It's cut into two "L" shapes. The long, thin ends can be placed adjacent to eachother, creating a size that is perfect for the new space, 2 ft. by 18 ft.

THE WORLD'S GREATEST DIE IS CAST PUZZLE

Although all four dice have the same relative orientation of spots, the three spots on the last die tilt from the lower left corner to the upper right corner.

When the other dice are rotated to this position, their three spots tilt from the upper left to the lower right corner.

THE WORLD'S GREATEST PLAYING WITH MATCHES PUZZLE

There are thirty-one matches. If one winner is to be found in thirty-two teams, then thirty-one teams must lose. Since each team can only lose once, the thirty-one losses result from thirty-one matches.

THE WORLD'S GREATEST COMPETING CLICK PUZZLE

It's Anthony. The actual period is 1 second less than the time given. Emily completes ten clicks in 9 seconds. Buzzy completes twenty clicks in 19 seconds. Anthony completes five clicks in 4 seconds. This gives us the approximate rates: Emily = 1.1 clicks/second, Buzzy = 1.05 clicks/second, Anthony = 1.25 clicks/second.

THE WORLD'S GREATEST ANOTHER PATTERN PUZZLE

The answer is four. The number in the center of each triangle results from dividing the product of the top two sides by the bottom side.

THE WORLD'S GREATEST VIVE LE FLAG PUZZLE

There are twenty-four combinations. If both the outside stripes are the same color, you'll have twelve possible combinations (4 x 3 =12).

If all three stripes are a different color, you'll have twenty-four possible combinations (4 x 3 x 2 = 24). However, these twenty-four flags are made up of twelve mirror-image pairs. Just rotate the mirror image one-half turn and you'll produce the other flag. This decreases the stripe combinations to only twelve.

Now let's add the two sets of possible combinations: 12 + 12 = 24 different color patterns.

THE WORLD'S GREATEST PIZZA CUT PUZZLE

See the pizza as four quarters. Since one quarter is gone, but four more people want to eat the same amount, cut a piece from each of the remaining three quarters to create the fifth portion.

THE WORLD'S GREATEST SLIP SLIDING PUZZLE

You'll get blocked if you don't place the coins in a specific order. Each coin must come to rest on the spot where the previous coin began its journey. Only in this manner can you then place all seven coins.

THE WORLD'S GREATEST A, B, SEE? PUZZLE

10	55	919	545
x10	+55	+191	+455
100	110	1110	1000

THE WORLD'S GREATEST SPARE CHANGE PUZZLE

The answer is $1.19. Jonathan has four pennies, four dimes, one quarter, one half dollar. Added together, they amount to $1.19.

THE WORLD'S GREATEST PUZZLING PRICE PUZZLE

The answer is $10. The trick is not getting fooled into thinking that the book is $5.
If the book is "p," then $5 + $\frac{1}{2}$p = p.
$5 = $\frac{1}{2}$p.
$10 = p.

THE WORLD'S GREATEST GUM DROP PUZZLE

There are 135 gum drops. If forty gum drops are left in the jar, the forty must represent two-thirds of the gum drops that were available when Britt appeared.

Therefore, the total number of gum drops before Britt took her share was sixty. Working with the same logic, you can figure out that before Tanya took her share of thirty, the jar had ninety gum drops. Before Michael took his share of forty-five, it had 135 gum drops.

THE WORLD'S GREATEST GO-CART CROSSING PUZZLE

The answer is 33.3 minutes. To travel 1 mile, go-cart A takes $\frac{1}{6}$ of an hour, go-cart B takes $\frac{1}{12}$ of an hour, and go-cart C takes $\frac{1}{15}$ of an hour. To travel one loop distance ($\frac{1}{3}$ of a mile), it would take each $\frac{1}{18}$, $\frac{1}{32}$, and $\frac{1}{45}$ of an hour, respectively. All three would meet at $\frac{1}{9}$ of an hour intervals. For five meetings to occur, five $\frac{1}{9}$-hour periods must pass. 5 x $\frac{1}{9}$ = $\frac{5}{9}$ of an hour, or about 33.3 minutes.

THE WORLD'S GREATEST TABLE MANNERS PUZZLE

There are two ways.

THE WORLD'S GREATEST WINNING SLIP PUZZLE

The contestant picks one of the slips. The slip is placed out of view (possibly eaten). The contestant then asks the MC to read the slip that was not selected. That MC's slip has the word "loser." When the audience hears "loser," they logically conclude that the contestant must have picked the winning slip.

THE WORLD'S GREATEST ANCIENT MAN PUZZLE

The answer is 60 years old. If his whole life is "X years," then:

His boyhood years = $\frac{1}{4}X$
His youth = $\frac{1}{5}X$
His adulthood = $\frac{1}{3}X$
His elder years = 13
$\frac{1}{4}X + \frac{1}{5}X + \frac{1}{3}X + 13 = X$
$X = 60$

THE WORLD'S GREATEST LIGHTS OUT! PUZZLE

He covers the window as shown here which meets both conditions.

THE WORLD'S GREATEST PENCIL PUZZLE

The answer is V. The layout is based on the sequence of letters found in the alphabet. The "twist" is produced by the extra pencil points aimed at certain letters. Each pencil point can be replaced by the words "advance one step."

Look at the letter L (either one). The L progresses to M. The M, however, does not advance to an N because two M pencil points converge on this next space. The letter then advances one extra step, resulting in an O.

With the same logic, the O leads to an R (advance three steps). The R leads to a V (advance four steps).

THE WORLD'S GREATEST SOUNDS LOGICAL PUZZLE

The answer isNiko. If Sheila picks rock 'n' roll, then according to (1) Ramon must pick jazz and according to (2) Niko must also pick jazz. These selections contradict (3). This rules Sheila out.

If Ramon picks jazz, then according to (1) Sheila must pick rock 'n' roll and the same contradictions surface.

The only person who can select either jazz or rock 'n' roll without any contradictions is Niko.

THE WORLD'S GREATEST TRIANGULAR TOWER PUZZLE

The answer is twenty balls arranged in four levels.

THE WORLD'S GREATEST CRISS-CROSSED PUZZLE

Place one coin on top of the corner coin.

THE WORLD'S GREATEST CRYSTAL BUILDING PUZZLE

The answer is twelve tennis balls. Place six in a circle around the middle of the ball. Place three on top and three on the bottom.

THE WORLD'S GREATEST TESTY TARGET PUZZLE

Two arrows struck the 8 region (16 points) and seven of them struck the 12 region (84 points). Total: 16 + 84 = 100 points.

THE WORLD'S GREATEST EIGHTH CENTURY ENIGMA PUZZLE

On his first trip, the man brings the goat over (leaving the cabbage and wolf behind). On his second trip, he brings over the cabbage. When he lands on the other side, however, he takes the goat back in his boat. When he returns, he drops off the goat and takes the wolf. He transports the wolf across the river and leaves it with the cabbage. He returns once more to ferry over the goat.

THE WORLD'S GREATEST PLANET ROTATION PUZZLE

The sun would now appear to rise in the west and set in the east. This change is caused by the switch in rotation spin. The switch in revolution does not affect the direction of the apparent sunrise or sunset.

THE WORLD'S GREATEST SHUFFLE PUZZLE

The straight is more probable. To select the four of a kind, you need to select "one card out of five cards" four times: $\frac{1}{5} \times \frac{1}{5} \times \frac{1}{5} \times \frac{1}{5}$, or 1 out of 625.

For the straight, the first card can be any card. Then, you'll need to select "one card out of five cards" three times: $\frac{1}{5} \times \frac{1}{5} \times \frac{1}{5}$, or 1 out of 125—a better probability.

THE WORLD'S GREATEST SOME EXCHANGE! PUZZLE

a. 14 and 9; the sum of all eight numbers is 60. Each column must have a sum equal to half that, or 30. To arrive at 30, you need to lessen one column by 5 and increase the other by the same amount. This is accomplished by exchanging a 14 for a 9.

b. 2, 1, and 3; as with the previous problem, you can add all nine numbers together, then divide that sum by 3. The result is 20:

THE WORLD'S MOST MIND-BOGGLING WORD PUZZLES

THE WORLD'S MOST MIND-BOGGLING WILLIAM'S PREFERENCE PUZZLE

William, whose name has a double letter, likes things with double letters in their names. (Thanks to Marilyn vos Savant.)

THE WORLD'S MOST MIND-BOGGLING IDK BAND PUZZLE

IDK are the initial letters of "I don't know."

THE WORLD'S MOST MIND-BOGGLING SNOWBALL PUZZLE

The daughter spoke a snowball sentence.

THE WORLD'S MOST MIND-BOGGLING NAME THE MONTH PUZZLE

Cover the top halves of each symbol and you will see the word JULY.

THE WORLD'S MOST MIND-BOGGLING WRONG CAPTION PUZZLE

Change hired to fired.

THE WORLD'S MOST MIND-BOGGLING TENNIS PLAYER PUZZLE

"Tennis, anyone?"

THE WORLD'S MOST MIND-BOGGLING FOUR SUIT PUZZLE

The symbols in order are Heart, Spade, Club, and Diamond.

THE WORLD'S MOST MIND-BOGGLING NAME THE STUDENT PUZZLE

Turn the page upside down and you'll see the sum turn into LIONEL.

THE WORLD'S MOST MIND-BOGGLING WHAT LETTER? PUZZLE

Give the page a quarter turn counterclockwise. Do you see the letter E?

THE WORLD'S MOST MIND-BOGGLING SAD KING PUZZLE

It's a word palindrome. The words read the same left to right and right to left.

THE WORLD'S MOST MIND-BOGGLING SHORT TEASER PUZZLE

Short

THE WORLD'S MOST MIND-BOGGLING NAME THE BOOK PUZZLE

In a dictionary

THE WORLD'S MOST MIND-BOGGLING WHERE? PUZZLE

The mnemonic that begins "Thirty days hath September..."(Thanks to Sol Golomb.)

THE WORLD'S MOST MIND-BOGGLING TWO DOOR PUZZLE

Hold the page upside down in front of a mirror.

THE WORLD'S MOST MIND-BOGGLING FAMILY TALK PUZZLE

The three-letter words are POP (or DAD), MOM, BOB, SIS, TOT, and PUP. The family owns A TOYOTA, and the photo was taken at NOON. When Bob first saw their brand-new Toyota, he shouted, "WOW!"

THE WORLD'S MOST MIND-BOGGLING NAME THE GIRL PUZZLE

Mary

THE WORLD'S MOST MIND-BOGGLING THREE SISTER PUZZLE

Dynamite (Dinah might)

THE WORLD'S MOST MIND-BOGGLING HOW MANY COOKIES? PUZZLE

1. Jim ate one, Joan ate one two.
2. If the children ate all but three, then three would be left.

THE WORLD'S MOST MIND-BOGGLING STOP AND SNAP PUZZLE

"Let's do the POTS and PANS (STOP and SNAP backwards)," said Mrs. Gardner to her son Martin.

THE WORLD'S MOST MIND-BOGGLING TOMMY'S TUMBLE PUZZLE

Tommy and his parents lived in France.

THE WORLD'S MOST MIND-BOGGLING HOW MANY PEACHES? PUZZLE

There were two peaches in the sack. Joy took one of them out of the sack. To take one peach (singular) is not to take peaches (plural) and to leave one peach is not to leave peaches.

THE WORLD'S MOST MIND-BOGGLING BABY CROSSWORD PUZZLE

S	A	M
P	I	E
A	R	T

THE WORLD'S MOST MIND-BOGGLING WHAT'S THE QUESTION? PUZZLE

The lady has asked the clerk how long her train will be in the station. His answer is, from: "Two to 2:00, to 2:22."

THE WORLD'S MOST MIND-BOGGLING CRAZY WORD PUZZLE

The professor is holding the sheet by the wrong edge. Give the sheet (page) a quarter turn counterclockwise and read the words vertically.

THE WORLD'S MOST MIND-BOGGLING DAY'S END PUZZLE

Yes, day starts with "d," and ends starts with "e."

THE WORLD'S MOST MIND-BOGGLING LISPING VERSE PUZZLE

The missing word is "wunth."

THE WORLD'S MOST MIND-BOGGLING IN THE MIDDLE PUZZLE

P is the middle letter of "the alphabet."

THE WORLD'S MOST MIND-BOGGLING MISSING LETTER PUZZLE

The missing letter is B, the first letter of BEATS. When my wife Charlotte checked this puzzle, she supplied three other answers: Nobody heats our apple pies; Nobody eats sour apple pies; and Nobody eats four apple pies.

THE WORLD'S MOST MIND-BOGGLING MISSING WORD PUZZLE

The word is "only."

THE WORLD'S MOST MIND-BOGGLING PUZZLING DOOR PUZZLE

Divided properly, the letters spell "To open door, push."

THE WORLD'S MOST MIND-BOGGLING CORRECT-THE-SPELLINGS PUZZLE

The proverb is illustrated by the picture. A bird in the hand is worth two in the bush.

THE WORLD'S MOST MIND-BOGGLING SHH! PUZZLE

Sure

THE WORLD'S MOST MIND-BOGGLING FOUR ARROWS PUZZLE

The words are anagrams of NORTH, SOUTH, EAST, and WEST. I found this puzzle in Marilyn vos Savant's popular *Parade* column.

THE WORLD'S MOST MIND-BOGGLING THREE-LETTER WORD PUZZLE

You can't put two, because then the sentence would have 3 three-letter words. So you must put the numeral 2.

THE WORLD'S MOST MIND-BOGGLING WYKMIITY AND WYLTK PUZZLE

Tom's letters are the initials of "Will you kiss me if I tell you?" and Susan's letters are the first letters of "Wouldn't you like to know?"

THE WORLD'S MOST MIND-BOGGLING ACE GIK MOQ SUWY PUZZLE

They are the letters at odd positions (1, 3, 5, 7...) in the alphabet. Note the remarkable fact that all five vowels, AEIOU, and the sometime-vowel Y, are included in the sequence.

THE WORLD'S MOST MIND-BOGGLING WHAT IS SANTA SAYING? PUZZLE

Read aloud the words Santa is speaking. They will spell the letters of MERRY CHRISTMAS.(Thanks to Mike Steuben.)

THE WORLD'S MOST MIND-BOGGLING YULETIDE REBUS PUZZLE

Silent night (knight), holy (holey) night (knight). (Thanks to Dexter Cleveland, who put this on his Christmas card.)

THE WORLD'S MOST MIND-BOGGLING THREE STUDENT PUZZLE

The students made the mistake of pinning their names upside down. Turn the page around to read the names: OLLIE, ELSIE, and LESLIE.

THE WORLD'S MOST MIND-BOGGLING RUTH'S CIPHER PUZZLE

If you divide the numbers like this: 9/12/15/22/5/25/15/21, the message decodes as "I LOVE YOU."

THE WORLD'S MOST MIND-BOGGLING MONKEY TALK PUZZLE

The monkey is saying, "I want a banana." Her name is Barbara, and the zoo is in Alabama. "I know how to spell banana," a little girl once said, "but I never know when to stop."

THE WORLD'S MOST MIND-BOGGLING CONCEALED CREATURE PUZZLE

Doe, ant, cat, fly

THE WORLD'S MOST MIND-BOGGLING HORSE JINGLE PUZZLE

One and two are the names of two racehorses. The poem reads:
> One was a racehorse.
> Two was one, too.
> One won one race.
> Two won one, too.

THE WORLD'S MOST MIND-BOGGLING SPELL THE CREATURE PUZZLE

Goldfish (Thanks to Charles Bostick.)

THE WORLD'S MOST MIND-BOGGLING NAGGING QUESTION PUZZLE

Nag...and also, a less nagging answer is, narwhal (a kind of whale).

THE WORLD'S MOST MIND-BOGGLING FREEZING FROG PUZZLE

Shift each letter of COLD ahead three steps in the alphabet. You arrive at FROG.

THE WORLD'S MOST MIND-BOGGLING THREE BUNNY PUZZLE

They must get "ears."

THE WORLD'S MOST MIND-BOGGLING OLD MOTHER HUBBARD PUZZLE

The nursery rhyme is missing the vowel "i."

THE WORLD'S MOST MIND-BOGGLING NAME THE POODLE PUZZLE

Did you notice that there was no question mark after the brainteaser's statement? The name of the poodle is "What."

THE WORLD'S MOST MIND-BOGGLING WHERE'S THE COMMA? PUZZLE

Did you see the lion eating, Herman?

THE WORLD'S MOST MIND-BOGGLING WHO DOES WHAT? PUZZLE

Sue — lawyer
Grace — dancer
Bridget — engineer
Patience — physician
Carlotta — used car saleswoman
Robin — thief

Ophelia — chiropractor
Wanda — magician
Sophie — upholsterer
Hattie — milliner
Octavia — musician
Carrie — waitress
Betty — gambler
Carol — singer
Faith — minister
Pearl — jeweler

THE WORLD'S MOST MIND-BOGGLING NAME THE TIME PUZZLE

1. 8 (ate) P.M.
2. 2:30 (tooth hurty)
3. Three after one
4. Time to get the clock fixed

THE WORLD'S MOST MIND-BOGGLING SPELL A NAME PUZZLE

MARCIA

THE WORLD'S MOST MIND-BOGGLING RIBBON LOOP PUZZLE

The word is leaves.

THE WORLD'S MOST MIND-BOGGLING PUZZLING LANDSCAPE PUZZLE

Sky

THE WORLD'S MOST MIND-BOGGLING GUESS THE PSEUDONYM PUZZLE

Martin Gardner

THE WORLD'S MOST MIND-BOGGLING ODE TO APRICOTS PUZZLE

The first three letters of each line are the abbreviations for the twelve months of the year.

THE WORLD'S MOST MIND-BOGGLING FILL THE BLANK PUZZLE

The number is seven.

THE WORLD'S MOST MIND-BOGGLING DO YOU DENY IT? PUZZLE

The word is "deny."

THE WORLD'S MOST MIND-BOGGLING WHERE TO DRAW THE LINES? PUZZLE

IN/DISC/RIM/IN/AT/I/ON

THE WORLD'S MOST MIND-BOGGLING HE! HE! PUZZLE

The word HEADACHE answers both questions.

THE WORLD'S MOST MIND-BOGGLING GUESS THE PUNCHLINE PUZZLE

1. Boyfriend: May I see it?
2. Waiter: There was, but I wiped it off.
3. Student: At the bottom.

4. Prisoner: I'll have a ham sandwich.
5. Psychiatrist: Next!
6. Doctor: That's what puzzles me.
7. Patient: Well, yes and no.

THE WORLD'S MOST MIND-BOGGLING WRONG WORD PUZZLE

The rooms were marked Ladies and Gentlemen.

THE WORLD'S MOST MIND-BOGGLING TYPEWRITER TEASER PUZZLE

Typewriter

THE WORLD'S MOST MIND-BOGGLING CHANGE 100 TO CAT PUZZLE

It's easy to do. Just work it out with toothpicks.

THE WORLD'S MOST MIND-BOGGLING MARRYING BACHELOR PUZZLE

Tim Rines is the MINISTER of the First EPISCOPAL Church.

THE WORLD'S MOST MIND-BOGGLING HIJKLMNO PUZZLE

H to O or H_2O, the chemical symbol for water — two atoms of hydrogen combined with one atom of oxygen.

THE WORLD'S MOST MIND-BOGGLING UNUSUAL WORD PUZZLE

Unusual

THE WORLD'S MOST MIND-BOGGLING CLOCK CONUNDRUM PUZZLE

IV (ivy)

THE WORLD'S MOST MIND-BOGGLING TEN BODY PART PUZZLE

Arm, leg, ear, toe, lip, hip, eye, rib, jaw, gum

THE WORLD'S MOST MIND-BOGGLING OPPOSITE PUZZLE

(Tim Tebbe contributed this to *Games* magazine.)

THE WORLD'S MOST MIND-BOGGLING ERGRO PUZZLE

UNDERGROUND

THE WORLD'S MOST MIND-BOGGLING ONE-LETTER CAPTION PUZZLE

J (jay), Q (queue), I (eye), B (bee), T (cup of tea), P (pea), C (sea), U (mirror-you)

THE WORLD'S MOST MIND-BOGGLING ANNOYED SIGN PAINTER PUZZLE

He changed the sign to THE BELLYACHE COMPANY.

THE WORLD'S MOST MIND-BOGGLING FOLD AND CUT PUZZLE

Believe it or not, the only word you can make is HEAD. (Thanks to magician Max Maven for this one.)

THE WORLD'S MOST MIND-BOGGLING IN AND OUT PUZZLE

1. exist

2. blank
3. center

THE WORLD'S MOST MIND-BOGGLING FROM Z TO A PUZZLE
The word ZEBRA

THE WORLD'S MOST MIND-BOGGLING WHAT CAN IT BE? PUZZLE
The letter L

THE WORLD'S MOST MIND-BOGGLING NUMBER ANAGRAM PUZZLE
One, Ten, and Six

THE WORLD'S MOST MIND-BOGGLING ENINYOS PUZZLE
Ten tiny tots

THE WORLD'S MOST MIND-BOGGLING NAME THE PAINTING PUZZLE
The Mona Lisa

THE WORLD'S MOST MIND-BOGGLING LOCKED SAFE PUZZLE
Psyche

THE WORLD'S MOST MIND-BOGGLING CHANGE THE SIGN PUZZLE
Private?
No! Swimming Allowed

THE WORLD'S MOST MIND-BOGGLING THREE B's PUZZLE
The word is "hubbub."

THE WORLD'S MOST MIND-BOGGLING HORACE SPENCER PUZZLE
"My age twelve years, height four feet ten, sir."

THE WORLD'S MOST MIND-BOGGLING WHAT'S THE NUMBER? PUZZLE
One

THE WORLD'S MOST MIND-BOGGLING NY, PA, AND OZ PUZZLE
Shift each letter of OZ one step backward in the alphabet and you get NY. Shift the letters of OZ forward one step (assuming a circular alphabet in which Z is joined to A) and you get PA.

THE WORLD'S MOST MIND-BOGGLING CURIOUS CARD PUZZLE
Mr. Curio changes the word to N-O-P-E.

THE WORLD'S MOST MIND-BOGGLING GHGHGH PUZZLE
The word is puff.

THE WORLD'S MOST MIND-BOGGLING HAL AND IBM PUZZLE
Shift the letters of HAL forward one step in the alphabet. They become IBM. Clarke claims that this was sheer coincidence. He never intended HAL to shift to IBM.

THE WORLD'S MOST MIND-BOGGLING TEN FLYING SAUCERS PUZZLE

Shift each letter of TEN one step forward in the alphabet and it becomes UFO.

THE WORLD'S MOST MIND-BOGGLING KUBLA KHAN PUZZLE

In each line the last two main words begin with the same letter. Critics call this "alliteration."

THE WORLD'S MOST MIND-BOGGLING MERRY CHRISTMAS PUZZLE

Not only do the first words of each line repeat the words of the first line, but the same line is repeated by taking the first word of the first line, second word of the second line, third word of the third line, and so on to the end.

THE WORLD'S MOST MIND-BOGGLING TWO WORD PUZZLE

The x word is drive, and the y word is park.

THE WORLD'S MOST MIND-BOGGLING BLIND BUS DRIVER PUZZLE

The "Blind Man" is the owner of a company that sells window blinds.

THE WORLD'S MOST MIND-BOGGLING LEWIS CARROLL PUZZLE

BIG FACED; in an 1877 letter Lewis Carroll gave this word teaser to Maud Stanton, one of his many child friends.

THE WORLD'S MOST MIND-BOGGLING CURIOUS SEQUENCE PUZZLE

The next pair is also TH. They are the last two letters of FIRST, SECOND, THIRD, FOURTH, and FIFTH.

THE WORLD'S MOST MIND-BOGGLING NAME TWO PUZZLE

Dwarf, dwell, and dwindle

THE WORLD'S MOST MIND-BOGGLING DECODE A NUMBER PUZZLE

Eighty-four

THE WORLD'S MOST MIND-BOGGLING MILES AND MILES PUZZLE

Smiles, smiled, smiler, and smiley

THE WORLD'S MOST MIND-BOGGLING AFTER AB PUZZLE

E comes after AB in "alphabet."

THE WORLD'S MOST MIND-BOGGLING ADD A LINE PUZZLE

ABODE

THE WORLD'S MOST MIND-BOGGLING DNE EHT PUZZLE

The End. Have a good day!